Josep Soler
Language Policy and the Internationalization of Universities

Language and Social Life

Editors
David Britain
Crispin Thurlow

Volume 15

Josep Soler

Language Policy and the Internationalization of Universities

A Focus on Estonian Higher Education

DE GRUYTER
MOUTON

ISBN 978-1-5015-2449-3
e-ISBN (PDF) 978-1-5015-0589-8
e-ISBN (EPUB) 978-1-5015-0585-0
ISSN 2192-2128

Library of Congress Control Number: 2018954425

Bibliographic information published by the Deutsche Nationalbibliothek
The Deutsche Nationalbibliothek lists this publication in the Deutsche Nationalbibliografie;
detailed bibliographic data are available on the Internet at http://dnb.dnb.de.

© 2020 Walter de Gruyter, Inc., Boston/Berlin
This volume is text- and page-identical with the hardback published in 2019.
Typesetting: Integra Software Services Pvt. Ltd.
Printing and binding: CPI books GmbH, Leck

www.degruyter.com

To Anthee

Acknowledgements

This book has benefited from the support of a great number of people and institutions, for which I feel extremely lucky and grateful and without which the completion of the project that led to the writing of this book would not have been possible. I would like to acknowledge in the first place the Mobilitas award, a fellowship granted by the Estonian Research Agency (Eesti Teadusagentuur) for the postdoctoral project 'The role and perception of English as a global language in academic research and higher education' (Mobilitas grant number GFLEE322MJ), a project hosted by the Department of Estonian and General Linguistics of the University of Tartu. Martin Ehala acted graciously as my host at the department, giving me the space and freedom to conduct the project, and providing scholarly guidance when needed, for which I am indebted. From a more practical and administrative point of view, Tiia Margus and Leelo Padari made sure that I had always what I needed on the day-to-day running of the project, as did Anne Tenno, my contact point regarding grant-related matters at the university. To all of them, a big thank you.

At the University of Tartu, additional key support came from other colleagues and friends of mine, including especially from Djuddah Leijen, Head of the Centre for Academic Writing and Communication at the university (AVOK, in its Estonian acronym), and Virve-Anneli Vihman, whose insider knowledge about recent developments in connection to the internationalization policies at the university proved extremely useful and helpful in my research project. A very special and heartfelt thank you to both of them. During the time when the project was being implemented, I was lucky enough to be able to travel with my ideas and preliminary findings to a good number of conferences and symposia. In them, I was able to engage in meaningful discussions and debates with colleagues who were working on related issues and who, as a result, ended up having an impact on my thinking about my own project. At the risk of missing many, I would like to thank the following colleagues: Beyza Björkman, David Block, Lídia Gallego-Balsà, Anna Kristina Hultgren, Merike Jürna, Kerttu Kibbermann, Kadri Koreinik, Maria Kuteeva, Heiko Marten, Taina Saarinen, and once again Virve-Anneli Vihman. With many of them, our discussions about shared interests led to further, more intense collaborations, ending in many cases in co-authored publications. Indeed, two of the chapters of this monograph draw directly on two such co-authored publications. Chapter 2 is derived in part from an article co-authored with Taina Saarinen and Kerttu Kibbermann, published in the *Journal of Multilingual and Multicultural Development*, 38(4), 301–314, copyright Taylor & Francis, and Chapter 3 is derived in part from an article co-authored with Virve-Anneli Vihman, published in *Current Issues in Language Planning*, 19(1), 22–41, copyright Taylor &

Francis. Permission to reuse the articles from the publisher and my co-authors is deeply appreciated. I am grateful to the Association for the Advancement of Baltic Studies (AABS) for the Emerging Scholar Grant award (2013) to conduct a study on the linguistic landscape of Baltic universities; Chapter 2 draws in part on data collected during that project.

In the final stages of my project, I was actively involved in the COST-funded network on New Speakers (Action IS-1306, www.nspk.org.uk). That involvement was particularly significant for my thinking and further reading about language policy issues. I would like to thank Bernadette O'Rourke and Joan Pujolar, the respective Chair and Vice-Chair of the Action, for giving me the opportunity to become a more active member of the network, and especially to Jeroen Darquennes, who co-led with me the working group of the network on 'new speakers and language policy'. In addition, also in connection with the last stages of my research, the writing of the book was completed when I had already joined the Department of English at Stockholm University. Conversations and discussions held with colleagues at the department have inevitably shaped the direction of my thinking about my object of study. I wish to thank, in that respect, Beyza Björkman, Kathrin Kaufhold, and Maria Kuteeva, for much collegial support. At De Gruyter Mouton, I would like to thank Lara Wysong for her continued assistance in the management of the project, and to Crispin Thurlow and David Britain, series editors of Language and Social Life, for their encouragement and support, especially in the early stages of the writing of this monograph. Finally, I would like this book to humbly pay homage to the memory of Professor Volli Kalm (1953–2017), the late rector of the University of Tartu, who passed away suddenly as the writing of this monograph was being finalized. As will become apparent, Professor Kalm was an invested interlocutor in the public discussion on the internationalization of Estonian higher education, and I can only hope the present monograph does some justice to his contributions to the debate.

Needless to say, it is impossible to complete any ethnographic project by oneself, and this project was no exception. I would like to thank all my informants and research participants who took time out of their busy schedules in order to sit down with me and talk about language-related issues at the university, or who allowed me to sit down with them in their academic English classes and record what was happening during class. Without them, the project and this book would simply have been impossible.

Last but not least, there is the emotional and personal support. This book is dedicated to Anthee, my partner in life and my endless source of inspiration. The fact that the book has actually been driven to an end, closely observing the foreseen schedule, is not a coincidence: Anthee and her coaching me and pushing me to focus on the writing project were essential in the latter stages of it. A big, big thank you to you, Anthee.

Preface

It was early September 2005 when I landed for the first time in my life in Estonia, then an Erasmus student, excited about the adventures and the new experiences that were to come. The country was in the middle of important transformations, barely one year after its accession to the European Union and NATO. One such important transformation pertained to the university sphere; one could say that, perhaps unknowingly, I was actually part of the changing scene of Estonian universities, together with the rest of exchange students that, from the year before onwards, would start arriving in the country in greater and greater numbers. Back then, though, there were still just a few of us. In fact, if my memory serves me well, I was the third Catalan student embarking on an exchange program at Tallinn University, after two of my compatriots had taken part in the program just the year before me. Some of us came to study languages, including Russian language and literature; for us, the university was in a relatively comfortable position to accommodate our needs and provide the number of exchange credits that we were looking for. For others, though, for those who were studying other kinds of degrees back home, the picture did not look quite as simple. Taking content courses in English was back then a complicated matter. Indeed, the university seemed to resort to offering its exchange students as many credit points as possible for courses on Estonian language and culture. For some of us, those like me and my friend and flatmate Ben, this was not a particularly bad arrangement, interested as we were in learning the language beyond something more than just a simple conversational level. Ben and I went to great lengths to study the language, investing part of our time and money to spend one and a half extra hours per week with a private language tutor just for the two of us. Together with the other four and a half hours a week we took of Estonian at the university, we did succeed in our enterprise reasonably well. Even so, one of my most vivid memories of my time at the university, especially during the first few weeks, is how challenging it felt to find out what was on the lunch menu every day at the cafeteria. Luckily for Ben, myself, and our course-mates, the waitress was kind and patient enough to try to explain what was on offer, despite her limited skills in English. This did prove useful in quickly learning some basic food vocabulary in Estonian, and altogether it was a rich experience.

After that first year, I managed to find a way to remain in Estonia for an extended period of time, until 2009, mainly teaching Catalan at the University of Tartu. I then moved away, and returned in 2012 to work on the postdoctoral project that this book is based on. Upon my return, I had the feeling that the country had experienced even more drastic transformations, including within the university sphere. In 2012, the offer of content courses in English, while still limited, was certainly wider than it had been a few years earlier, certainly not just restricted to Estonian language and culture. Reading off from the material landscape, even the Estonian-only menu boards at the university cafeterias had been reshaped to now include bilingual signs, in Estonian and English. So, the language guessing games were gone for current exchange students, who were now a much larger group than we had been just seven or eight years before. The university cafeteria example is just an anecdotal one, of course, but it serves to illustrate the point that the whole institutional machinery of Estonian higher education was undergoing important transformations, with changes that were reflected in the sociolinguistic configuration of universities, both physically and conceptually. In fact, much like I now have the feeling that, in 2005, I was perhaps part of the unfolding changes in Estonian higher education, part of the increasing number of Erasmus students arriving in the country, now too, in 2012, one could say my arrival was a symptom of the ongoing changes within the Estonian university system. In addition to starting my postdoctoral project, I was going to teach in English in the intercultural communication track within the BA and MA programs in Communication Management at Tallinn University.

This book, then, offers an account of the changing language-ideological landscape of Estonian universities over the past few years. It is not, by any means, an exhaustive account and in fact, as will become apparent, there are a number of pieces and elements that are missing and that could have enriched the analysis in very relevant ways. The book is, certainly, my interpretation of what I think are the key themes and the central discourses surrounding the field of Estonian higher education and the associated language policy issues connected to its internationalization agenda. In scholarly terms, I am interested both in the sociolinguistics of higher education and in Estonia as a rich site for sociolinguistic research. I am aware that readers might not equally share both interests at the same time and to same extent, but I can only hope that the account presented here will prove relevant and attractive to readers with different trajectories and expectations, whether their focus is on the sociolinguistics of higher education generally or on the sociolinguistics of Estonia more particularly.

Contents

Acknowledgements —— VII

Preface —— XI

List of Figures —— XVI

List of Tables —— XVII

1		**Sociolinguistic and language policy perspectives on the internationalization of higher education. An introduction to the volume** —— **1**
1.1		Introduction —— 1
1.2		Language policy as social action: The discursive turn in language policy research —— 9
1.3		The Estonian context —— 14
1.4		Overview of the book —— 19
2		**Language policy responses to the internationalization of higher education: Conceptual and material discourses in place** —— **23**
2.1		Introduction: English-taught programs in European higher education —— 23
2.2		Multilevel policies in Finland, Estonia, Latvia, and the EU: Conceptual discourses in place —— 25
2.2.1		Finland —— 29
2.2.2		Estonia —— 31
2.2.3		Latvia —— 33
2.2.4		EU —— 35
2.2.5		Multilevel policies and conceptual discourses in higher education. Final remarks —— 38
2.3		Higher education institutions in the Baltic context: Material discourses in place —— 41
2.3.1		Physical and online spaces of higher education in Baltic universities —— 45
2.4		Conclusion —— 55
3		**University language regimes in Estonia: (Re)creating discourses in place** —— **57**
3.1		Introduction —— 57

3.2	Internationalization trends in Estonia and at the University of Tartu —— 58	
3.2.1	State and institutional (language) policy documents in Estonia —— 62	
3.2.2	The members of the institution – debating A2020 —— 69	
3.2.3	A public debate: The Pärnu Leadership Conference media discussion —— 72	
3.2.4	Celebrating twenty years of English-language studies at the University of Tartu —— 75	
3.2.5	Discursive orientations towards language in higher education: Nationalizing and globalizing tensions —— 80	
3.3	Conclusion —— 83	

4 Language ideologies and the internationalization of higher education in Estonia —— 85
4.1 Introduction —— 85
4.2 Transnational scholars' views on the internationalization of Estonian higher education —— 86
4.3 Local scholars' views on the internationalization of Estonian higher education —— 100
4.4 Conclusion —— 112

5 A historical perspective on language choice and attitudes in academia and higher education in Estonia —— 114
5.1 Introduction —— 114
5.2 A historical perspective on languages in academia and higher education in Estonia —— 114
5.3 Ideas about academic English among teachers and researchers in Tartu —— 129
5.4 Students' language attitudes towards English-medium instruction: A view from Tallinn —— 136
5.4.1 Focus-group discussions and in-depth interviews —— 142
5.5 Conclusion —— 147

6 Language policy discourses at the internationalizing university: Estonian perspectives on a global issue —— 149
6.1 Introduction —— 149
6.2 Applying discourse approaches to language policy —— 149

6.3 Language ideology and language policy: The case of Estonian higher education —— **153**
6.4 The sociolinguistics of higher education: A look from Estonia and a note for further research —— **158**

Bibliography —— **162**

Index —— **172**

List of Figures

Figure 2.1	Bilingual Estonian–English signs at the UT historical campus	49
Figure 2.2	Multilingual signs at the VU historical campus	49
Figure 2.3	Bilingual Estonian–Russian signs at UT	50
Figure 2.4	Monolingual signs in the state language at UT, UL, and VU, respectively	51
Figure 2.5	Monolingual signs in English at UT	51
Figure 2.6	Multilingual signs at UL	52
Figure 3.1	English-medium degree programs, University of Tartu 1993–2013	61
Figure 4.1	Erasmus mobility in Estonia – Incoming students and staff 2000–2014	86
Figure 4.2	List of tongue-twisters in Estonian included in the Welcome Guide (p. 10)	98
Figure 4.3	Glossary of terms included in the Welcome Guide (p. 38)	99
Figure 5.1	Theses defended at the Faculty of Theology 1802–1918	117
Figure 5.2	Theses defended at the Faculty of Law 1802–1918	117
Figure 5.3	Theses defended at the Faculty of History and Philology 1802–1918	118
Figure 5.4	Theses defended at the Faculty of Physics and Mathematics 1802–1918	118
Figure 5.5	Candidate of Science theses (*kandidat nauk*) at Tartu State University, 1946–1959	120
Figure 5.6	Candidate of Science theses (*kandidat nauk*) defended at the Estonian Academy of Sciences, 1954–1972	120
Figure 5.7	Habilitation theses (*doktor nauk*) defended at the Estonian Academy of Sciences	121
Figure 5.8	Publications of members of the Estonian Academy of Sciences – Astronomy and Physics	122
Figure 5.9	Publications of members of the Estonian Academy of Sciences – Informatics and Engineering	122
Figure 5.10	Publications of members of the Estonian Academy of Sciences – Biology, Geology, and Chemistry	123
Figure 5.11	Publications of members of the Estonian Academy of Science – Humanities and Social Sciences	123
Figure 5.12	PhD theses defended at UT, 1991–2017: Faculty of Science and Technology	124
Figure 5.13	PhD theses defended at UT, 1991–2017: Faculty of Medicine	125
Figure 5.14	PhD theses defended at UT, 1991–2017: Faculty of Social Sciences	125
Figure 5.15	PhD theses defended at UT, 1991–2017: Faculty of Humanities	126
Figure 5.16	Students' reported percentage of EMI courses	139

List of Tables

Table 2.1	Higher education (language) policy documents in Finland, Estonia, Latvia, and the EU —— 28
Table 2.2	Overview of comparisons of Finland, Estonia, Latvia, and the EU —— 37
Table 2.3	Composition of the population in the Baltic states according to ethnic affiliation (%) —— 43
Table 2.4	Mono-, bi-, and multilingual signs at the University of Tartu (N=869) —— 47
Table 2.5	Mono-, bi-, and multilingual signs at the University of Latvia (N=609) —— 47
Table 2.6	Mono-, bi-, and multilingual signs at Vilnius University (N=762) —— 47
Table 2.7	Languages and items available per language on the UT, UL, and VU websites —— 53
Table 3.1	Number of instances of each theme in the analyzed documents —— 65
Table 3.2	Overview of comments submitted by UT members in preparation for A2020 —— 69
Table 4.1	Features of the transnational scholars interviewed at UT —— 87
Table 4.2	Features of the transnational scholars interviewed at UT (focus-group discussion) —— 88
Table 4.3	Features of the local scholars interviewed at UT —— 100
Table 5.1	Historical chronology of the University of Tartu —— 116
Table 5.2	Students' attitudes towards EMI courses and English as an academic language —— 140
Table 5.3	Students' perceptions of the degree of difficulty/easiness in studying their subjects in English as compared to their L1 —— 141

1 Sociolinguistic and language policy perspectives on the internationalization of higher education. An introduction to the volume

Public university brands are probably the most undermonetised asset in the American economy. The way we have gone about it has been very limiting, and that is move students across borders, bring them to the United States, bring them to the source of knowledge, and that has given them a great cultural experience, and it is something which we should continue to do. But to go to scale, to offer the quality of an American brand to the whole world is now possible and inevitable.

(Randy Best, founder and chairman of Academic Partnerships)

The difficult questions regarding the future of Estonian higher education are tied to the competitiveness of Estonian higher education compared to English higher education. Master's and doctoral studies are inevitably becoming more English-based. Students will increasingly go abroad for niche disciplines [...] We are often unaware of the price of preserving Estonian-language higher education.

(Volli Kalm, late rector of the University of Tartu)

1.1 Introduction

This book is about the sociolinguistic dimension of what has come to be known as the internationalization of higher education, a process in which many universities around the world find themselves engaged in. Over the past few years, the terms 'internationalization' and 'higher education' have been paired together more and more frequently, with universities immersed in processes of trying to become internationally competitive, more attractive to larger numbers of foreign students at both graduate and undergraduate levels, aspiring to climb higher up in the popularized university rankings, and struggling to find additional sources of funding. Very often, discussions around the internationalization of higher education have revolved around the economic dimension of it, as the quote above from Randy Best illustrates. In this brief but revealing statement, Best synthesizes one common view of why American public universities need to become more international. In the short clip,[1] he continues to explain what becoming

---

1 https://www.youtube.com/watch?v=4k8ehqG3Bko (accessed 5 October 2017).

https://doi.org/10.1515/9781501505898-001

more international might mean for American public universities: "a substantial and sustainable and growing revenue stream", something that will "change the flavour of universities". Even though it can be argued that universities have historically been international by nature (Altbach 2004), it is precisely the economic angle that distinguishes present-day internationalization trends at universities more distinctively (Holborow 2015). Needless to say, this kind of discourse is not exclusive to American universities, but has now permeated higher education systems around the world (Qiang 2003).

Indeed, in recent years the role of universities has evolved into something of a double bind. In late-capitalist contexts, universities seem to have entered a 'post-national' stage (Bull 2004, in Mortensen and Haberland 2012), increasingly seen as "international businesses competing as economic agents in an open and lucrative market" (Hultgren et al. 2014: 7). In that position, universities are supposed to strive for excellence and competitiveness in the global sphere. At the same time, however, higher education institutions are also perceived as essentially national entities "integral to the national culture and with certain obligations towards the nation state", institutions largely funded by taxpayers' money and on which members of the public can place legitimate demands (Hultgren et al. 2014: 7). This situation puts universities in a somewhat contradictory position, especially those from outside anglophone contexts (e.g. Cots et al. 2012; Vila and Bretxa 2015). Such a contradictory position is well illustrated by the second quotation included in the opening above by Volli Kalm, the rector of the University of Tartu from 2012 until 2017. At a conference in Pärnu in 2012, shortly after the start of his appointment, Kalm expressed doubts in connection to the sustainability of a higher education system functioning in Estonian. In view of the increased use of English in Estonian universities, Rector Kalm publicly wondered how feasible it would be to continue offering higher education in Estonian, something that provoked a somewhat heated media debate in the subsequent weeks (a debate we shall analyze in more depth in Chapter 3). In a similar way to companies and other for-profit organizations, universities seem to be hard-pressed, caught between global discourses of profit and national discourses of pride, a commodification of authenticity (Heller and Duchêne 2012; Heller 2011; Thurlow and Aiello 2007). Quite clearly, language plays a central role in shaping the discourses of the internationalization of universities. Not only do there exist contradictory discourses around universities (seen as international enterprises and national institutions at the same time), but each of these discourses is also presented as linked (inevitably) to different languages: English, on the one hand, and a local (national) language, on the other. This is despite the fact that language per se is not always explicitly recognized as a problematic issue in discussions of higher education internationalization (Saarinen 2012). It is either invisibilized (i.e. intentionally not referred to as a problem) or simply erased (not recognized as a potential problematic issue).

Certainly, then, universities today are increasingly prone to ambiguities and paradoxes produced by and through language, and as such, they are rich sites for exploring contemporary sociolinguistic tensions (Haberland and Mortensen 2012; Cots et al. 2014). However, the awareness that higher education and scientific research constitute a domain of potential political and sociolinguistic struggle is not something new (cf. Ammon 2001), although it is true that in recent years, the double-sided nature of universities (as both flagship national institutions and business-like international companies) has become more of a tangible reality for all kinds of groups and collectives, from students to teachers and researchers (local and international), to administrative staff, high-tier university officials and lawmakers (Hultgren et al. 2014). The difficult position of present-day universities can be summarized briefly thus: on the one hand, they need to remain locally relevant and nationally leading institutions (a function that sometimes they are required to fulfil by law, as in the case of the University of Tartu that will be analyzed in this volume); on the other hand, they are also required to pursue an international agenda, competing side by side with other universities from abroad at a global scale for key resources such as international students and staff, which can subsequently generate increased revenue for their institution. This kind of paradox leads to an apparent sociolinguistic conundrum. Briefly put, the national scale and its concomitant nationalizing discourses will likely require universities to work in a local or national language, whereas the global scale and its associated globalizing discourses will often be linked to a global language, nowadays almost exclusively English.

The above discussion should not make us lose sight of the fact, mentioned already, that the for-profit nature of universities is not at all something entirely new, neither is it something that universities based in anglophone countries are exempt from, quite the contrary, even if such paradoxes might be more relevant for universities in non-anglophone contexts (cf. Vila and Bretxa 2015). In fact, Fairclough (1993) already remarked on the marketisation strategies employed by public universities in the UK and their accompanying discursive practices: "Institutions of higher education come increasingly to operate (under government pressure) as if they were ordinary businesses competing to sell their products to consumers" (Fairclough 1993: 143). More recently, and in the aftermath of the 2008 financial crisis, discourses of austerity and entrepreneurship have been more and more prominent. Holborow (2015) presents empirical materials from the context of Irish universities to illustrate how the discourse of the university as an enterprise has come about and gained force in recent times, and how this discourse in turn is mobilized in order to hide the economic reality of reduced funding and budgetary cuts (Holborow 2015: 98); in the US, Rhoades and Slaughter (2004: 37) find that higher education institutions (particularly those more vulnerable to losing state support) "now develop, market, and sell a wide range of products commercially in the private sector as a basic source of income", a range of products that touch upon universities' core activities, that is, educational, research, and service functions (see also Slaughter and Rhoades 2004 for a lengthier analysis of the notion of 'academic capitalism').

Still, returning to the point of higher education institutions in non-anglophone contexts, it seems indeed that the current economic context has linked internationalization demands with an increased presence of the English language, whose growing importance, in turn, is key in shaping particular policies and practices of university members. Documenting the situation of Korean universities, Piller and Cho (2013) find that neo-liberalism and its associated set of ideological tenets acts as an implicit language policy baseline, channelled through the English language, in particular through the introduction of English-medium instruction (EMI) as a means to affect university rankings and for institutions in the country to climb up those rankings in a cost-effective manner at the expense of the social suffering and stress of university members (Piller and Cho 2013: 25). Even though this may be a specific feature of the Korean context (Hultgren 2014 does not find a determining correlation between the use of English by Danish universities and their position in university rankings), what seems more and more established is that internationalization and its accompanying globalizing discourse are inextricably linked to the English language.

In line with Piller and Cho (2013), Fabricius et al. (2017) are critical of this fact, and they insightfully point out several contradictions that the taken-for-granted connection between English and internationalization might provoke. Importantly, if internationalization is to entail university models designed to bring together students and staff from a range of different cultural and linguistic backgrounds, and in so doing foster successful intercultural milieux, then language policies should be designed in a way that can lead to this kind of objective. However, at present, and with the Danish context in mind, Fabricius et al. emphasize that language policies "act as structural obstructions to this kind of internationalization, because they institutionalize a non-integrated perspective on the local and the transnational" (2017: 592). The kind of language policy that the authors have in mind is what has come to be popularly known in the Nordic countries as "parallel language use", a concept whose "practical applications remain unclear, and to this day it largely remains an unoperationalized political slogan" (Kuteeva 2014: 333). Indeed, discussions on what internationalization really is and how institutions are to apply it in practical terms have not been thoroughly conducted, beyond the idea of the potential economic gains and benefits, as Fabricius et al. (2017: 590) have pointed out as well.

So, language policy, understood in its more classical sense as a means of affecting the status, use, and acquisition of a certain language(s) in a given context, is in this case also a resource that universities, public officials, and administrators have in order to craft specific agendas associated with internationalization goals, while at the same time responding to nationalizing anxieties. This type of double-edged sword associated with language practice and ideology is not exclusive to universities, but is observed in other areas as well, including the tourism industry (e.g. Heller et al. 2014). Even if not in the exact same terms, both the sociolinguistics of tourism and the sociolinguistics of higher education highlight how mobility (of people and resources) disrupts previously conceived markets and creates new ones, emphasising the key role that language plays in this process. Whether it is globally-minded airlines producing visual meanings that are highly localized while appealing to an international market (Thurlow and Aiello 2007), or whether it is locally produced souvenirs in a Sámi village that can circulate globally with some degree of ease (Pietikäinen and Kelly-Holmes 2011), so too universities in increasingly more geographical areas seem to be experiencing similar processes of discursive tension.

In fact, Gallego-Balsà and Cots (2016), from the perspective of universities in Catalonia, propose precisely a reading of the internationalization of Catalan universities in the framework of the discourse of tourism, showing how universities mobilize a discourse of the commodification of the Catalan language as a way to increase the value of a particular university and to potentially attract more foreign students; for their part, however, international students may not be fully receptive to this strategy, and tensions associated with their position as tourists versus sojourners may arise throughout their exchange period. Initially, universities will tend to portray students as tourists, a position that would not require them to engage extensively with the local language and culture; on the contrary, the local language and culture might be initially presented to students as a means of performing cultural authenticity (Gallego-Balsà and Cots 2016: 18), tasting local foods, enjoying tours to tourist attractions, and so on. However, quickly following a short period of adaptation, universities might expect students to adopt a sojourner position, one that demands a more intense engagement with the local language and culture (particularly for teaching and learning purposes, and for academically related activities, where stakes are certainly higher). These two positions may generate feelings of discomfort and tension in the students and their teachers. While these tensions can be smoothed out with the passage of time, as Gallego-Balsà's (2014) ethnographic study illustrates, Gallego-Balsà and Cots (2016) reveal important sociolinguistic tensions and anxieties associated with and emanating from language; these issues, however, are unlikely to be exclusive to the Catalan context, and can be observed in increasingly more universities across Europe and elsewhere.

In a context full of contradictions, then, universities are particularly rich sites for exploring tensions and ambiguities around language policy matters from a language ideological perspective, which is the angle that will be developed in this book. As already noted, the growing trend towards becoming more international and the rising demands placed on universities to function as global companies is normally accompanied by an increased use of English. In parallel, the view of universities as quintessentially state institutions emphasizes a discourse of protection and promotion of the national language, which is to be academically cultivated and developed. How are these two discourses encompassed? How is English constructed both as a friend and a foe in the context of a growing number of universities at present? How is the protectionist discourse presented? What is at stake for the relevant stakeholders in these debates? How do they position themselves vis-à-vis the two broad discourses mentioned above? These are some of the broad questions that guide the exploration and inquiry presented in this book.

Even though these questions are, of course, not entirely new, in recent years, there has been a surge of publications on the topic of the role of the internationalization of higher education from a sociolinguistic perspective, including a number of journal thematic issues and edited collections (e.g. Cots et al. 2014; Doiz et al. 2013; Haberland and Mortensen 2012; Hultgren et al. 2014; Liddicoat 2016; Saarinen 2017; Vila and Bretxa 2015). However, the interest in sociolinguistic issues in the context of higher education and scientific research goes back at least several years further, namely to the turn of the century, in the context of a then-solidifying body of work on issues of language and globalisation (e.g. de Swaan 2001; Maurais and Morris 2003). Ammon's (2001) collection of essays is one of a kind, for its inclusion of perspectives from a variety of countries with different degrees of presence of English in their respective academic traditions. The angle taken in that volume is already visible in its title: *The dominance of English as a language of science*. In short, already at the turn of the century, before the Bologna process had reached full speed in many European countries, there was a realisation among some linguists that academia – that is, higher education – deserved to be analyzed sociolinguistically. In particular, it was the role of English that seemed to be most worthy of analysis, a role which for some was problematic in different ways, notably in the advantage that native speakers of English enjoy vis-à-vis non-native speakers. Ammon takes this advantage as "self-evident" (2001: vii). Whether or not this is the case is a question that has gained more attention since the early 2000s and the debate has evolved in different directions, including analyzes of English as a lingua franca in academic settings that show how speakers in micro-level situations work to achieve communicative effectiveness (e.g. Björkman 2013). While the analysis presented in the current volume does not engage specifically with this particular question (i.e. the advantage/disadvantage of native/non-native speakers of English), the point to take from this discussion is that it is the English language and its role in academia and higher education that have fuelled the debate in recent years in sociolinguistics and applied linguistics circles.

The presence of English in higher education today tends to be seen in binary, opposed, terms: as a language that facilitates global contacts and international collaboration, "international English", or as a language that poses a serious challenge (or even a threat) to the presence of other national/local languages in academia, "global English" (Bull 2012). The former tends to be associated with the globalizing, entrepreneurial discourse described above, and the latter with the nationalizing, protectionist discourse. The coexistence of English with national languages in higher education is certainly of a complex nature, and some authors have attempted to capture such complexity from the point of view of language policy analysis with discourse-analytical tools (e.g. Dafouz and Smit 2016; Hult and Källkvist 2016). The conceptual framework provided by Dafouz and Smit (2016) takes as its point of departure a set of theoretical standpoints from recent sociolinguistic research, particularly considering language as a set of resources with different indexical values that are shaped and affected by globalisation flows (Blommaert 2010). Inspired by a language-ecological perspective (Haugen 1972), Dafouz and Smit (2016) suggest that language policy-making is of a multi-sited nature, which eludes simple dichotomies of macro and micro levels. Their framework highlights the fact that different languages fulfil different functions within the domain of higher education, from teaching to conducting and communicating research, to the languages used in more informal situations.

In an earlier and well-considered model along the same lines, Hamel (2008) outlines three different spheres with a number of different activities and sub-activities within these spheres in the context of higher education. Depending on the context, each of these activities can be carried out more frequently in one language or another. In Hamel's model, the three main spheres in higher education consist of (a) scientific research or knowledge production, (b) diffusion and communication or knowledge consumption, and (c) scientific training. Haberland (2014) adds a fourth dimension to Hamel's model: administration, which is now increasingly seen as another key part of universities' language ecologies in the context of higher education internationalization (Llurda et al. 2014; Siiner 2016). All these different spheres are context-dependent and they may entail different linguistic practices and ideologies (Haberland 2014: 253–254).

When conducting research, for example, everyday conversations in laboratories and departments, discussing project developments and so on, can be certainly done in languages other than English in non-anglophone universities (e.g. Bretxa et al. 2016). Scientific communication (diffusion) and knowledge consumption is increasingly dominated by English, a trend that is discipline-specific (Kuteeva and Airey 2014: 539) and more recent in the humanities than in the natural sciences. In terms of scientific training (i.e. education), again there is field-specific variation, as well as degree-level variability, with more English being used in the hard sciences and in graduate courses than in the humanities and in undergraduate degrees (Wächter and Maiworm 2014).

So, there are a variety of situations and contexts, and the variability in the languages used in them is contingent on a great number of factors. Going back to the broad questions previously outlined, this makes it all the more challenging for language policy-makers and university officials to manage the tensions and ambiguities resulting from current trends in the context of the internationalization of higher education. From a policy-making perspective, the approach taken in a number of non-anglophone university settings where English has made important inroads has been informed by a parallel-linguistic framework, especially in the Nordic countries (Linn 2010); as seen above, such a framework has been problematized and criticized by scholars because of its unclear practical applicability (e.g. Kuteeva 2014) and because of the contradictions that it enhances, with the potential of creating more language barriers than it dissolves (e.g. Fabricius et al. 2017). Still, many universities in Sweden, prompted by the passing of the Language Act in 2009, have written their own language policies, taking parallel language use as their point of departure. In an analysis of several such documents, Björkman (2014: 353) has found that "these language policy documents have as their (explicit) point of departure the worry that Swedish is losing ground with the widespread use of English". In addition, Hult and Källkvist (2016) show how the notion of 'parallel language use' is discursively constructed with different meanings, and depending on the scale on which it is projected (local, national, global) it can be interpreted with different meanings: more Swedish (and potentially other languages), or more English.

These and related issues are explored in detail in the current monograph, issues of language policy-making in connection to the internationalization of higher education. The angle taken is grounded in ethnographic and discursive approaches to the study of language policy, investigating how discourses circulate across the language policy cycle (Canagarajah 2006; Johnson 2013b) and how different actors position themselves vis-à-vis prevailing discourses about language in a given context. The role of language ideology is particularly relevant in exploring how spaces of language policy creation, implementation, adaptation, and/or resistance are constructed, and to dig deeper into understanding what resources are at stake in each context and for whom. These are the overarching goals that I set myself to explore in the current volume. In the next section I develop these theoretical underpinnings further and continue afterwards with a description of the site from which the empirical materials for my investigation comes: Estonian higher education. I conclude this introductory chapter with a brief overview of the organization of the book and of the content of the different chapters that constitute it.

1.2 Language policy as social action: The discursive turn in language policy research

With the above discussion in mind, it should be apparent that universities today are characterized by phenomena taking place at multiple levels and at different scales that affect their sociolinguistic configuration and can be observed in day-to-day, micro-level interactions that in turn feed into larger, more global layers of reality (Ljosland 2015; Saarinen 2017). In this book, the main objective is to portray and to analyze the set of contradictions and paradoxes, the tensions, ambiguities, and anxieties experienced by universities and their primary members, key stakeholders, in the context of the internationalization of Estonian higher education. These tensions and ambiguities are both implicitly and explicitly played out in and through language; that is, *in* language as an object of contention (Should any language(s) be named official or be given priority by the institution? What should be the language(s) of instruction at different levels of the curriculum? etc.) and *through* language as the vehicle of discursive struggle (What is meant by the internationalization of higher education? How are different positions by key stakeholders discursively constructed in this process? etc.).

In the book, the chosen framework to conceptually examine the object of study will be heavily informed by discourse-analytical tools, specifically by nexus analysis (Scollon and Scollon 2004) and its application to the study of language policy issues (Hult 2010; 2015). In this framework, policy is seen as social action, as something that "happens while you're busy doing something else" (Saarinen 2017: 553). Inspired by the work of Scollon and Scollon (2004) and taking the argument further, one could posit that language policy is best conceived as a verb, as something that people do in situated social settings. The central idea, then, is to focus on people and their actions, and then interpretively read from those situated actions the series of discourses of different scope and breadth that intersect them and shape those policy actions in particular ways. In short, the goal is to capture the patchwork of 'layered simultaneities' (Blommaert 2005) that co-occur in a given social setting connected to a language policy action, and to try to present them in a logical and coherent way, in a manner that helps understand the different discursive positions taken by the social actors involved in that context, and the stakes that are at play as well. Hult (2015: 222) emphasizes that such a discourse-analytical approach to the study of language policy differs from ethnography and discourse analysis more generally in that the focus here is on policy actions, that is, on actions taken by policy stakeholders (broadly defined: from policy- and lawmakers to individual speakers) in connection to de jure or de facto language policies. This is an important point that we should keep in mind in order to understand the nature of nexus analysis studies of language policy situations.

Such a discourse-analytical approach to the study of language policy is in line with recent developments in the field such as the ethnography of language policy, on which I elaborate further below. Whether inspired by nexus analysis or grounded in the framework of the ethnography of language policy, in recent years authors have emphasized the need to trace how different discourses about language circulate across the language policy cycle, and in this circulation, how these discourses are shaped and (re)created, and how they are appropriated or contested by the different social actors involved in the process (Johnson 2009). Briefly put, this has been the approach and the spirit taken in this volume in order to find out about the different discourses circulating the field of Estonian higher education and its internationalization trends, and in this way to try to discover the different positions and interests that are at stake for the different actors in this field.

Recently, then, a 'new wave' of language policy and planning (LPP) studies has emerged under ethnographic and discursive analytic approaches (e.g. Blommaert et al. 2009; Hult 2010; Johnson 2013a; McCarty 2011; Johnson and Ricento 2013; Halonen et al. 2015; Barakos and Unger 2016). The ethnography of language policy (Johnson 2009), sometimes known as 'new language policy studies', understand "language policy not as a disembodied text but as situated sociocultural processes" (McCarty 2011: 335). This new thrust in language policy studies builds on more established theories in LPP that see the implicit dimension of language policy-making (e.g. Shohamy 2006) and that regard language policy as an emerging feature at the intersection of speakers' language beliefs and attitudes, language planning strategies, and actual language practice and behaviour (Spolsky 2004; 2009). Needless to say, the roots of these more traditional language policy theories can be traced back even further in the discussions on language planning (e.g. Cooper 1989; Kaplan and Baldauf 1997), which already emphasized the complex dimensions of language policy decisions, with a multitude of social agents playing key roles in the development of both explicit and implicit arrangements about language use, status, and acquisition.

The key point of the new strand of LPP scholarship, which has more decidedly incorporated ethnography and discourse analysis into the LPP research agenda, is the idea that language policy is a multilayered phenomenon (Halonen et al. 2015), something that social actors constantly recreate through their complex discursive interaction (Barakos and Unger 2016: 1). This increasingly solidified line of research in language policy scholarship draws, at least implicitly, on two main ideas: the idea of language governmentality (Pennycook 2006) and the idea of policy as discourse (Ball 1993), understood as "a complexity of human interactions, negotiations and productions mediated by interrelationships in contested sites of competing ideologies, discourses and powers" (Hélot and Ó Laorie 2011: xv, in Brown et al. 2017: 5). Indeed, Pennycook (2006) usefully illustrates how a framework grounded in postmodernism can be applied in language policy studies, taking language governmentality as a point of departure. Understood as how language use, thought, and action are regulated, and how the decisions about languages in a range of different institutional settings are managed (Pennycook 2006: 65; see also Blommaert et al. 2009), language governmentality provides a basis for a discursively oriented view on language policy analysis. A postmodern take on language policy also emphasizes the need to deconstruct preconceived ontologies such as language, policy, mother tongue, and so on, thus questioning taken-for-granted concepts, and also recognising the role of the researcher and their positionality within the analysis.

By and large, the main thrust for the motivation of current multilayered frameworks of language policy analyzes is the perennial need to bridge the gap between the traditionally conceived dichotomy of the macro versus the micro levels of society, a gap that has consistently been seen as problematic in language policy research (Ricento and Hornberger 1996). Typically in ethnographic and discourse approaches to language policy, the goal is to find connections between critical discourse studies (traditionally focused on macro-level structures of power domination), interactional studies (typically aimed at highlighting the agency of individuals and their capacity to provide a counterweight to macro domination), and studies of micro practices and attitudes towards languages 'on the ground'. Thus a methodological and theoretical framework is proposed in order to investigate "the agents, contexts, and processes across the multiple layers of language policy creation, interpretation, and appropriation" (Johnson 2013a: 44). One of the strengths of the ethnography of language policy (ELP) is the capacity to show how ideological spaces for the protection, promotion, and development of (minority) languages can be either fostered or hindered, and under what societal conditions that happens (Hornberger and Johnson 2007).

From the point of view of theory, ELP has the merit of emphasising the power of ideological constructs in a given language policy setting. By carefully tracing how discourses circulate from layer to layer in the LPP cycle (Canagarajah 2006), researchers can demonstrate the ways in which broader-level discourses on language policies are created and how they are then interpreted and appropriated or resisted locally in situated encounters. When grounding their work in (long-term) ethnographic fieldwork, scholars are able to detect such circulation of discourses and to examine them critically. In addition to that, ELP has the capacity not only to critically describe and analyze a particular language policy setting, but also to empower practitioners 'on the ground' in order to bring about meaningful social change and possibly redress power inequalities (Johnson 2009; McCarty 2015). As Pérez-Milans (2018) notes, ELP has the merit of having placed ethnography clearly in the agenda of language policy research, a call that in LPP scholarship goes back at least to the 1990s (cf. Ricento and Hornberger 1996; Ricento 2000).

Still, ELP is not without its limitations, and following Pérez-Milans (2018), there are at least four aspects that ethnographic studies of language policy can and should consider in more detail. According to that author, the items that need further inquiry include the reproducing of dichotomies (agency/structure), a focus on explicit commentaries on policy documents, an event-based entry point to data collection/analysis, and a tendency towards presenting participants in rather superficial ways. Pérez-Milans calls for more trajectory-based ethnographic analyzes of language policy in action, investigating social actors' self-reflexive strategies and socialisation trajectories. In a similar way, Saarinen (2017: 557) emphasizes that "while dichotomies such as macro–micro, discourses–practices, structures–agents, ideals–realities are necessary in making policy issues visible and understandable, they also tend to (over-)simplify the multi-sited issues they represent". A key challenge, Saarinen continues, is to overcome, theoretically and methodologically, these dichotomies and reflect, in the analysis, on these concepts (cf. Halonen et al. 2015).

Indeed, the management of this multiplicity of layers of human activity constitutes a formidable difficulty. To overcome the demanding task of tracing the connection between different scales and ordered realities, more and more language policy scholars are turning to ethnographic and discourse approaches for their analyzes, as already noted. In particular, nexus analysis (Scollon and Scollon 2004) has been usefully appropriated in recent language policy studies in multiple contexts, from minority language situations (e.g. Lane 2010) to the production of university policy documents, as noted already in the previous section (e.g. Källkvist and Hult 2016). Given its well-delineated structure, in combination with a certain degree of flexibility that allows the researcher enough room for analytical manoeuvring, nexus analysis seems well situated to tackle the difficulties of tracing the circulation and intersection of the different discourses by multiple agents in the context of a given language policy cycle. Thus, nexus analysis is the overarching theoretical and methodological framework that I shall follow in the current volume; I shall do so in a slightly eclectic manner, namely without a strict order of finding out about the different components of the nexus analysis and with an emphasis on 'discourses in place' and on 'historical bodies' rather than on 'interaction orders'. However, in the following chapters there are sufficient materials and analyzes to look at the intersection between the different discourse types so as to obtain a precise view of language policy discourse in the context of Estonian higher education. Before that, let us first elaborate a bit further on the theoretical framework of nexus analysis and see how it can be applied to language policy studies. In what follows, I draw on Hult (2015) and his elaborate explanation of the use of nexus analysis in language policy research.

As a theoretical and methodological framework, nexus analysis tries to connect three well-established research traditions in sociolinguistics and discourse studies: the ethnography of communication, interactional sociolinguistics, and critical discourse analysis. The goal of nexus analysis is to trace a map of how discourses from multiple layers intersect in a social phenomenon, the "nexus of practice" (Hult 2015: 218). Any nexus of practice consists of different social actions that take place in particular physical spaces and in specific temporal scales. In the context of language educational policy, for example, relevant social actions would include state legislature, professional teacher training programs, schools, teacher-student interaction in classrooms, and so on. Social action is the entry point for analysis, and the goal is to trace how discourses mediate a given social action, placing it within the nexus of practice as a whole (Hult 2015: 218).

In line with the ethnographic, interactional, and critical traditions on which nexus analysis draws, Scollon and Scollon (2004) propose three types of discourses to investigate: the historical body, the interactional order, and the discourses in place. The *historical body* refers to the embodied life experience of the individuals that participate in a given social action; as such, it underlies the phenomenological nature of human experience and highlights human agency. The *interactional order* relates to the actual observed behaviour among the individuals involved in a given social action, looking at the different modes and modalities with which interactants co-construct meaning. *Discourses in place* has to do with the available beliefs and ideologies present in the setting at the moment when the social action takes place, both conceptually (ideational space) and materially (physical space). Nexus analysis, in this way, follows from Gee's (1999: 13) conceptualisation of big 'D' Discourse, of how language relates to "ways of thinking, acting, interacting, valuing, feeling, believing, and using symbols, tools, and objects in the right places and at the right times" (see Hult 2015: 218, see also Gee 2011);

this has a clear Foucauldian resonance, connecting thus language policy studies to issues of governmentality and language regimentation, which underlie current debates in language policy theory, as mentioned before.

The broad questions that this book sets out to explore have already been presented earlier in this chapter. However, it is necessary to narrow them down further, and here too nexus analysis offers a useful framework to work with, focusing on both the big picture of language policy-making at large, while remaining attentive to speakers' everyday practices and interactions. Considering different scales and actors involved in a range of social actions, nexus analysis can help us distinguish the different layers of reality and bridge connections between them. Thus, one can examine the position of different languages in policy documents and the relationship that is established between them in such documents, followed by an inquiry of how such documents are perceived and experienced by individual speakers in daily, routine interactions. One can elicit explicit perceptions about such policy documents in interviews, combined with observations of real-life interactions that can provide more implicit and indirect understandings of the policies in place. In the chapters that make up the current volume, I develop an analysis that is structured precisely around this point of departure. I begin with an investigation of language policy documents in the context of higher education in different states in Europe, followed by a more in-depth examination of language policy documents in Estonian higher education and reactions to them by different key and primary stakeholders. I also provide and analyze direct narratives of speakers on the ground about their lived experiences of language in Estonian higher education, in the current trend towards internationalization goals, coupled with more indirect observations of classroom interaction and attitudinal surveys. The analysis also presents a historical account of the evolution of different language regimes in Estonian higher education, with the goal of tackling the temporal dimension of discourse formation in this field. A more detailed, chapter-by-chapter overview of the volume at hand is provided below, but before we turn to that, I shall elaborate more on the selection of the research site, Estonia, and the particular intricacies of this context and its higher education system.

1.3 The Estonian context

At the time of regaining its independence in 1991, Estonia's demographic composition was significantly different from what it had been half a century earlier. In 1945, Estonians comprised 97.3% of the population, whereas in 1990 their proportion had been reduced to 61.7%. By and large, that change had been brought about by the important influx of working-class migrants that arrived during the Soviet period and settled in the growing industrial areas of the country, particularly the capital region of Tallinn and in Ida-Viru county, bordering Russia in the northeast. At present, in terms of self-declared ethnicity, the 2011 census indicates that of the approximately 1.3 million inhabitants of Estonia, 68.7% are Estonian, 24.8% are Russian, and 1.7% are Ukrainian (Statistics Estonia, n.d.). The demographic transformation of the country was accompanied by a series of policies during the Soviet period that produced significant inequalities between speakers of different languages (Skerrett 2010): at the same time that the functional and symbolic status of Estonian decreased, that of Russian increased rapidly (Rannut 2008), which produced an asymmetric bilingualism between speakers of different first languages (L1s). The profound sociopolitical changes in 1991 led to significant modifications in the legal and educational spheres devised in order to reverse this situation. From the language political point of view, the 1992 Constitution establishes Estonian as the single official language of the country and declares all languages other than Estonian to be foreign languages. Language legislation in the country is strictly regulated: there are over 400 laws and lower legal and normative acts (Rannut 2004: 7). The Language Act (Government of the Republic of Estonia 1995, renewed 2011) features most prominently among such laws, as it regulates linguistically all the state apparatus, including the language of public administration, language rights, and requirements of proficiency in Estonian. It also regulates the state supervisory authority, the Language Inspectorate, which (among other competencies) has the right to check on the use and knowledge of Estonian and foreign languages, including among employees of private companies operating in the service industry.

Officially, Estonia recognizes only one single state language; however, Estonia has been a multilingual country for a significant part of its contemporary history (Verschik 2005) and it continues to be one, something that has brought some sociolinguists in the country to point out that Estonia is monolingual from above and multilingual from below (e.g. Zabrodskaja 2014). In that respect, the situation of extensive contact between at least three languages is not new for the country. In the early twentieth century, Estonian, Russian, and German were societal languages, considered indeed as three local languages (Marten 2017), although they occupied different niches and fulfilled different roles. At present, one could argue that German has gradually lost importance against English, but multilingualism is not restricted to Estonian–Russian–English. In Tallinn in particular, there is a strong effect of tourism, and Finnish especially can frequently be heard in the city center and in the commercial malls (Verschik 2012).

In line with other northern European countries, the foreign language skills of Estonia's inhabitants are well above the European average. In fact, it is one of the few countries in the European Union (EU) whose average citizen has practical skills in at least two foreign languages, fulfilling the long-term EU objective of "mother tongue plus two" (European Commission 2012b: 13). However, the latest Eurobarometer survey (European Commission 2012a) also shows some noticeable shifts, and these data do not offer a completely positive reading for Estonia. The percentage of the population that claims to have mastered at least one foreign language is at present 87% (a decline of two points since 2008), at least two foreign languages is 52% (a decline of six points), at least three languages is 22% (a decline of two points), and none is 13% (a gain of two points). Overall, the changes are not particularly important, apart from the six-point reduction in the population claiming to be able to speak at least two foreign languages. Lauristin et al. (2011) offer more quantitative data regarding the self-estimated skills in Estonian, English, and Russian of the country's population by age group, contrasting it with the data obtained in 2002. In brief, the younger age groups of L1 Estonian-speakers are becoming more bilingual in Estonian and English, whereas the older groups still maintain their Estonian–Russian bilingualism. In contrast, younger L1 Russian speakers' Estonian skills are increasing, compared to the older age groups, who tend to be more monolingual in Russian. The English language skills of the L1 Russian-speaking community are also clearly on the rise, particularly among the younger groups. The different directions that bilingualism is taking among the country's different language groups had already started to take shape in the 1990s; in fact, in 1992, just one year after independence, Russian had already been replaced by English as the most commonly taught first foreign language in Estonian secondary schools (Estonian Ministry of Education and Research 2013: 13). This trend seems to have solidified and as a consequence, encounters between L1 Estonian and L1 Russian speakers in the country take place increasingly in English, especially among younger age groups (Soler-Carbonell 2014b), something that may well have consequences for the country's integration policies in the long run.

With this legal, demographic, and linguistic background, the Estonian language ecology differs from that of the neighbouring Nordic countries in an important aspect: its Soviet past and its post-Soviet present. Certainly, Russian continues to be a key element in the Estonian sociolinguistic context; so far, the vast majority of language policy scholarship from and on Estonia has been dedicated to analysing relevant issues in connection to the Russian-speaking minority in the country, issues of integration and language education in schools (e.g. Skerrett 2014), as well as the role of Russian-language media and its consumption by the Russian-speaking part of the population (Vihalemm and Hogan-Brun 2013). Indeed, the sociolinguistic study of the Russian-speaking population in Estonia from a variety of angles continues to be one of the central issues for

Estonian sociolinguistics. Even if Russian is considered a foreign language in Estonia, in many professions in Tallinn (particularly in the service industry) it is considered an important asset, a "commodified" resource that can be exploited to make a profit (Heller and Duchêne 2012). In that regard, some authors have argued that there is a revival of interest in the Russian language among younger Estonians (Siiner and Vihalemm 2011: 135–137), although, arguably, it is still too incipient to be significantly observable (at least considering the data provided by Lauristin et al. 2011).

That said, it is also increasingly clear that the Estonian language ecology transcends its Soviet/post-Soviet temporal dimension, as well as its East–West spatial border dimension. Siiner et al. (2017) convincingly explain that up to this point, most language policy research in Estonia has been framed around these two dimensions; at present, however, an insistence on these parameters might have the consequence of missing important questions that sociolinguists and language policy scholars should be asking. Given current conditions of globalisation, mobility, and transnationalism, an increasing number of settings in Estonia need to be explored from a new perspective, taking into account the temporal and spatial dimensions mentioned above, but transcending and going beyond them, as Siiner et al. (2017) suggest. Higher education and its changing environment is a paradigmatic example of this, and that is precisely the setting to be further investigated in the current volume.

At present, as we have already noted and as we will see in more detail in the forthcoming chapters, debates within and about Estonian higher education are not infrequently formulated around language issues. Typically, one of the key challenges that is mentioned is how to find and maintain a balance between Estonian and other, foreign languages, chiefly English. However, historically, Estonian higher education has had to face other important difficulties, in particular the reforms that began with the restoration of independence during the early 1990s and continued throughout the beginning of the twenty-first century (Saar and Mõttus 2013). Important among those reforms was the rise of private higher education institutions, in particular the Estonian Institute of Humanities (EHI, Eesti Humanitaarinstituut), established in 1988 as a counterweight to the ideologically biased higher education institutions of that time, especially in the field of the humanities. EHI was created on the initiative of the Estonian Writers' Association, and it was a pioneer institution in Eastern Europe. The creation of such an institute was a catalyst for the establishment of several other private institutions. Moreover, it led to other important developments in the public sphere as well, such as the fact that in 1989 the Council of Tartu State University decided to withdraw the word 'State' from its official name, and declared the university to be academically autonomous (Tomusk 2001: 204). Since 1992, several important reforms have followed, from which can be highlighted the merger of institutions among themselves (private and/or public) and the renaming of higher education establishments. Taking EHI again as a prototypical example, it has been a part of Tallinn University since 2005 and operates as an autonomous department within the university. In 2005, Tallinn University underwent several structural reforms, illustrated by the changing of its name: from Tallinn Pedagogical University (1992–2005) to Tallinn University. Similar changes occurred in the majority of other universities and colleges (public and private) in the country (see Tomusk 2001 and Vaht et al. 2010). Currently, taking into account the size of its population (slightly below 1.3 million), Estonia has a wide variety of higher education institutions, with six public universities and three private ones, ten state institutions of professional higher education and twelve private institutions in this category, and two state vocational education institutions offering professional higher education. With the exception of EuroAcademy (Euroacadeemia), all public and private universities offer degrees up to doctoral level (Vaht et al. 2010: 49–94).

Until recently, work on the sociolinguistics of higher education has placed the focus on areas such as Scandinavia and the Nordic countries, analysing the linguistic practices and ideologies at universities in these countries (e.g. Hultgren et al. 2014). This focus on the Nordic countries has arisen because of the important and consistently growing presence of English in recent years in the field of higher education in those countries, particularly in Denmark, Sweden, and Finland (Wächter and Maiworm 2014). This is, of course, related to the fact that English has made important inroads at societal level in general in those countries, becoming what Hult (2012) has termed a "transcultural language"; so, one cannot read the growth of the presence of English in higher education contexts in Nordic countries without looking at the linguistic ecologies of these countries more broadly (cf. Haberland and Preisler 2015). The Baltic states, in general, and Estonia, in particular, have been less explored (but see, e.g., Bulajeva and Hogan-Brun 2014; Klaas-Lang and Metslang 2015; Soler-Carbonell et al. 2017), even though here too the use of English as a language of instruction has increased especially significantly in the past few years (Klaas-Lang and Metslang 2015), with a 516% increase between the years 2007 and 2014 in Estonian higher education (Wächter and Maiworm 2014: 48). In addition, recent surveys are consistently showing that knowledge of the English language in the general population is very high (Education First 2015), which demonstrates that English has been making important inroads into society at large in Estonia too, following the Scandinavian path (cf. Hult 2012). Therefore, issues of language policy and planning at universities in countries like Estonia merit more attention, considering the steep increase in knowledge of English and the role of English on the one hand, and the continued presence of unresolved societal concerns about language, on the other (Rannut 2008; Verschik 2005; Klaas-Lang and Metslang 2015).

Examining issues of language policy-making in Estonian higher education is, of course, the topic of this entire monograph, so at this point I shall just briefly introduce some key ideas. First of all, by and large, Estonian continues to be the most commonly used language in Estonian higher education across all its different spheres (Klaas-Lang and Metslang 2015), with English being used (mostly in parallel with Estonian) in upper-level degrees (Master's and PhD studies). In fact, Estonian is used as the language of instruction in universities in an even higher proportion today than 25 years ago: in 1993, students in Estonian-medium higher education programs comprised 82% of the total, in 2014 they represented 92%. Conversely, students in Russian-medium higher education comprised 17% of the total in 1993; today, they represent only 3%. As for students studying in English-taught programs, they have gone from 1% in 1993 to 5% in 2014 (Klaas-Lang and Metslang 2015: 168). Importantly, in 2013, a higher education reform was put in place by the government by which full-time students enrolled in Estonian-language curricula would not have to pay for their education. In compensation for that, the reform stipulated that foreign-language-taught curricula would require a fee from students. Clearly, this has opened the door for the development of English-taught programs and for higher education institutions in the country to compete in order to attract more fee-paying foreign students. The introduction of English-taught programs is not entirely new, but since 2005, shortly after the country's accession to the EU, it has progressively been on the rise (Vihman and Tensing 2014). As just stated, on the one hand this is economically motivated, but on the other, it is also spurred by the progressive demographic decrease of home-student populations, something that is not exclusive to Estonia, but also observed in neighbouring Latvia, with a similar (although by no means identical) situation (Kibbermann 2017). Clearly, then, language matters intertwine with issues of a social, demographic, and economic nature. These and related issues will be treated more extensively in the forthcoming chapters. In what follows, I present an overview of the organization of the volume and a more detailed, chapter-by-chapter, description of what will be presented in each part.

1.4 Overview of the book

Chapter 2 provides a wider view of the internationalization of higher education across different contexts in Europe, with the aim of situating Estonian universities in terms of these broader and more general contexts. In the chapter, I adopt a comparative outlook to see how internationalization developments are similar or different in Estonian universities compared to other nearby contexts: the other Baltic states (Latvia and Lithuania); the Nordic countries (with a focus on Finland); and the European context. The chapter draws on data from different sources and types in order to map the different (conceptual and material) discourses in place (e.g. pictures of the linguistic landscape of different universities, and the analysis of policy documents). The results of this overview show that, broadly speaking, each context is sensitive to its own specific historical and sociological developments, which account for its particular sociolinguistic and language policy formation both at the university and the state levels; so, any intent to generalize possible claims has to be read from that point of departure. Interestingly, however, it appears that state-level policy documents orient themselves towards state (national) ideologies, placing emphasis on the need to protect and promote the national language, whereas university policy documents sometimes deviate from that stance, adopting a more pragmatic approach to the language question and arguing more explicitly in favour of adopting the English language for instrumental purposes. However, turning to the more specific context of Baltic universities, their material linguistic landscape, seems to align institutions more with nationalizing discourses, with a dominant presence of national languages. This first glimpse, then, shows the complex intricacies of circulating discourses at higher education institutions and it highlights the need to dig deeper into trying to disentangle these discourses.

In chapter 3, I begin the narrowing effort and present an analysis of how university language regimes in Estonia are constructed and reinforced by different agents in the field. First and foremost, I consider a set of official policy documents written in order to regulate the internationalization of the Estonian higher education system (university and state language strategy documents, state language policies, etc.). In addition to that, I consider other sources of data: a set of comments produced by university members during the drafting and discussion of a university policy document; a public debate and the comments made by members of the university community in public media during a number of weeks in autumn 2012; a speech offered by the then Minister of Education and Research of Estonia, Prof. Jaak Aaviksoo, at a conference held in October 2013 to commemorate twenty years of studies in English at the University of Tartu; and an intervention at that same conference by Prof. Rector Volli Kalm at a round-table discussion. These materials, in combination with the analysis of the policy documents, allow me to trace the creation and development of institutional discourses on language policy issues within the country's internationalizing higher education system. Chapter 3, then, combines an analysis of (conceptual) discourses in place with historical bodies, and it begins to offer a perspective of how language ideological constructs are at play in the analyzed setting.

Chapter 4 turns to speakers' ideas and beliefs about languages at a higher education institution. The chapter presents the results of fieldwork conducted at Tartu University in 2013–2014 when a series of in-depth interviews and focus-group discussions were conducted in order to find out more about individual speakers' reactions to and knowledge of the university's formal language policy, and to examine their lived experiences of language policy issues at the university. The chapter focuses on the discourse of two main groups: Estonian scholars, on the one hand, and transnational academics, on the other. The starting point for all interviews was a conversation on the speakers' linguistic trajectories, their language biographies, followed by a discussion of how they perceived their sociolinguistic environment, what languages they used on a daily basis, in what ways they saw the university adapting sociolinguistically to its current challenges, and so on. The analysis of their opinions reveals important results and nuances in connection to how speakers feel about different languages in a context of growing trends of internationalization. There were, for example, important disciplinary differences, in that scholars from technical disciplines felt language issues of a political nature were not crucial to them; historians, on the other hand, argued they would need more linguistic support not just in Estonian, but also in Russian and German, two key languages in their field in particular. Finally, transnational scholars presented a set of different opinions, ranging from a lack of motivation to learn Estonian to actually acquiring the language after some years in the country; they also expressed frustration at times towards the institution for not keeping to their promised English-taught PhD programs, which for some informants seemed to generate more resistance towards Estonian. Chapter 4 delves deeper into issues of the historical body and shows how language ideologies can be shaped by speakers' linguistic trajectories. It also includes a component of the interaction order, indicating how different stances towards sociolinguistic issues can emerge.

Chapter 5 takes a slightly different perspective, in that it first aims to show the historical evolution of language choice and the different language regimes in place in academia and higher education in Estonia, combined with a present-day view of students' attitudes towards language and towards learning in English. Firstly, then, the chapter explores how, at different points in time, different languages have been used with varying degrees of intensity in the Estonian higher education sphere. Data on the languages in which PhD theses were written from the nineteenth century until the present are offered to illustrate that in the nineteenth century, German was the dominant language of science, with a minor turn to Russian after 1895. The convoluted first decades of the twentieth century brought a decrease in scientific activity in the country, which was only reversed during the Soviet period. At that time and in Soviet Estonia, Estonian dominated as the language of scientific output, with Russian used to some degree as well, particularly during the 1970s. The 1990s show a drastic shift towards producing PhD theses in English. To illustrate the more recent period and this shift to English as the preferred language for publishing research, I collected data from a number of members of the Estonian Academy of Science about their scientific production. The turn to English, I argue, is the result of changing language regimes impacting the Estonian higher education and scientific fields directly. The chapter then turns to the present, with an analysis of how those who find themselves immersed in the context of Estonian universities feel about adapting to their changing environment. In order to do that, the chapter first considers another key component of fieldwork, conducted in autumn 2013: classroom observations of two courses on English for academic purposes. The observations in those courses and the transcriptions of the recordings of them reveal additional important nuances about language, in particular about English, shown by members of the university community, namely researchers and teachers. Following that, the focus shifts slightly, with an analysis of students' reported attitudes towards learning in and using English for academic purposes more frequently and intensively in their courses. A survey was delivered to, and a series of focus-group discussions were conducted with, students at another major university in the country: Tallinn University. This was done in order to counterbalance the weight placed on Tartu University through the majority of the study, and to explore relevant issues in other higher education settings. The discussion in chapter 5 ties in once again with issues connected to the historical body and conceptual discourses in place, and in this chapter in particular there is an explicit effort to historicize current language ideologies in the context of higher education.

Chapter 6, the concluding chapter, contains the discussion of the material presented in the previous chapters in light of the theoretical framework developed above. In this chapter, I reconsider the main issues presented in the book and offer an interpretive reading of them. I attempt to highlight what makes the Estonian higher education system unique from the perspective of current debates around issues of a sociolinguistic and language policy nature at universities. At the same time, I also offer an appraisal of the methodology used in the book and the theoretical import of nexus analysis and ethnographic approaches to the study of language policy. These reflections are geared towards emphasising the role and the significance of language ideologies in any language policy setting. The chapter concludes with a brief overview of some of the issues that the volume was not able to tackle with enough depth and breadth, issues that can be further explored in subsequent empirical studies.

2 Language policy responses to the internationalization of higher education: Conceptual and material discourses in place

2.1 Introduction: English-taught programs in European higher education

Higher education and internationalization have in recent years been increasingly related, and as noted in the introductory chapter, the English language has been assumed to be the language for universities' internationalizing goals. In their 2014 report, Wächter and Maiworm summarize the development trends in connection to the presence of English in European higher education, with a particular focus on English-taught programs (ETPs) at Master's level. Their conclusions are concise and straightforward, showing a steady trend of growth in ETPs since their first survey in 2002: in that year, 821 institutions reported offering 725 ETPs; in 2007, 2,218 institutions reported 2,389 ETPs; and in 2014, 2,637 institutions reported offering 8,089 ETPs (Wächter and Maiworm 2014: 15–16). It is particularly interesting to note that looking beyond the Nordic countries, where levels of ETPs have consistently been high (together with the Netherlands), a 'new' leading geographic area in providing ETPs in 2014 has emerged: the Baltic region. In the 2007 report, there were 18 ETPs in total identified in Estonia; by 2014, that number had grown to 59. (It might be useful to note that in Wächter and Maiworm's terminology, ETPs are Master's programs that are taught fully through the medium of English.)

There are several reasons why institutions decide to introduce English-taught programs, including a willingness to remove language barriers to incorporate more international students and to foster 'brain gain' (Wächter and Maiwrom 2014: 18). In other cases, ETPs are introduced by universities in order to offer local students the possibility of conducting their studies in English and having the experience of studying in a foreign language, which for many students in low-income countries might be the only possibility of obtaining a sense of a study-abroad experience; the latter can also work towards a policy of preventing 'brain drain', retaining highly qualified local students and scholars, and helping them build international careers. Finally, there is an economic and demographic motive for the introduction of ETPs, fuelled by the need for universities to cover a lack of newly enrolled (local) students by attracting international (sometimes full-fee-paying) students. This motivation seems to be the strongest factor in the

Baltic area (Kibbermann 2017); in Latvia, for example, local students represent 94% of those enrolled in ETPs (Wächter and Maiworm 2014: 21).

Importantly, even if the number of ETPs has continued to grow in recent years, the proportion of students enrolled in these kinds of programs is still low or very low, with the exception of the Nordic countries (particularly Finland, with 12.4% of its student population enrolled in ETPs). In the Baltic countries, the average is 1.7% of total students enrolled in ETPs, with 1.5% in Estonia and Lithuania, and 2.2% in Latvia (Wächter and Maiworm 2014: 40). This is despite the quite significant growth in total numbers of ETPs identified from 2007 to 2014 (from 56 to 345), representing a 516% increase in the area. Proportionally, in 2007 only 1.7% of the total number of programs were offered in English, while in 2014 this percentage had grown to 10.3%; in 2007, 25% of institutions in the Baltics offered ETPs, whereas in 2014, it was 38.7% of them (Wächter and Maiworm 2014: 48–49). The relatively low number of students enrolled in ETPs across the Baltics might be explained by the relative youth of these programs in the area (33% of them have been introduced only since 2011, according to Wächter and Maiworm 2014: 19), but also because of what was mentioned in the paragraph above: the fact that these programs aim at recruiting local students, rather than international ones, places them in competition with other programs run in the local language, which might be more established and enjoy a more stable flow of student intake. The point is that it is also crucial to see ETPs and their numbers in perspective, without unnecessarily inflating their impact and significance (Haberland 2014), which might be particularly the case in areas such as the Baltic countries.

In terms of language matters, Wächter and Maiworm's report notes that institutional coordinators and program directors do not find students' proficiency in English to be problematic; they do highlight, however, that the different levels of command of the language by the students can be challenging, particularly when it comes to classroom management. In addition to that, many report an unmet expectation that foreign students will master the domestic language, which is something that, according to Wächter and Maiworm (2014: 22), has been reported consistently since 2002. This means that, when thinking about language support measures, institutions have tended to focus more on finding ways to support the learning of the local language rather than English. However, in this respect the Baltic region looks slightly different: since ETPs are more geared towards recruiting local students, English language support has been a priority of many institutions in the region (Wächter and Maiworm 2014: 23). Inevitably, then, this begs the question of how institutions adapt themselves to this changing environment, in particular what language policy initiatives emerge, and what goals do these policy strategies aim to fulfil. This chapter will explore this question in more detail from two broad perspectives: from the point of view of the initiatives reflected in a series of documents at different levels and in different countries, which will allow us to have a sense of the policy and the political context from which higher education institutions operate, and from the angle of the physical and online spaces in three universities in the Baltic states, which will complement the policy analysis with the perspective of the material discourses in place.

2.2 Multilevel policies in Finland, Estonia, Latvia, and the EU: Conceptual discourses in place

The management of language issues connected to the internationalization of higher education has increasingly become a topic of a complex nature, where language ideological premises have become entangled with political and economic conceptualisations of the nature of universities (Coleman 2006; Haberland and Mortensen 2012; Hultgren et al. 2014; Woodfield 2010). In particular, the growing use of English for teaching and research publication purposes has drawn the attention of many stakeholders, voicing worries in connection with the fact that local (national) languages might be losing ground in state-funded universities (cf. Philipson 2015). This seems to be a particularly prescient debate in the Nordic countries (cf. Hultgren et al. 2014), recalling earlier, more vivid debates, about the sustainability of their respective languages in tertiary education (Salö 2014). This might not be all that surprising given that English enjoys a stable presence in these countries outside academia (for an overview of the case of Sweden, see Hult 2012). In Finland, higher education internationalization policies were already promoted in the 1980s (Nokkala 2007; Saarinen 2014), which indicates the long-term engagement of thinking about what it means for universities to become more international.

In the present climate, and in their key role within the "knowledge society", universities tend to be increasingly seen as assets that states can make use of for economic profit (Saarinen 2012). In that respect, debates about language can be linked to other, strictly non-linguistic, issues. Importantly, as introduced in the previous chapter, the presence of English in higher education today tends to be seen in binary terms: as a language that facilitates global contacts and international collaboration, "international English", or as a language that poses a serious challenge (or for some, a threat) to the presence of other national/local languages in academia, "global English" (Bull 2012). Oftentimes, different agents can show different kinds of alignments with one type of idea of English; Hultgren (2014) shows that in the case of Denmark, state institutions are perhaps more inclined to the idea of "global English", thus emphasising the need to protect and promote the national language, while universities align themselves more with "international English" as a means to promote the international dimension of their institution. It is, therefore, important to understand how English is conceptualized in policy documents, and what its relationship to national languages is expected to be. This can give us a first sense of the conceptual discourses in place (Hult 2015) that are prevalent in today's European higher education arena.

The main purpose in this part of the chapter is to provide an analysis of several key higher education policy documents on the institutional and state level in Finland, Estonia, and Latvia, in order to see how the language question at higher education is handled in these three neighbouring countries, exploring in this way one specific component of nexus analysis: conceptual/ideational discourses in place (Hult 2015: 224). Three cases are chosen for detailed analysis: Finland, Estonia, and Latvia. These countries are geographically close and relatively small non-anglophone states that share historical, cultural, and political links. Finland has commonly been looked at in the Nordic context, and Estonia and Latvia in the Baltic comparison; slightly altering this traditional division might provide new insights. Additionally, Estonia and Latvia often compare themselves with and position themselves among the Nordic countries; this is particularly true of Estonia. Whereas Finland has been at the forefront of internationalization for a while now, the recent growth in English-medium teaching has been particularly rapid in the Baltic countries. When taking into account the share of universities in each country that offer programs in English and the share of total student enrolment in them, the Nordic countries as well as the Baltic countries stand out in Europe (Lam and Wächter 2014: 17).

The analysis will also take into consideration one EU higher education policy document, in an attempt to map the different discursive constructions around the language question by a variety of relevant stakeholders in the field, complementing in this way the multilevel analysis that will be presented, with policy investigation of state, national, and supranational orders. The goal is to consider the fact that language policy and language policy-making is a multilayered process, taking place at different levels (e.g. Halonen et al. 2015). The analysis highlights the interconnectedness and circularity of language policy-making by tracing the recurring themes that appear in the documents produced by these different institutions, highlighting commonalities and differences. This approach makes visible the apparent frictions and potential contradictions between different policy sectors and levels, highlighting this particular nature of policy-making: rather than approaching (language) policy as a linear continuum, we acknowledge the temporally and spatially fluid nature of policy (Halonen et al. 2015).

The supra-state level is represented by the European Commission document *European higher education in the world* (2013), which contributes to the objectives of the Europe 2020 strategy from the point of view of internationalization of higher education. State-level document data, on the other hand, consist of documents on higher education and internationalization strategies. As non-binding documents, but rather strategically steering ones, these papers are all the more relevant to the present analysis, since they are likely to contain more politically oriented views on the issues to be discussed. The Finnish state-level documents are (1) the *Internationalization strategy for higher education 2009–2015* (2009; henceforth *Internationalization strategy*), which was drafted just prior to the renewal of the Universities Act (2009) and (2) the *Development plan for education and research 2011–2016* (2011; henceforth *Development plan*), which is a steering document accepted every four years by the Council of State for the next five-year period. Estonian documentation consists of (1) the *Estonian higher education internationalization strategy 2006-2015* (henceforth *Internationalization strategy*) and (2) the *Estonian lifelong learning strategy 2020* (henceforth *Lifelong learning strategy*). Both are authored by the Ministry of Education and Research. Unlike Estonia and Finland, Latvia has not yet drafted a strategy for the internationalization of its higher education system. The Latvian state-level data include (1) the *Concept of the development of higher education and higher education institutions for 2013–2020* (henceforth *Concept*) by the Council of Higher Education and (2) the *National development plan of Latvia for 2014–2020* (henceforth NDP) authored by the Cross-Sectoral Coordination Centre and approved by the parliament in 2012. The NDP is the highest national-level medium-term planning document that aims to summarize the state priorities and main areas of action.

Finally, the analysis includes institutional language policies from multidisciplinary universities that have a significant role in the higher education system of the respective countries. The *Language principles of the University of Helsinki: From guidelines to practice* (2014) have their starting point in the particular role of the University of Helsinki as the academic flagship organization of bilingual Finland. The *Language principles of the University of Tartu 2009–2015* (henceforth, *Language principles*) were produced as part of the *University of Tartu strategic plan 2009–2015*. The *Language policy of the University of Latvia* was adopted by the University of Latvia in 2010. Most documents were directly accessible in English, with official translations available at the time of analysis; here, text examples have been drawn from the English versions. Only in the case of the Latvian *Concept of the development of higher education and higher education institutions for 2013–2020* and the *Language policy of the University of Latvia* were no official translations available; here, the equivalent keywords in Latvian were used instead. Table 2.1 summarizes the document metadata.

Table 2.1: Higher education (language) policy documents in Finland, Estonia, Latvia, and the EU.

	Year of publication	Length in number of words
Finland		
Development plan for education and research 2011–2016 (Development plan)	2012	25662
Internationalization strategy for higher education 2009–2015 (Internationalization strategy)	2009	13952
Language principles of the University of Helsinki: From guidelines to practice	2014	n.a.
Estonia		
Estonian higher education internationalization strategy 2006–2015 (Internationalization strategy)	2006	6133
Estonian lifelong learning strategy 2020 (Lifelong learning strategy)	2014	9861
Language principles of the University of Tartu 2009–2015 (Language principles)	2009	898
Latvia		
Concept of the development of higher education and higher education institutions for 2013–2020 (Concept)	2013	30267
National development plan of Latvia for 2014–2020 (NDP)	2014	23432
Latvijas Universitātes valodas politika (Language policy of the University of Latvia)	2010	570
EU		
European higher education in the world	2013	6478

A qualitative content analysis (Mayring 2000) of all the documents was conducted, following a 'directed' approach (Hsieh and Shannon, 2005). In line with Mayring (2000), a deductive analysis of the selected documents was conducted looking for the keywords pertinent to the analytical goals. The specific keywords (or categories, following Mayring 2000) that were deemed relevant for each particular document were references to particular national and other languages: Finnish, Swedish, English, Estonian, Latvian, Russian, (minority) language(s), multilingualism, plurilingualism, and so on. This allowed for the attainment of the relevant themes in connection to language(s) for each document, and to focus on what is explicitly discussed in connection to them. At the same time, an inductive analysis of the documents was implemented (Mayring 2000), particularly when looking for absences of the above categories, and thus when issues connected to the research questions were formulated in an indirect manner.

2.2.1 Finland

In the documents analyzed, the Finnish language – one of the two national languages – is seldom mentioned. Of the 47 explicit mentions of 'language' in the *Development plan*, Finnish is not mentioned once. Swedish, by contrast, is mentioned in the *Development plan*; mostly in a steady discourse of protecting its status in the formally bilingual system: 'The status of the Swedish language will be guaranteed in integration education.'

In the *Internationalization strategy*, Finnish (the language) is mentioned twice. The first mention is, in fact, an illustrative quote, made to stress the importance of Finnish for foreign staff. It seems that credibility is sought for the strategic goals by presenting 'eyewitness accounts': 'I do not feel there is a place for me as a teacher or a professor at the university unless I speak Finnish very well.' (from a university researcher). The second reference to Finnish is in connection with Swedish; incidentally, this is the only mention of Swedish in the *Internationalization strategy*. This echoes the constitutional coinage of the two equal national languages (see Pöyhönen and Saarinen, 2015): 'The monitoring of the program pays particular attention to activities supporting transition to labour markets, study programs aimed at non-Finnish students and the teaching of Finnish and Swedish.' An exceptional example is a quote used to illustrate the internationalization strategy, construing the stress on national languages as 'self-congratulatory': 'We should move away from a self-congratulatory homogenic culture to genuine appreciation and recognition of the importance of internationality, language skills, and multiculturalism.' This quote in effect says the opposite of the Estonian and Latvian documents (see below) with regard to the local languages, framing 'homogenic culture' as something unwanted in Finland.

'Foreign languages' is an interesting coinage in Finnish language education policy. The study of foreign languages (at that time, mostly English, German, and French) in Finnish secondary and tertiary education began to decline in the 1990s, but the term 'foreign languages' remained to refer to languages other than Finnish and Swedish. 'Foreign' gets several mentions in both documents, but as previous work by Saarinen (2012, 2014) shows, in higher education contexts foreign mostly refers to the programs offered for international students, which are in practice conducted in English. 'English', in turn, is only rarely mentioned explicitly in either of the national-level documents. It is mentioned twice in both documents, mainly from the point of view of its dominance over other foreign languages: 'In proportion to the size of our higher education sector, there is an exceptionally large amount of teaching available in English.' (*Internationalization strategy*).

The *Development plan*, however, has a somewhat paradoxical relationship to English. On the one hand, the dominant position of English in the comprehensive and upper secondary school is discussed as a problem: 'In view of this, language learning in the comprehensive and upper secondary schools has been overly focused on the English language' (*Development plan*). On the other hand, as subject teacher training is discussed, it is proposed that while the number of subject teachers should be reduced, English and physical education are exceptions. Thus, it seems that while the dominance of English is construed as potentially (ideologically) problematic, English is simultaneously seen as a practical requirement that needs to be supported politically.

At the institutional level, the situation becomes slightly different. In the *Language principles of the University of Helsinki* from 2014, bi- and multilingualism are seen as a resource and strength to all actors. An equal starting point is the university's stated responsibility for the national languages, Finnish and Swedish. The third starting point introduces English into the language palette by framing it as the lingua franca of international academic cooperation, while at the same time reminding the reader about the value of 'other' languages. The goals of the *Language principles of the University of Helsinki* focus on three main aspects. First, the language sensitivity of university actors needs to be increased, meaning that the use of languages needs to be flexible and sensitive to circumstances, and languages need to be used in a parallel fashion. Second, the position of national languages needs to be secured as languages of teaching and communicating about research. And third, the language policy responds to the challenges of internationalization, and outlines practices for teaching and research in different languages. While English is not mentioned explicitly in the goals, it is obvious from the presentation of the background that it is the first language of internationalization. From the viewpoint of internationalization, then, English is framed as the de facto third language of the university. Teaching is construed as multilingual (Finnish, Swedish, and English), and it is also expected that in many situations these can be used simultaneously. However, while the policy states the university's responsibility for the national languages, only Swedish is explicitly referred to as needing 'securing'.

The three documents form a relatively clear continuum in that Swedish, in particular, but also the 'national languages' are presented as needing 'securing' (though Finnish is not explicitly mentioned in this context). This is in line with the longer historical continuum of construing Swedish in need of support and security (see Pöyhönen and Saarinen, 2015, for a discussion of the 'protection discourse'). The Finnish language, on the other hand, is even more rarely mentioned, implying perhaps that it is the norm that does not need specific protection. It seems that on the political level, Finnish is not perceived to be in an endangered position even where internationalization is concerned. Here, Finland seems to differ from Estonia and Latvia (see below). Finally, the position of English as the academic lingua franca becomes more explicit as we move towards the institutional level. Even at this level, where English becomes explicit, it is framed as a practical question rather than a political one.

2.2.2 Estonia

Both the *Internationalization strategy* and the *Lifelong learning strategy* share one common goal: the protection, promotion, and development of the Estonian language. The *Internationalization strategy*, for instance, states: 'in opening up Estonian higher education and introducing the international dimension into every curriculum, we must ensure the preservation of the Estonian language as the primary language of teaching and research at institutions of higher education.'

The other feature that the two documents share is a lack of explicit references to English, much like we have seen above in the case of Finnish. It is only explicitly referred to in the *Internationalization strategy* three times, and not a single time in the *Lifelong learning strategy*. Instead, the keyword 'foreign language(s)' is much more frequently used in the *Internationalization strategy* (19 times), and it also appears in the *Lifelong learning strategy* (3 times). This would seem to imply that 'internationalization' in Estonia is not equated to English only, but instead a more open attitude towards several foreign languages prevails. However, many times the implied 'foreign language' is just one. This is the case, for instance, when reference is made to the need to develop foreign-language curricula, since there are almost no curricula offered in a foreign language other than English.

Finally, one important difference between the *Internationalization strategy* and the *Lifelong learning strategy* is in connection to the Russian language. In the former document, it is not explicitly mentioned at all, whereas in the latter, it appears four times. When it is mentioned, it is used to refer to the fact that graduates from Russian-medium schools in the country do not have sufficient Estonian language skills to be competitive in the labour market or to continue their education further at universities or higher education institutions. The document mentions that special support should be given to students graduating from these schools and for students who speak a different 'native' language (a category that is also absent from the *Internationalization strategy*).

Turning to the *Language principles of the University of Tartu 2009–2015*, the first observation to be made is that this document, unsurprisingly, is much more clearly geared towards language matters at university. Of relatively short length, the document's goal is to set out the guidelines that should govern the status of the different languages at the University of Tartu. Similarly to the two other documents analyzed above, the *Language principles* seems to concentrate thoroughly on the need to protect, promote, and develop the Estonian language, to prevent a full transition to a different language in any field of knowledge, to develop the necessary specialized terminology in Estonian for all areas, and to give the opportunity to all members of the university whose L1 is not Estonian to learn the language.

Indeed, the keyword 'Estonian' (with reference to the language) appears 25 times in the document, whereas 'English' and 'foreign language(s)' appear 8 times each; and 'Russian' is not mentioned in the document. In effect, the absence of explicit mentions of Russian means that the discourse presented in the *Lifelong learning strategy* in connection to the challenge posed by graduates from Russian-language schools to Estonian universities is not picked up in the *Language principles* document. Interestingly, however, although 'English' and 'foreign language(s)' are mentioned explicitly the same number of times, 'English' appears more times in this shorter document than in the other two documents analyzed above, which are much longer. Indeed, one of the basic standpoints of the *Language principles* states that "Language competence – fluency in the native language, the official language, and various foreign languages – is a key competence necessary for professional success; in the academic world, the English language has become the lingua franca".

Thus, when English is mentioned explicitly, the *Language principles* document refers to it as an important language, which university graduates and employees should know in order to be competitive in the labour market. At the same time, it is sometimes also mentioned in connection to the idea that 'English is not enough', and that multilingualism with English and other languages is an objective to be pursued: "Create the conditions to enable students to study at least one foreign language in addition to English".

Finally, as in the case of the *Internationalization strategy*, 'foreign language(s)' remains here an ambiguous label. Indeed, although it is used in the plural, in many cases its meaning is once again rather singular, such as when talking about the need to 'promote the development of curricula in foreign languages on all levels'. Apart from the relatively reduced number of curricula in, for example, Germanic, Romance, and Slavonic philologies, all other curricula at the University of Tartu in a foreign language are officially English-taught programs.

All in all, although the analysis presented here is centerd on the three documents that were examined, the trends that can be detected are in line with the bulk of (language) policy documents in the country (for a more detailed policy analysis of other documents in Estonian higher education, see Soler-Carbonell 2015). In sum, policies regulating language and education issues in the country, especially regarding the internationalization of higher education, are particularly concerned with the protection, promotion, and development of Estonian. In other respects, the language question does not appear as clearly and explicitly formulated, and indeed, the use of the 'foreign language' label produces more ambiguities rather than clarifying anything.

2.2.3 Latvia

In the *National development plan of Latvia for 2014–2020* (NDP), 'language' is seldom mentioned in the document – only 17 times. 'Latvian' is mentioned 5 times and 'foreign language', 3 times. Foreign languages are not named. Similarly to Estonian policy, Latvian governmental policy also construes the Latvian language as the language in need of state-aided protection, promotion, and development. The NDP views Latvian as 'the fundamental national treasure', and Latvia as 'the only country in the world where the Latvian nation, language and culture can exist and fully develop'. In addition, Latvian is defined as the language that could and should unite society in Latvia. Social integration based on Latvian has been a long-term aim of the state language and integration policy. Although minority language speakers, who constitute about thirty per cent of the total population, have a good command of Latvian (only ten per cent of the inhabitants do not speak any Latvian), both Latvians and minorities often opt for Russian in everyday interethnic communication (Latvian Language Agency, 2016, in press). Thus, the acquisition and use of Latvian should be further promoted in order to provide the basis for social integration, a goal not yet reached, the NDP implies. As a result, the NDP stresses that a 'coordinated system for the acquisition of the Latvian language for children and adults' should be created that would 'encourage the use of Latvian in public' and strengthen 'the position of Latvian in everyday communication'. At the same time, the NDP also claims that the strength of Latvia lies in the knowledge of other languages too. Thus, it stresses that Latvian as well as foreign languages 'are the pillars of the education system', and children should have 'the knowledge of at least one foreign language'.

When it comes to higher education, internationalization is set as a goal to reach. Here too, the NDP points out the value of the Latvian language, which is to remain the main language of instruction in higher education. In addition, other official languages of the EU are encouraged to be used. Interestingly, the previously mentioned 'foreign languages' become 'the official languages of the EU' in higher education, excluding Russian from becoming a potential medium of instruction at tertiary education:

(In 2020) Latvia has internationally competitive colleges and universities employing internationally recognized and qualified academic staff. Higher education has become a widely coveted export service of Latvia. Study programs are provided in accordance with the language policy of Latvia as a national state: primarily in Latvian and in one of the official languages of the European Union.

The *Concept of the development of higher education and higher education institutions for 2013–2020* (2013) has been drawn up to work towards the long-term aim of the Latvian higher education policy that is defined in the same document. The aim is to create a system that would ensure the development of the state, its economy, and higher education (parallel to developments in Europe). Connecting the tertiary education of Latvia to that of Europe raises many language-related questions that remain largely ignored on the 110 pages of this document. Language (Latvian 'valoda' and its derivatives) is rarely mentioned – only 9 times (among which only one mention of Latvian is found, 'latviešu valoda').

The *Concept* discusses the internationalization of higher education thoroughly, arguing that internationalizing Latvian higher education at different levels (including the language of instruction) is crucial for its development. However, the document does not discuss in greater detail the language-related issues of internationalization. The remaining mentions of language ('valoda') have to do with stating that internationalization has to take place according to the official language policy of the state – studies at universities should be carried out mostly in Latvian and partly in other official languages of the EU. The *Concept* stresses that it is important to develop programs in the official languages of the EU, although, at the same time, foreign students' interest towards Latvian language and culture should be stimulated by creating special scholarships. Neither the NDP nor the *Concept* name the official languages of the EU which are encouraged to be used, hinting that all the official languages of the EU are equal in that sense. Although the *Concept* rarely mentions language issues at all, it draws attention to the need to draft a strategy for the internationalization of Latvian higher education.

The state documents do not say in much detail how to find a balance between internationalization and the accompanying influx of English, and the maintaining and developing of Latvian as the language of higher education. In order to deal with questions that rise in everyday practice, the University of Latvia has adopted its own language policy guidelines – the *Language policy of the University of Latvia* (2010) – that focus on connecting national and international interests. In this short document, there are 48 mentions of language (Latvian 'valoda' and its derivatives), 23 mentions of the Latvian language ('latviešu valoda' and its derivatives), 8 mentions of English ('angļu valoda' and its derivatives) and 5 mentions of foreign language ('svešvaloda' and its derivatives). Thus, the main focus of this document is on Latvian; however, in comparison to the previously analyzed state documents, the language policy guidelines of the university explicitly refer to English, and leave the implicit phrase of 'the official languages of the EU' entirely out of its text. The main aim of the document is to search for a balance between the use of Latvian, that is, the official language, and English, whose importance is defined through its status as an internationally acknowledged scientific language.

The aim of the language policy of the University of Latvia is to:

> 1.1. enhance the skills of its academic staff and students in the Latvian language, i.e. the official language, and the English language, i.e. the internationally acknowledged language of scientific communication.

Thus, Latvian is defined as being important because it is the official language of the country, and the University of Latvia as the national university is responsible for its maintenance and development. Whereas the language policy guidelines of the university mostly speak about Latvian as a language which use has to be maintained and guaranteed, English is often put in a light in which its acquisition and use has to be enhanced, expanded, and broadened. Altogether, language skills, especially in English, are depicted as a necessary prerequisite for professional development in today's world, just as in Finland and Estonia.

2.2.4 EU

The EU policy document analyzed here (*European higher education in the world*, European Commission, 2013) is a rather short document (slightly above 6,000 words), and the language question does not appear as particularly prominent in it. 'English' is explicitly mentioned 4 times, 'language(s)' 9 times and 'multilingualism' only once. By contrast, 'higher education' appears 54 times, and 'internationalization' 40 times. The document is clearly about the internationalization of higher education, but language does not seem to play a very significant role for EU policymakers in the context of higher education internationalization. This, however, is nothing new, and it has been observed in other European higher education policy documents, such as the Bologna Declaration (e.g. Phillipson 2015).

The document, however, explicitly acknowledges the relevance of English in the context of the internationalization of higher education, and although it also emphasizes the promotion of multilingualism, defined as a 'European asset', this explicit reference to English is not so frequently found in EU policy discourse

(Nikula et al. 2012). This is a somewhat surprising direct reference to English in the context of an EU policy document:

> On the one hand, proficiency in English is de facto part of any internationalization strategy for learners, teachers and institutions and some Member States have introduced, or are introducing, targeted courses in English (especially at Masters level) as part of their strategy to attract talent which would otherwise not come to Europe. On the other hand, multilingualism is a significant European asset: it is highly valued by international students and should be encouraged in teaching and research throughout the higher education curriculum.

In this document, mobility seems to be an issue of particular concern, and when it comes to 'language', it can be read in two different directions: mobility that is motivated by languages, and languages (or language teaching and learning) that is motivated by mobility. In other words, on the one hand, mobility leads to the acquisition of different skills and competences, including linguistic ones; on the other hand, institutions need to be aware of the importance of catering for good services for mobile students and scholars, including linguistic services too:

> Mobility concerns more than students: staff mobility brings manifold benefits to the institution and individual. It is an instrument for the acquisition of new competences, languages and teaching methods and forges international networks.

> Mobility, and in particular credit mobility, should be used as a strong incentive for improving the quality of European higher education. HEIs [higher education institutions] should develop better services to send and receive international students or researchers, including individual counselling to advise on career paths and to facilitate integration into the city/region/country, with language training where appropriate.

Finally, and as in many of the other country documents analyzed here, the EU policy document contains several vague references to 'language(s)', as seen in the previous two extracts as well as in the following example: 'Integrating an international dimension in curricula highlights the importance of languages.' Which language in particular, for what purposes, and so on, is something that is left unmentioned, and this, as with the 'foreign languages' label, is likely to lead to more ambiguities and uncertainties. The same ambiguity is present in the country cases described above, supporting Harder's (2012) observation of 'soft multilingualism'; that is, language policy where "all languages should be allowed and none prescribed". This contradicts the explicit language policy of the EU where the languages of the member states are supported over others (Nikula et al. 2012). Table 2.2 summarizes the analysis of the languages mentioned, the status of the national language(s) in the documents, and the motivations for mentioning other languages.

Table 2.2: Overview of comparisons of Finland, Estonia, Latvia, and the EU.

	Languages mentioned explicitly	Motivation for national languages	Motivation for other languages
Finland			
Development plan for education and research 2011–2016	Swedish, English	Swedish in need of protection	Dominance of English, but also need for English; "Foreign" as euphemism for English
Internationalization strategy for higher education 2009–2015	Finnish, Swedish, English	Finnish and Swedish as national languages	Dominance of English; "Foreign" as euphemism for English
Language principles of the University of Helsinki: From guidelines to practice	Finnish, Swedish, English	Finnish and Swedish as national languages; Swedish in need of protection	English as academic *lingua franca* Value of "other" languages
Estonia			
Estonian higher education internationalization strategy 2006–2015	Estonian, English	Estonian in need of protection	"Foreign languages" implied as not only English
Estonian lifelong learning strategy 2020	Estonian, Russian	Estonian in need of protection	"Foreign languages" implied as not only English; Russian natives in need of language support
Language principles of the University of Tartu 2009–2015	Estonian, English	Estonian in need of protection	English as *lingua franca*; Value of "foreign languages"
Latvia			
Concept of the development of higher education and higher education institutions for 2013–2020	Latvian	Latvian as language of higher education	Study programs in official languages of the EU needed

(continued)

Table 2.2 (continued)

	Languages mentioned explicitly	Motivation for national languages	Motivation for other languages
National development plan of Latvia for 2014–2020	Latvian	Latvian as official language; Strengthening the use of Latvian	Importance of "foreign languages"; Study programs in official languages of the EU needed
Latvijas Universitātes valodas politika (Language policy of the University of Latvia)	Latvian, English	Latvian as official language	Balance between Latvian and English
EU			
European higher education in the world	English	EU policy of multilingualism	"Additional" European languages promoted with an employment motivation

2.2.5 Multilevel policies and conceptual discourses in higher education. Final remarks

The present analysis, while indicating no particular contradictions between the continuum from supra-state to state to institutional language policies in the national cases, showed differences between the conceptualisations of languages particularly in the state-level analysis, and to a smaller degree on the institutional level. The national-level documents understandably focus on the formal and explicit ideologies of the state, whereas the institutional policies often refer to 'practical' needs, thus showing a different kind of (more implicit) ideological stand where internationalization (represented by English-language study programs) is more prevalent.

One aspect of the analysis focused on the position of the national languages in higher education. In Finland the position of the national languages (i.e. Finnish and Swedish) seems to be more or less the same across the levels, which reflects the strong (hygienic even, see Pöyhönen and Saarinen 2015) position of societal (rather than individual) bilingualism in Finland. The bilingual Finland's state-level documentation refers to Swedish more often than Finnish, discursively constructing the position of Swedish as a minority language more in need of 'protection'. Finnish, in turn, which is spoken as a first language by approximately 90 per cent of the population, is not construed as in need of protection. This puts Finland in a different position from Estonia and Latvia, which have large minority populations and present policies concerned with the 'protection, promotion, and development' of Estonian or strengthening and maintaining the position of Latvian in the country and as an official language of the EU. In line with Bulajeva and Hogan-Brun's (2014) analysis of Lithuanian higher education internationalization policies, we can observe here a clash between the need to reconcile ethnocentric approaches to language-in-education policies in the country (in place since re-independence in the early 1990s) with Eurocentric and global trends (becoming a member of the EU in 2004, joining the Bologna process, etc.). This results in important identity dilemmas: on the one hand, supporting and celebrating multilingualism and multiculturalism, and on the other hand, strengthening and maintaining the position of the country's official language in higher education.

On the state level, English seems to be construed as 'foreign' both in Finland and Estonia, indicating that while it has a strong position in both countries, the relationship is not unproblematic. At times, 'English' is construed as 'dominant' and possibly problematic. The reference to 'foreign' may also indicate a genuine need to support 'other' languages. This is what Harder (2012) calls 'soft' multilingualism: there are no explicit policies on promoting some languages of internationalization over others, which leads to a strengthening of an already strong language, in this case English. 'Multilingualism' becomes a label for anything that's not national or (hegemonic) English (Harder 2012).

Latvia, on the other hand, only very generally mentions the use of the official languages of the EU in the internationalization process, with the main aim being to avoid the influx of Russian in its state-funded higher education market. Russian, although a widespread language in Latvia and spoken by almost everyone, is not once mentioned. It becomes totally invisible, it is construed neither as a threat nor as an opportunity. A similar situation can also be observed in the case of Estonia, where neither the state documents nor the institutional documents explicitly refer to Russian in connection to higher education issues (although the Russian language does appear in state-level documents when it comes to the challenge of preparing the Russian-speaking minority well enough linguistically at the end of their obligatory education). While both countries are still sensitive about their recent historical developments and prefer not to discuss Russian explicitly in (language) policy matters around higher education, it seems that Russian-language programs are being promoted to attract fee-paying Russian students: Russian is prohibited as a language of instruction in state-funded higher education in Latvia (except for Slavic language and culture studies), but private institutions of higher education teach approximately one-quarter of their programs in Russian (Kibbermann 2014).

English, however, becomes more explicit on the institutional level, reflecting the problematic relationship between language 'policy' and language 'practice' (see Björkman 2014). At the University of Helsinki, English is framed as an academic lingua franca, making the University of Helsinki de facto a trilingual university. In Estonia, the 'foreign languages' label still appears in the University of Tartu *Language principles*, but 'English' becomes more explicitly visible, considered as a functional need. In Latvia, the situation is similar on the university level: the language policy of the University of Latvia presents a practical need to deal with language issues, and 'the official languages of the EU' become concretized as 'English and other foreign languages'. English is viewed as an opportunity and never framed as a threat at the institutional level in Latvia, it offers the university a source of prospective students that are very much needed in the light of decreasing number of local students. These results are in line with Hultgren's (2014) analysis of the Danish case, where 'parallel language use' tends to be interpreted as 'more Danish' by state-level institutions, and 'more English' by university policy makers. In other words, university officials seem to be more legitimized to frame the need for more English in practical terms and, in so doing, avoid taking a political stance in connection to the language.

Thus, on the institutional level, Finland, Estonia, and Latvia resemble each other more than on the national level. The universities apparently deal with issues of internationalization relating to practical questions of language choice, whereas on the state level, the issue is more about following national needs and policies. In this, the Latvian state-level ideology differs substantially from Estonia and Finland. Consequently, we can see that different national policies may still lead to similar institutional reactions. The differences on different policy levels also reflect that agents have different agendas. State-level public officials are likely to be more concerned about the political effects which language policy and planning decisions may have when it comes to language-and-identity debates. University officials, on the other hand, are likely to be more concerned about making their institutions more competitive on the international scene (although, as we shall see in the next chapter in more detail, they are by no means immune to language-and-identity debates in the broader society). The consequences of these ideological and discursive tensions are certainly at the core of the tensions and ambiguities felt by stakeholders in the field of higher education. Having such seemingly opposed directions on the language question at university may lead to further struggles in the field, with state officials being more attuned to national discourses about languages (which explains the difference between Finland versus Estonia and Latvia at that level), and university officials more in tune with the internationalizing needs of their institutions and campuses (which explains the similarities between the three).

The EU document, which was drafted as part of the work for the European Union 2020 strategy, is surprisingly explicit in its promotion of English – EU language policies tend to promote 'multilingualism', which often refers to the equal position of the official languages and a special role for the autochthonous languages of the union (Nikula et al. 2012). Thus, it would appear that the EU level feeds into the ideology of the institutional level rather than the national one. The tripartite connection between EU-level, national-level, and institutional-level policies deserves further exploration with a more fully fledged treatment of policy at the EU level than could be developed in this chapter.

In sum, language policy and planning in higher education takes place in the context of a complex interaction between different agents and competing ideologies in the field. Policies (in this case language policies) have different inputs from different policy sectors, and looking at an individual sector gives only part of the picture (see Saarinen 2017 and the articles in the special issue of *Higher Education* on 'language' indexing higher education policy). The state-level documentation reflects national policies with national needs, and links carefully to national ideological debates. The institutions, on the other hand, take their ideological impetus from internationalization as well as from national ideologies, making the institutional level an interesting meeting place of official and unofficial views of policy and practice. Language policies are not linear and hierarchical continua that neatly follow the same logic, but rather they produce different outcomes depending on the actors and interests that surface in different contexts. One of the sites where these interests inevitably surface is in the built environment or the linguistic landscape of universities, where some language may have a more prominent presence than others, and from which we may be able to read potential policy effects. We turn to this issue in the following section.

2.3 Higher education institutions in the Baltic context: Material discourses in place

Sociolinguistic and language policy issues in the Baltic states have increasingly been at the center of scholarly debates in recent decades. Although usually framed in spatio-temporal frameworks (e.g. Eastern European, post-Soviet) (Siiner et al. 2017), the interest in the Baltic region as a fruitful geographical site to explore relevant sociolinguistic questions arises because of several features. Amongst these features, the changing language regimes that have been in place in the region during recent historical periods is one of the central defining characteristics. In the twentieth century alone, six such changes have taken place, starting with the Russification period of Tsarist times at the beginning of the century, to a recovery of full sovereignty and an exclusive official status of the local languages at the end of the century (Hogan-Brun et al. 2007: 470). Between the two poles, different periods of more or less intense domination by authoritarian regimes were experienced. In this context, and for the less familiar reader, it might be useful to present in some more detail the vicissitudes and historical changes in the region, before delving in more detail into the material discourses in place in three universities in the three Baltic states.

The period of Soviet occupation is of central relevance in the sense that it strongly shaped the social and demographic configuration of the Baltic region. During that period, policies were aimed at fostering the spread of the Russian language and promoting asymmetric bilingualism, whereby the Russian-speaking population would be able to function monolingually across the Soviet Union (Rannut 2004). Although Article 36 of the Soviet Constitution provided an official declaration of respect for and promotion of the languages and cultures of other nationalities within the Soviet Union, this was more symbolic rather than having any practical consequences. Certainly, the fact that nationalities with languages other than Russian were able to keep important domains for their languages (e.g. education) helped them resist Russification attempts, although by the end of the Soviet period, even in the more resistant communities such as those in the Baltic, the situation was one of minoritized languages in need of political and legal support (Rannut 2008).

In Estonia and Latvia, the outcome of the Soviet period was particularly felt in demographic terms. The proportion of Estonians and Latvians in the 1920s and 1930s decreased from 92.4% and 73.4% to 61.5% and 52% respectively in 1989. In the case of Lithuania, the decline in percentage of Lithuanians was not as significant (from 84.2% to 79.6%) (Gerner and Hedlund 1993: 74), and in this country, Poles constitute a minority of similar size to Russians. In recent years, the situation has reached a certain stability in terms of the relative weight of the different main groups: titular nationals, Russians (and Poles in Lithuania), and other groups. However, a decline in the percentage of Russians in Latvia and a corresponding increase in Latvians can be observed. Table 2.3 summarizes the composition of the population in the three republics, with data from the last two censuses (2000 and 2011).

Table 2.3: Composition of the population in the Baltic states according to ethnic affiliation (%).

	2000	2011
Estonia		
Estonians	67.9	68.7
Russians	25.6	24.8
Others	6.5	6.5
Latvia		
Latvians	57.7	62.1
Russians	29.6	26.9
Others	12.7	11
Lithuania		
Lithuanians	83.5	84.2
Russians	6.3	5.8
Poles	6.7	6.6
Others	3.5	3.4

Sources: Estonian Census (2000 and 2011), Latvian Census (2000 and 2011), and Lithuanian Census (2000 and 2011).

Legislating around language was seen as an important step in all three Baltic states in order to overturn the asymmetric bilingualism that had been brought about by the Soviet occupation of the region (Rannut 2008). Soon after regaining independence, all three states took decided action in order to put in place official language policies that were aimed at strengthening the status and the position of their respective national languages. Specifically, the three laws that were passed in Lithuania, Latvia, and Estonia, are the following:
– Lithuanian Law on the State Language (Republic of Lithuania, 1995)[1];
– Latvian State Language Law (Republic of Latvia, 1999)[2];
– Estonian Language Act (Republic of Estonia, 1995, renewed 2011).[3]

All three official language laws declare the national (state) language as the official language of the respective republic. Article 2 of the Lithuanian Law on the State Language states that "the Lithuanian language is the state language of the Republic of Lithuania"; "in the Republic of Latvia, the state language shall

---
[1] https://www.uta.edu/cpsees/lithlang.htm. Accessed 01 August 2018.
[2] http://www.minelres.lv/NationalLegislation/Latvia/Latvia_Language_English.htm. Accessed 01 August 2018.
[3] https://www.riigiteataja.ee/en/eli/506112013016/. Accessed 01 August 2018.

be Latvian", declares Article 3 of the Latvian State Language Law; in Estonia, the Language Act enshrines Estonian as the official language of the republic, together with Estonian Sign Language (Article 3 of the Estonian Language Act).

In connection to education matters, which are of more central concern in the current analysis, the Lithuanian Law on the State Language establishes that all citizens in Lithuania have the right to acquire education in the state language at all levels of education, including higher education (Articles 11, 12, and 13). The same is stated in connection to Latvian by the Latvian State Language Law (Article 14). In Estonia, language and education matters are covered by the Education Act (passed in 1992); the law states that all public institutions shall teach the Estonian language, including those in which instruction is in a different language. When it comes to Estonian higher education, language use is regulated by the Universities Act (1995), which states that the language of instruction at universities is Estonian; however, the law leaves ample room and autonomy for university councils to determine the use of other languages for teaching purposes. All in all, the main goal of the language laws in Estonia, Latvia, and Lithuania is the protection of their respective state language, securing its status as the official language in each country respectively. Since the laws were passed by the parliaments in the 1990s following re-independence, no significant changes have taken place, not even in the case of the Estonian Language Act, which was originally passed in 1995 and was subsequently renewed in 2011.

The three universities that will be the focus of further analysis and scrutiny in the following section have naturally lived through the changing linguistic regimes that the three countries have experienced throughout their histories. Each historical period has been characterized by particular ideas about language and about the role that different languages should fulfil socially and, of course, within the university system. The University of Tartu (Estonia), the University of Latvia, and Vilnius University (Lithuania) are taken in the following section as paradigmatic examples of how universities look, physically and materially, and what sociolinguistic environments emerge from their built spaces, an environment that will have been influenced by both long-term, historical past and more recent, synchronic events. Of the three of them, only the University of Latvia was founded in the twentieth century (in 1919); the University of Tartu and Vilnius University were established centuries earlier (in 1632 and 1579 respectively). Particularly relevant in the current context is the fact that, starting in the 1920s, achieving the status of being used as an academic language was seen as an important objective for Estonian, Latvian, and Lithuanian, in terms of these national languages gaining a prestigious domain. In the case of Estonian, for example, this would happen during the first period of independence (Verschik 2005), although naturally, during that period, other languages played a relevant role in the higher education contexts of the three republics, including German, Russian, French, and

English (the latter two to a lesser extent). However, the national languages were strengthened during the interwar period thanks to continuing linguistic work by prominent philologists and linguists, who helped complete the standardisation processes for Estonian, Latvian, and Lithuanian (Hogan-Brun et al. 2007: 497). Additionally, at least in the Estonian case, universities continued to operate in the national language to a significant extent during a large part of the Soviet period, judging by the fact that a substantial number of PhD theses in the 1950s and 1960s were written in Estonian (we will return to this in more detail in Chapter 5, where a more extended historical account of the developments in higher education in Estonia will be elaborated).

At present, as already noted above, the dilemmas experienced by universities and higher education systems across the Baltic around language issues seem quite noticeable. It is also important to add here that the analysis in this chapter focuses on three public universities, and public and private institutions may have different approaches to language issues, with private ones for example making more active use of both Russian and English (see the discussion above on the more extensive use of Russian by private institutions of higher education in Latvia). In any case, what follows is a linguistic landscape analysis of three public universities in the three Baltic states with one main goal in mind: mapping how the three institutions adapt to and react to the current tensions and dilemmas present in the higher education systems of all three countries, dilemmas and paradoxes nicely captured by Bulajeva and Hogan-Brun (2014: 328) in their analysis of Lithuanian higher education and its internationalization trends. Indeed, the need to reconcile ethnocentric approaches to language educational policies (firmly in place since the 1990s) with Eurocentric demands to accommodate multilingualism decidedly and actively would seem to require substantial effort by university officials and key stakeholders, and this might be reflected not only in their written policy documents, but also in the physical and online environments, and in the material and linguistic landscapes of the universities. This is what I set out to explore in more detail in the following section.

2.3.1 Physical and online spaces of higher education in Baltic universities

As indicated in the previous chapter, language policy-making does not happen in a vacuum, it takes place in real contexts and social spaces, be they physical or virtual ones. Looking at the material side of where social action takes place makes sense in attempting to provide a fuller, more complete picture of the discourses circulating in that space, and in considering how the material context may foster or hinder the presence and use of different languages and varieties

(Hult 2015: 224). With that goal in mind, in May and June 2014 I took a short trip to visit the universities of Tartu (in Tartu, Estonia), Latvia (in Riga, Latvia) and Vilnius (in Vilnius, Lithuania) in order to map and analyze the use of languages in their public spaces, considering which languages are used, how often, and for what. Much has been written in recent years about the linguistic landscape (LL) as a method and tool to investigate issues of interest in bi- and multilingual settings (e.g. Gorter 2006; Shohamy, Ben Rafael, and Barni 2010; Shohamy and Gorter 2009). Critical voices have also been raised with regard to the 'traditional' approach to the study of LL; Blommaert (2013a), for instance, sees the quantitative side of LL research as too superficial, erasing the historical trajectories of signs in place. One possible way to remedy this shortcoming is to look at specific signs in more detail and try to find out more about their indexical values: what do the signs point to, what underlying meanings and messages can we read from them? Scollon and Scollon's (2003) ideas of 'emplacement' (where a sign is actually situated in space) and 'dialogicality' (a sign's connection and relationship to other signs in a given setting) provide useful starting points to read beyond the textual and graphic layers of a given sign. In other words, the realisation that signs point in different directions is also important to include into the analysis (Blommaert 2013a): signs point to the past, or to their authors; to the present, or to other signs they connect with; and to the future, or to their intended readers. Looking at these different layers in specific signs might grant us access to the social and cultural layers of meaning of the sign and retrieve richer nuances from them. Here, I first of all take quantitative LL data as a way of providing a general overview and as complementary to other sources of information, with the goal of mapping the distribution of different languages in the public space of the three universities investigated. I then offer an in-depth analysis of a selection of signs that, in my reading of them, are indicative of interesting and relevant sociolinguistic meanings.

Tables 2.4, 2.5, and 2.6 summarize the results of the linguistic landscape fieldwork conducted respectively at the University of Tartu (UT; Table 4), the University of Latvia (UL; Table 5), and Vilnius University (VU; Table 6). In processing the data from all three universities, I categorized the signs as being monolingual (in the state language, in English, or in another language), bilingual (in the state language and English, in the state language and Russian, and other types of bilingual signs, e.g. Spanish language courses advertised in Estonian and Spanish), or multilingual (with multiple options being possible, e.g. handwritten signs by students in several different languages). I also distinguished different sources of authorship and categorized the signs as being produced by the respective university, by outside companies or organizations, or by individuals (students or staff).

Table 2.4: Mono-, bi-, and multilingual signs at the University of Tartu (N=869).

Author	Monolingual signs			Bilingual signs			Multilingual signs
	Estonian	English	Other	Est–Eng	Est–Rus	Other	Multiple combinations
UT	296	23	5	41	1	7	8
Outside companies	362	35	3	8	10	0	2
Individuals	23	41	3	1	0	0	0
Total	681	99	11	50	11	7	10
%	78.36%	11.39%	1.26%	5.75%	1.26%	0.80%	1.15%

Table 2.5: Mono-, bi-, and multilingual signs at the University of Latvia (N=609).

Author	Monolingual signs			Bilingual signs			Multilingual signs
	Latvian	English	Other	Lat–Eng	Lat–Rus	Other	Multiple combinations
UL	264	5	6	3	0	2	1
Outside companies	181	42	11	16	2	7	9
Individuals	44	11	1	0	0	0	4
Total	489	58	18	19	2	9	14
%	80.3%	9.5%	2.95%	3.11%	0.32%	1.47%	2.3%

Table 2.6: Mono-, bi-, and multilingual signs at Vilnius University (N=762).

Author	Monolingual signs			Bilingual signs			Multilingual signs
	Lithuanian	English	Other	Lit–Eng	Lit–Rus	Other	Multiple combinations
VU	252	13	4	52	0	4	1
Outside companies	140	45	1	4	0	0	0
Individuals	18	65	0	1	0	0	0
Total	572	123	5	57	0	4	1
%	75.02%	16.14%	0.65%	7.48%	0%	0.52%	0.13%

The above tables provide a general overview of the main features of the linguistic landscape in the three universities. This first overview tells us that the university space in these settings is prototypically monolingual, with signs being mostly in monolingual Estonian, Latvian, and Lithuanian respectively. One sees also that monolingual signs in the state language are typically produced either by the institution itself or by outside companies (particularly in the cases of UL and VU). In contrast, signs authored by single individuals are more likely to be monolingual in English, not the state language (especially in the cases of UT and VU). A very common example of this type of sign was conference posters displayed in the corridors of some departments (I elaborate more on this below). An important insight from this first point is that agents at the macro and meso layers (e.g. institutions and private companies) may tend to reinforce state monolingualism, whereas agents at the micro level (e.g. individual researchers) may be more ready to engage with languages other than the official state one, and particularly with English.

There are, however, more nuances that need to be presented in this kind of analysis, and we can only reach these fine-grained details by taking a closer look at specific individual signs. What we can notice, in this detailed analysis, is that the signs in the linguistic landscape of the three universities index different kinds of meaning drawing on a variety of linguistic and semiotic resources. As noted above, one way to start looking at the indexical values that signs can point to in the settings surveyed here is to analyze them in view of their actual physical position (emplacement) and their connection to other signs and objects around them (dialogicality). In this meaning-making process, the interaction (real-time or imagined) between actors arranged in different positions, with a set of resources and affordances, will determine the type and shape of sign that is observable.

Signs authored by the university – that is, institutionally authored signs – tend to be prototypically monolingual in the respective state language. However, in the cases of UT and VU, the two universities are seen as part of the cultural and historical heritage of their countries and of the two cities, Tartu and Vilnius, respectively (see Figure 2.1 and Figure 2.2). So, much like what happens in other tourist sites elsewhere (cf. Heller et al. 2014), here too language is employed strategically for both practical and symbolic purposes, and bilingual signs are used in order to make sure that larger audiences can be reached; in this way, not just international students and scholars, but also all kinds of visitors, can connect to the place and have a closer experience of it. This is a relevant point that we will return to below and in the more general discussion in the final chapter of the book. This type of bilingual sign was prototypically found in the historical centers of the universities, seamlessly merging their campuses with the bilingual signs from the town center. Thus, the historical campuses of UT and VU become yet another attraction that Tartu and Vilnius offer, sites for tourists to visit, enjoy, and consume.

Conceptual and material discourses in place — 49

Figure 2.1: Bilingual Estonian–English signs at the UT historical campus.

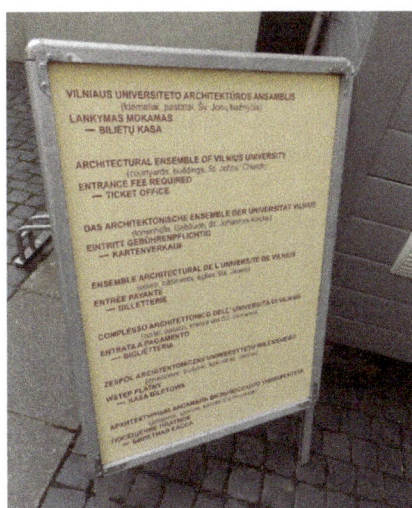

Figure 2.2: Multilingual signs at the VU historical campus.

In both cases, therefore, UT and VU seem to construct their city center campuses as relevant locations of cultural importance and make them available as sites attractive to tourists. In the case of VU, multilingualism is more prominently used in its historical campus; the photo on the left in Figure 2.2 features seven languages in total: Lithuanian, English, German, French, Italian, Polish, and Russian. In the photo on the right, we see two parallel monolingual signs with the same information, in Lithuanian and English, and a monolingual sign in Lithuanian authored by the EU. This kind of sign, with slight variations in the text inserted in the blue box on the top part of it, was found repeatedly in several campuses of the university. The fact that it is authored by the EU and is monolingual in Lithuanian is relevant and will be discussed below.

Bi- and multilingual signs on other campuses of the two universities were less frequent (and they were rare in general in the case of UL). A particular case is the absence of bilingual signs in the state language and Russian, which seems motivated by a conscious erasure (Irvine and Gal 2000) of the language by policy and sign makers. Only at UT were a number of signs composed bilingually in Estonian and Russian, from a single driving school (see Figure 2.3, left), which might indicate that the company wishes to attract Russian-speaking clients. Also at UT, there was one sign in Estonian and Russian which, given its font and general appearance, gives the impression of being a sign from a more distant past that has not been removed, and this is supported by the marginal position it occupies on the campus where it was found, hidden in a corner of a departmental corridor (see Figure 3, right). Present-day signs with safety instructions, such as evacuation plans or instructions in emergency situations, are monolingual in the state language – this was observed across all three universities (see Figure 2.4).

Figure 2.3: Bilingual Estonian–Russian signs at UT.

Conceptual and material discourses in place —— 51

 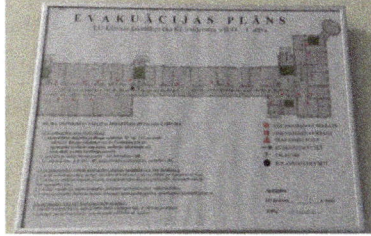 

Figure 2.4: Monolingual signs in the state language at UT, UL, and VU, respectively.

Monolingual signs in languages other than the state language (particularly signs in English) were also found in all three universities. This type of sign is especially (but not exclusively) used in cases where the authors of the signs are outside companies or individual agents (e.g. universities from abroad offering study programs at their institutions, or scholars showcasing their research in posters presented at international conferences). Sometimes, the university itself also produces signs monolingually in English, as when advertising English-taught programs newly offered in some of its departments. These types of sign are exemplified in Figure 2.5 – the examples here are from the data set collected at UT, but similar instances were recorded at UL and VU.

 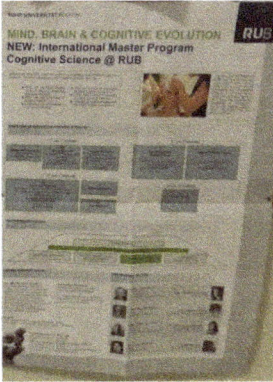 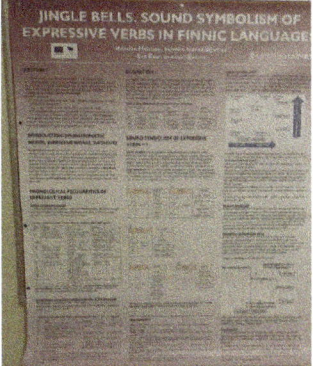

Figure 2.5: Monolingual signs in English at UT.

Finally, multilingual signs, with multiple combinations of languages, were rare at all three universities. At both UT and UL, signs of this kind were found in the Faculty of Humanities where foreign language courses were advertised – the only difference was that at UT these signs were authored by the institution, whereas at UL they had been authored by outside companies (see, for example, the sign on the left in Figure 2.6, an Italian–English bilingual sign). At UL, a multilingual sign was found in the Faculty of Humanities written by what would seem to be exchange students; this type of more organically produced sign, with temporary scribbling, co-exists interestingly next to a sign in the official language Latvian, produced in a more stable and durable kind of material, a sign with information for emergency situations, which, as we have seen above, is produced in the official language of the state.

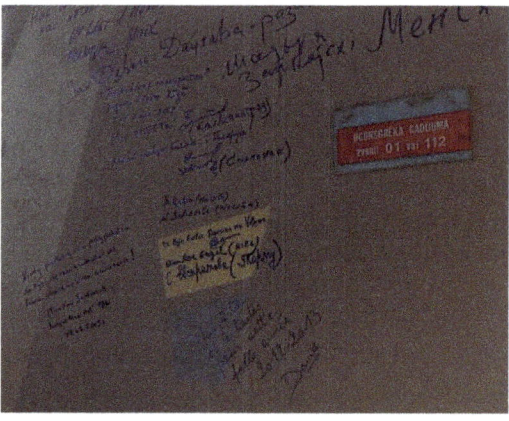

Figure 2.6: Multilingual signs at UL.

Turning now from the physical to the online space of the universities, the websites of the three institutions are yet another rich source to find out about the 'discourses in place' and the spread and distribution of the different languages at play in a given setting. Although there are certainly important qualitative differences in terms of how information is presented in one language or another, without translations being fully representative of the original content (Greenall 2012), a quantitative display of the number of items available per language can help us gauge the relative importance of each language in each institution (see also Soler-Carbonell and Gallego-Balsà 2016). Here, the 'site map' of each university's website was explored in order to count the items available in each of the languages: Estonian, English, and Russian at UT, Latvian, English, and Russian at UL, and Lithuanian and English at VU (the latter does not have a Russian-language version of its website). Table 2.7 summarizes the results obtained from this exploration.

Table 2.7: Languages and items available per language on the UT, UL, and VU websites.

	Estonian/Latvian/Lithuanian	English	Russian	Total
University of Tartu	495 (53%)	387 (41%)	53 (6%)	935
University of Latvia	655 (67%)	300 (31%)	15 (2%)	970
Vilnius University	227 (73%)	86 (27%)	-	313

If we consider just the number of items available in each of the three languages (national, English, Russian) at the three institutions, this gives us a slightly different image of each of them, as they emerge as slightly more bilingual or multilingual spaces – more markedly so in Tartu than in Riga and Vilnius. Indeed, UT and UL here appear to have a more bilingual outlook than VU, although in equally quantitative terms, we saw earlier that the latter university presented a higher percentage of bilingual signs (Lithuanian–English) than the former two (in their national languages and English). In any case, and percentages aside, the point here is that when moving from the physical, built environment, to the online and virtual space, universities seem to find it easier to incorporate a greater use of other languages, particularly English. This is not all that surprising, given that it is relatively easier to do so, as opposed to using other languages in physical space. Indeed, in the online space, there might also be an awareness by the institutions that their potential reach, and therefore the intended audience of their websites, transcends the more local (national) spaces, potentially reaching viewers from other parts of the world and speakers of a great variety of languages, whose numbers might not necessarily be that significant in their university corridors and auditoriums. Finally, it is again clear here that the institutional use of the Russian language is very minimal, with very low percentages at both UT and UL, and not an option at VU; this is in line with what we saw above in connection to the presence of Russian in the physical space, the material linguistic landscape. The (significant) absence of Russian from the universities' physical and online spaces can give us further clues about the institutional stance towards the role of this language in particular; leaving aside qualitative differences in terms of what information is given in which language (which, as noted above, can be a relevant element to consider in the discussion), not including Russian in their physical and online spaces might imply a de facto lack of recognition of the language and a de-legitimisation of its presence and use by the university, implicitly acknowledging a language hierarchy by which institutions are to function first and foremost in the national language, and secondly, in English, with Russian having an almost symbolic position only in UT and UL.

Bringing the argument to a close, in connection to the actual physical spaces of the universities – their linguistic landscapes – we see here a strong correspondence with the states' dominant monolingual language ideologies. It seems, indeed, that the three universities (UT, UL, and VU) function in their state language – in Estonian, in Latvian, and in Lithuanian, respectively. All kinds of information, from information about courses and programs to signposts indicating the internal organization of a given building, is predominantly given in the state language. English, however, is used as well, although it is noticeably more common on the historical campuses and buildings of the universities (particularly in the case of UT and VU). Not incidentally, these historical buildings are also located in the city centers, where the physical spaces and the linguistic landscapes are already bilingual to a significant degree. The effect of this is that the historical university sites appear to be more tourist oriented; indeed, the tourist framework is an important idea we shall return to in the concluding chapter. Of course, English does appear on campuses outside the historical city centers, but when it does, it is found in non-institutionally authored signs: more frequently than not, the English found outside historical campuses and buildings appears in signs authored by outside companies (e.g. foreign universities advertising their English-taught programs) or by individual members of the university community (e.g. researchers displaying conference posters in English in their departmental corridors).

In light of this, drawing definite conclusions seems a difficult, if not risky, task. One might say that institutions operate more with a national framework in mind, at least in their physical spaces and less so in their virtual environment, whereas individual members (e.g. teachers and researchers) also have an international framework in mind, exemplified by their display of their research in posters presented at international conferences. Interestingly, what we see here is that in their recontextualisation of particular signs (in this case, academic posters), researchers are in effect crafting new meanings with new implications for those signs. Signs originally created to be exhibited at a conference by members of a particular discourse community are reframed in a new context, their departmental corridors, with a new set of potential meanings. What was originally a sign for colleagues from different institutions outside their own is now a sign for colleagues and other members in their home university, with different indexical values. The posters, originally thought of as pointing to their work and its relevance in the international research front, may now be used to point to their authors and their potential individual or collective achievements. We see here, then, a complicated intersection of different discourses as we observe signs travelling through space and time. Effectively, one of the possible consequences of the re-emplacement of the conference posters discussed here is the shifting orientation of the university space from a national to a more international one. Even if only ad hoc instances, the researchers' individual decisions and actions seem to de facto drive internationalization initiatives, localising international practices into the very corridors of their university departments.

2.4 Conclusion

This chapter has offered a first overview of the reactions and adaptations to current trends in the internationalization of higher education from a broad, regional (Baltic) perspective. Conceptual and material discourses in place in the higher education systems of Finland, Estonia, Latvia, and Lithuania have been investigated by looking at a series of language policy documents and by examining their physical and online spaces, studying their material and virtual linguistic landscapes. The chapter started by noting that the presence and role of English in European universities is, obviously, not the same everywhere. The tendency, as we have seen, is for English to become more commonly adopted as a language of instruction in more and more programs; this is particularly true for studies at Master's level in the Nordic countries and the Netherlands. The Baltic states, of particular interest in this volume, have more recently joined these European 'powerhouses' of English-taught programs (Wächter and Maiworm 2014), although the introduction of ETPs in the Baltics seems to be primarily motivated by the progressive decrease in the local student population (Kibbermann 2017). At any rate, the consequences of an increased level of heterogeneity in the context of higher education are felt across the board and by the different stakeholders involved in this area. We have seen in this chapter that state and institutional (university) sectors can react differently to the language question, sometimes emphasising more state/national needs and priorities, and other times more institutional and particular ones. These different needs and different points of view on the role of language in higher education are far from being simply organized and transparently observable, but are instead complicated matters. For universities and their members (from students to teachers and administrators), the tension between the 'nationalizing' and the 'globalizing' discourses can be acutely felt (Soler and Vihman 2017), and as seen above, universities in the Baltic countries are particularly prone to experience these tensions due to their ethnocentric approach to language-in-education policies, combined with their more recent need to engage with internationalizing goals and agendas (Bulajeva and Hogan-Brun 2014). In the next chapter, we will delve deeper into the Estonian context, looking at how different stakeholders in the higher education system align themselves more with one type of discourse or another, and how they negotiate their position in the field.

3 University language regimes in Estonia: (Re)creating discourses in place

3.1 Introduction

On 10 October 2013, the Language Forum, organized by the Estonian Language Council, took place in Tallinn. It was a one-day conference event dedicated to examining the implementation of the *Development plan of the Estonian language 2011-2017* (Estonian Language Council 2011). A particular emphasis was put on the issue of the Estonian language in Estonian higher education policy, and judging by the title of the concluding round-table discussion ("The Estonian language – friend or foe of innovation?"), one gets the impression that the topics discussed were anything but neutral and problem-free. Moreover, the opening of the event was an address by the then Estonian President Toomas Hendrik Ilves, a sign that adds to the understanding that this conference had great symbolic importance and that the matters discussed there were of major relevance. The following day, on 11 October 2013, the University of Tartu (UT) organized a one-day seminar in Tartu, this time, however, to celebrate the twentieth anniversary of the first English-taught program at the university and, indeed, in the country. In this case, the focus was on the English language and its decisive role in the internationalization process of the country's universities, with a particular focus on the University of Tartu, naturally. Key top-level government officials also took part in that seminar, including an opening address by the Minister of Education and Research, Professor Jaak Aaviksoo, and a closing speech by the rector of the University of Tartu, Professor Volli Kalm.

We shall return to some of the presentations at the seminar in Tartu later in this chapter, given the importance and relevance of the topics discussed there. The point to emphasize here is that these two contrasting examples, the event in Tallinn and the seminar in Tartu, held on adjacent days, are particularly revealing of the increasing discussion in the country regarding language and higher education issues at that particular moment (Tensing and Vihman 2014). I attended both events, and the initial impression I was left with was that they neatly represented the two approaches that, while perhaps contradictory, might be the source of the language-related tensions and ambiguities in higher education: the need to incorporate a growing use of English for almost all purposes, while at the same time maintaining a significant space for Estonian in the country's higher education system. Even more important than that, the two events can be read as two excellent examples of how discourses about language(s) and about the internationalization of higher education are shaped and developed, of

https://doi.org/10.1515/9781501505898-003

how discourses in place are produced and circulated, emphasising certain kinds of ideas and making others less prominent. Events like these are important in that they provide the conditions for certain ideological frameworks to emerge, while actively contributing at the same time to these very ideological frameworks from which social actors interact (Johnson 2009).

The goal of this chapter is to provide a closer look at the ideas that are implicitly or explicitly formulated by different stakeholders in connection to language(s) and the internationalization of Estonian higher education. The chapter analyzes how university language regimes are constructed and reinforced by different agents in a given field. First and foremost, the chapter looks at a set of official policy documents written in order to regulate the internationalization of the Estonian higher education system (university and state language strategy documents, state language policies, etc.), some of which we have already seen in the previous chapter. In addition to that set of documents, two other sources of data are considered: (a) written material from an online forum discussion of the University of Tartu's 2020 strategic plan, as well as media texts relating to a short-lived debate in late 2012 about the internationalization of Estonian higher education; and (b) spoken data with key extracts from participants at the aforementioned seminar celebrated in late 2013 at the University of Tartu to commemorate the twentieth anniversary of English-taught courses there – as already stated, participants in the seminar included UT Professor and Rector Volli Kalm and Professor Jaak Aaviksoo, then the Estonian Minister of Education and Research and a former rector of UT. These pieces of spoken, mediatized data, in combination with the analysis of the policy documents and comments about them by members of UT, allow the possibility of tracing the creation and development of institutional discourses on language issues within the country's higher education system. Importantly, they show how certain ideological frameworks are (re)created, how certain ideas about language and about the internationalization of higher education are packaged and circulated to the wider community. The main goal of the chapter is, in short, to offer a possible explanation of the discourses in place in the context of the internationalization of Estonian higher education. Before moving on to the details of the analysis, some general introductory remarks about recent internationalization trends in Estonia and at the University of Tartu more specifically are in order, to which we turn first in the next section.

3.2 Internationalization trends in Estonia and at the University of Tartu

Considering the upheavals which took place in the 1990s in the former Soviet Union, sweeping through political, economic, and cultural spheres, the countries which regained independence faced the task of rebuilding their nations both materially and morally. After regaining its independence in 1991 following the downfall of the Communist regime in Eastern Europe and the Soviet Union, important changes took place in Estonia at all levels of society, and higher education (HE) was not immune. Many of these changes and developments related to a range of different areas encompassing higher education: funding, quality assurance, equity, links to the job market, and so on (Saar and Mõttus 2013: 11). A noteworthy example that can illustrate these changes and the developments during the 1990s is the number of institutions offering HE programs. In 1990/91 there were six public universities in the country. In contrast, by 2002 there were 49 institutions offering HE provision, both public and privately owned. At present, there are 34 such institutions, divided into two main groups: universities, on the one hand, and professional HE institutions, on the other. However, instead of providing more opportunities to attain a higher education, this expansion of the number of offerings has led to increased inequality within the population in Estonia, with socially disadvantaged students suffering more difficulties in securing a place at a HE institution (Huisman et al. 2007). Indeed, another key development that can be highlighted from the last two decades is the drastic increase in students paying tuition fees: from 7% in 1993 to 49% in 2011 (Saar and Mõttus 2013: 13–14). This supports the argument that those students who can afford to pay for higher education studies can attain that level of education, whereas those who cannot pay for it are more likely to struggle.

Zooming in to the situation at the University of Tartu, during the Soviet occupation of Estonia, the university offered both Estonian-medium and Russian-medium curricula and drew a student body from across the Soviet Union in certain fields (such as sports medicine), but these students were classified as domestic (Soviet) students rather than international, though they hailed from outside Estonia. Full curricula were not taught in English, and attracting international students from beyond the borders of the USSR was not legally possible. Hence, the development of English-medium courses and programs, and the recruitment of international students, has taken place entirely in the quarter-century since the collapse of the Soviet Union in 1991. As this involved a shift in attitudes, ideology, and preparedness, the movement towards English-language study did not take place immediately, but has more recently seen faster growth. This has been supported by a growth in global student mobility and funding for the increased internationalization of higher education. However, as noted by Klaas-Lang and Metslang, the proportion of students studying in Estonian is higher now (92% in 2014) than two decades earlier (82% in 1993), because of the decrease in Russian-medium studies (Klaas-Lang and Metslang 2015: 168). Note that the dwindling importance in the role of Russian overall in

Estonian HE is in line with the shifting sociolinguistic situation in Estonia and the Baltic states overall since 1991 (for lengthier analyzes of these changes, see Hogan-Brun et al. 2008; Skerrett 2014).

The initial impetus for offering English-language courses, however, occurred immediately after the reestablishment of Estonian independence, when UT joined ISEP (International Student Exchange Programs; www.isep.org) in 1992 and welcomed the first ISEP students and other visiting and exchange students who spoke neither Russian nor Estonian. They were not fee-paying students, but it was crucial to offer courses in English for them, not least because this reciprocally enabled the university's own students to study abroad. So it was that in 1993, UT developed a full semester program in regional studies in English for international students, "Semester in the Baltics". This module became a regular semester program the following year, 1994, and has been offered continuously since then.

Two years later, UT's integrated (six-year) program in medicine launched two years of English-taught studies for international students, following which the students could join the regular Estonian-taught program under the same conditions as domestic students. Because of the difficulty of learning the Estonian language in such a short time, and alongside their medical studies, the two years of English-language studies were designed primarily with a Finnish cohort in mind. Finnish and Estonian are closely related languages, and students from Finland had little trouble learning enough Estonian to continue their studies with domestic students after two years. For twenty years, the English-medium medical program mostly attracted Finnish students, helping make Finns the most numerous nationality in the international student population at UT.

A lengthy plateau followed the initial launch of these programs, with little support for further development, either among academic departments or in the administration. Meanwhile, the university joined the European Union's Socrates Erasmus mobility program in 1998, which slowly but surely moved internationalization into the university's core activities. The increasing importance of international developments at UT was flagged by official moves such as the founding of a Centre for Baltic Studies to coordinate English-language courses in social sciences in 1999; a centrally funded competition to develop international courses in 2000; and the establishment of an International Relations Office in 2004, in addition to the already existing International Student Service.

The University Development Plan (A2008, adopted at the end of 2003) named four 'breakthrough' areas, including both internationalization and the strengthening of the national university (as the university is officially designated to be under the University of Tartu Act 1995). This led to a new push towards

English-based program development, resulting in the first full international Master's degree program launched in 2005, based on the existing 'Semester in the Baltics' program. Funding schemes were opened both within the university and on the national level to support the development of English-medium teaching. New MA programs were launched nearly every year from 2007 to 2014, as summarized in Figure 3.1. The program names are difficult to read, but visually, the document captures very well the steep increase in English-taught programs at UT since 2005, following the relatively long period of inactivity at that level mentioned above, of about ten years, from 1995 to 2005. This diagram comes from a document was distributed to the attendees of the seminar to celebrate the twentieth anniversary of English-taught programs at UT in October 2013, mentioned at the start of the chapter, to which we shall return later with the analysis of some key contributions from that seminar.

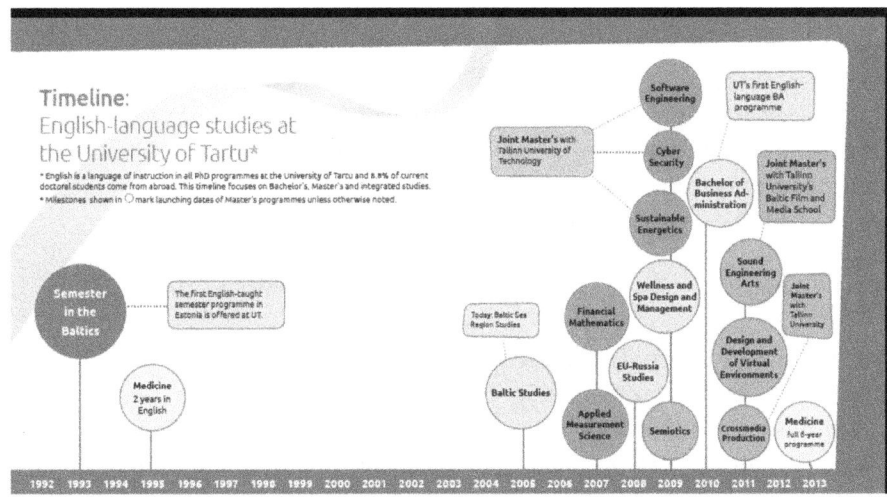

Figure 3.1: English-medium degree programs, University of Tartu, 1993–2013.

Vihman and Tensing (2014) give a more detailed overview of the early period of international program development at UT, and of the speed and impetus taken since 2005, with strategic changes adopted by the university administration, which we shall analyze in more detail below. Initial experiences with the complexity of recruiting students to a little-known destination such as Estonia showed that this activity required innovation and investment. English-language teaching grew extensively during this period, not only in the framework of degree programs, but also in individual courses, bolstered by international staff and funding for visiting scholars and exchange students requiring more English-language courses.

From 2009/10 to 2012/13, the proportion of courses taught in English rose from 6% to 10% in just three years. Vihman and Tensing (2014) show that academic units varied in how much teaching took place in English, but English-taught courses accounted for 5–18% of all courses in most faculties. English-taught courses were also attended by domestic students.

With this important background information in mind, let us now turn to the materials to be analyzed in more detail in this chapter, consisting of two kinds of data. On the one hand, there are written materials, which comprise: (a) state and institutional (language) policy documents; (b) university members' comments to an online forum to discuss the UT strategic plan for 2020; and (c) a media debate on the role of language and identity in the internationalization of Estonian higher education. On the other hand, there are also spoken materials, comprising the speeches and contributions to the seminar celebrating twenty years of English-taught programs at UT. Altogether, the corpus consists of a varied data set from which we will try to trace the perspectives of at least three different key stakeholders (state and institutional officials, other members of the university, and members of the public), each invested to varying degrees in both the creation and discussion of the sociolinguistic situation in Estonian higher education. Let us turn, in the next section, to the first set of materials: state and institutional (language) policy documents in Estonia.

3.2.1 State and institutional (language) policy documents in Estonia

The first set of materials analyzed in the chapter consists of a series of policy documents from approximately 2003 to 2014 that contain relevant passages relating to the issue of language in the context of higher education. These documents can be roughly divided into two types, according to their authorship or scale of application: state-level documents, on the one hand, and institutional-level documents, on the other. The state policy documents included in this analysis are:

- *Estonian higher education strategy 2006–2015*, authored by the Ministry of Education and Research;
- *Strategy for the internationalization of Estonian higher education 2006–2015*, authored by the Ministry of Education and Research;
- *Agreement on good practice in the internationalization of Estonia's higher education institutions*, authored by the Council of Rectors of Estonian Universities;
- *Development strategy for the Estonian language 2011–2017*, authored by the Estonian Language Council in collaboration with the Ministry of Education and Research.

As for the institutional-level documents, four key policy documents adopted by the university in order to outline its strategic developments were analyzed:
- A2008 – *University of Tartu strategic plan 2008*;
- A2015 – *University of Tartu strategic plan 2009–2015*;
- A2020 – *Strategic plan for the University of Tartu 2015–2020*;
- *Language principles of the University of Tartu*.

The state-level documents have different goals and different agendas, reflected in their different sets of priorities and measures. The *Strategy for the internationalization of Estonian higher education 2006–2015* places a strong emphasis on measures to push forward an internationalizing agenda for Estonian universities, while the *Development strategy for the Estonian language 2011–2017* takes a more protectionist stance in safeguarding the position of Estonian in the context of higher education. A similar thing happens with the institutional-level documents. A2008, A2015, and A2020 are institutional strategic documents. The *Language principles* is a separate document drafted to support and supplement the aims of A2015, addressing all questions related to language, from the political issue of aiming for a "balance between higher education in the Estonian language and the development of an international study environment" to questions of foreign-language teaching and the provision of services in Estonian and other languages. All these documents, state and institutional, contain passages which are relevant for language-related issues, and they are key to investigating the positions of the different languages at play within the university.

A content analysis of all the documents was conducted to find out relevant goals and measures related to language(s) and the internationalization of higher education, as well as to analyze the position of languages in the documents (Saarinen 2012). More particularly, the documents were analyzed using a qualitative content analysis, which Hsieh and Shannon (2005: 1278) define as "a research method for the subjective interpretation of the content of text data through the systematic classification process of coding and identifying themes". Initially, a line-by-line reading of the documents was conducted in order to identify passages with content relevant to the research aims, namely passages with language- and sociolinguistic-related issues. A conventional content analysis (Hsieh and Shannon 2005) was then implemented, highlighting keywords and phrases of each passage that were then linked to the emerging themes detected from each document. In the final stage, a summative content analysis was conducted to identify the number of instances of each theme in the document, assisting thus in the overall interpretation of it (see also Björkman 2014 and Soler et al. 2017 for a further elaboration of similar methodological procedures with similar kinds of data).

Moving beyond content-analytical strategies, in line with the discursive approach of nexus analysis adopted here, the analysis was influenced by recent developments in the field of language policy research (e.g. Ajsic and McGroarty 2015; Hult and Källkvist 2016; Johnson 2009). Texts are viewed as cultural products that emerge at the intersection of different layers of historical, geographical, and sociocultural elements (Scollon 2008). As a result of the analysis, there were four emerging themes that were identified as the most salient from this set of documents, summarized as follows:
- Theme 1: Estonian language and culture has to be protected, promoted, and developed in the context of Estonian higher education;
- Theme 2: English is important for practical purposes; university students and staff need to have a good command of it;
- Theme 3: English needs to coexist with other languages in the context of Estonian higher education; a balance needs to be met; multilingualism should be promoted;
- Theme 4: University students and staff should have a good command of other foreign languages; education programs in foreign languages should be developed.

Essentially, the four themes capture the already mentioned tension between securing a safe space for Estonian language and culture in the context of higher education while at the same time opening up that context to international influences, namely through an increased use and presence of English. The tension that exists is visible in the different ways of referring to English that the documents choose and the need to incorporate the language into the higher education domain: Theme 2 represents a more explicit engagement with English, while Theme 4 is a seemingly more implicit one. Indeed, it is difficult to decide, from the reading of some passages in the documents, whether they truly refer to 'foreign languages' when they use this label, or whether this is a proxy for not having to name an explicit 'foreign language', that is, English. This ambiguity is hard to work through completely, but this is not exclusive to the Estonian case: Saarinen (2012) reports that a similar strategy is used in Finnish university policy documents (see also Saarinen and Nikula 2013). Indeed, in the Finnish context, Lehikoinen (2004: 44) explains that "[W]e try to avoid speaking about English-language education; we always say foreign language education, and everyone knows that in practice it means English, only English."

In sum, documents may adopt different stances towards the language question in higher education, leaning to either one pole of the continuum or the other: the need to protect, promote, and develop the Estonian language, and the need to incorporate an increased use and presence of English. To have an overview of where the different documents stand, Table 3.1 provides a summary of the number of instances of each theme detected in the different documents.

Table 3.1: Number of instances of each theme in the analyzed documents.

	Theme 1	Theme 2	Theme 3	Theme 4
Higher education strategy	4	1	0	0
Internationalization strategy	4	2	0	10
Agreement on good practice	2	2	0	2
Development strategy: Estonian language	10	0	0	1
A2008	4	8	0	6
A2015	8	6	0	0
A2020	4	0	0	0
Language principles of UT	9	4	2	7
Total	45	23	2	26

As can be seen, Theme 1 is the most prominent in both state and institutional documents, and therefore represents a persistent idea which recurs through the years, from 2003 to 2014. So, the idea that Estonian needs to be protected, promoted, and developed in the context of higher education appears across all documents. The protection of Estonian is understood in the sense that institutions need to "ensure the preservation of the Estonian language as the primary language of teaching and research at institutions of higher education" (*Internationalization strategy*); promotion of the language is usually interpreted as the idea that institutions will "provide opportunities for learning Estonian to members of the academic staff of the University of Tartu who do not speak Estonian as their native language" (*Language principles*); and the development of Estonian is linked to terminological and field-specific initiatives: "in cooperation with the national government, implement measures to develop scientific terminology in Estonian and promote disciplines studying Estonian language and culture" (A2015).

Clearly, then, all stakeholders, both national and institutional, seem to support the idea that Estonian needs protection, and that it needs to be promoted and developed in the area of higher education. At the institutional level, all three strategy documents (A2008, A2015, and A2020) and the *Language principles* note that they are based on the premise that UT, as Estonia's national university, has the legal duty and responsibility to carry out research and teaching in Estonian and to safeguard the position of the language across the domain of higher education:

> The national university considers as of vital importance the research into the Estonian language, literature and history and appraises such aspects of Estonian nature, environment,

society, economy and culture that through distinguishing and emphasizing the Estonian *alma mater* among the European and world universities will secure its international position. (A2008)

The University of Tartu as a national university of Estonia bears the responsibility for solving problems faced by the society by ensuring the continuity of Estonian intellectuals and language and culture and by contributing to the development of education, research, and technology and other creative activities throughout the world. (A2020)

Interestingly, although UT's mandate as the national university is codified in law (University of Tartu Act 1995), there remains ample room for interpretation, as demonstrated by these two extracts. In 2003 (see extract from A2008 above), the concept of the national university is equated with the subject of research relating to the Estonian nation. The extract from A2020, on the other hand, demonstrates that by 2014, when the A2020 document was finalized, the concept had been broadened to include not just research connected to Estonia, but also the development of Estonian intellectual life and research, making the very notion of the national university more compatible with a globally oriented institution.

More remarkable is how the different documents indicate a change in orientation towards linguistic trends and globalisation at the university. Produced in 2003 at the cusp of the first push towards internationalization, A2008 is the most extensive of the four institutional documents, almost three times as long as A2020. A2008 presents a more detailed treatment of the internationalization dimension of the university. Indeed, 'international' and its derivatives ('internationalization', 'internationally', etc.) appear 30 times in the document. In A2020, there are 13 mentions of 'international', but 'internationalization' is not mentioned once. 'English' is explicitly mentioned 4 times in A2008, always in the context of expressing the need to expand the use of English; for example, "increase the proportion of the academic staff from abroad and those teaching in English", "develop interdisciplinary programs taught in English with the aim of offering them on the international education market". A2020 has no explicit mentions of 'English' or 'foreign languages'. It seems that either the thrust towards internationalization and the explicit role of English has waned in the intervening years, or else the authors of the strategy document are responding to a shift in attitudes. There are, of course, several possible reasons for this decrease in the number of explicit mentions of 'English' or 'internationalization'. In that respect, it is also relevant to note that the *Language principles*, drafted in 2009 as part of the A2015 strategy plan, has not been renewed in the subsequent A2020 plan. The *Language principles*, although the shortest of all documents, is probably the most balanced of them in terms of the different themes, despite still giving more weight to the protection, promotion, and development of Estonian (Theme 1). The *Language principles* underscores the theme of the practical importance of English (Theme 2), giving this emotionally loaded issue a functional justification. This idea appears in the context of giving students and staff the necessary skills in English in order to be well positioned for employment in the job market. Finally, it is the single document to mention the idea that English needs to coexist with other languages (Theme 3), pointing at the notion of 'parallel language use' without explicitly referring to it as such.

All in all, we see a degree of intertextuality within same-level documents (e.g. between the *Language principles* and A2015) as well as across levels (e.g. between the *Language principles* and the *Internationalization strategy*). Explicit or not, intertextuality in policy documents is always a relevant feature to detect, as it can help in understanding the underlying meanings of documents and their intended messages (Johnson 2015). A case in point among the documents analyzed here occurs between the *Strategy for the internationalization of Estonian higher education 2006–2015* and the *Development strategy for the Estonian language 2011–2017*. As seen in Table 3.1, the *Internationalization strategy* seems to lean more heavily towards a less protectionist stance in connection to the language issue in higher education. Indeed, there are more instances of Theme 4 (the importance of developing 'foreign language' programs and curricula) than of Theme 1 (the importance of protecting, promoting, and developing the Estonian language). As a reaction to that and in a dialogic way, the *Development strategy* comments negatively on the *Internationalization strategy* by explaining that "the Strategy for the Internationalization of Estonian Higher Education 2006-2015 diminishes the role of Estonian-medium education by further removing the requirement of the existence of Estonian-medium education from doctoral education."

With statements like the following, it does indeed seem like the *Internationalization strategy* places a lot more emphasis on the importance of opening up the system of higher education in the country than being worried about the position of Estonian in it:

> The presence of international students and academic staff members adds to the attractiveness of every living environment. It is very important that local government bodies become more aware of the significance of this factor, and take it into consideration. In cooperation with the local authorities, institutions of higher education will also try to facilitate the emergence of an international environment off campus. The goal is to provide foreigners with all essential information and access to community services and medical care in English, to help them to integrate their professional and personal lives (schools, kindergartens, student clubs) etc. (*Internationalization strategy*)

Even so, the *Internationalization strategy* includes elements of Theme 1 too. In fact, after the passage above, it continues:

> Institutions of higher education and the national government will cooperate to provide elementary language training to foreigners, to ensure they have a sufficient knowledge of

Estonian to manage in everyday situations. Each international student and academic staff member must have the opportunity to participate prior to or during the study period in free courses on the Estonian language and culture (*Internationalization strategy*)

So, one has the impression that the authors of the document want to remain careful in the formulation of their text, while still leaning more in favour of pushing Estonian higher education towards internationalizing goals. It is probably not a surprise that the *Internationalization strategy* places more emphasis on the need to support internationalization initiatives in the country, and that the *Development strategy for the Estonian language* pitches the need to protect, promote, and develop the Estonian language in the context of higher education and elsewhere. What is more relevant to read in this instance of intertextuality is the observation that official bodies or organizations from the same level (in this case, national agencies) can have different views on language policy matters, in our case in connection to the language question in higher education. Although stemming from the same organization – here, the Ministry of Education and Research – stakeholders can have different views, responding to the different agendas that they may wish to promote. In that respect, it is probably not by chance that the *Internationalization strategy* makes extensive use of the label 'foreign language' rather than naming any explicit foreign language in particular (e.g. English), resulting in a more prominent presence of Theme 4 than Theme 2 in the document. This might be a strategy employed by the authors of the document to avoid being seen as too open to English, which could be interpreted as a threat to Estonian language and identity.

Indeed, in the *Language principles of the University of Tartu* (i.e. at the institutional level), the 'foreign language(s)' label (Theme 4) is also strategically employed by the document's authors. Although it is the shortest of all the documents analyzed here, it has the highest number of instances of this term (7 times). Once again, an interesting degree of intertextuality between two equal-level documents, A2008 and the *Language principles*, can be noted. Whereas A2008 refers to developing "interdisciplinary programs taught in English with the aim of offering them on the international education market", the *Language principles* notes the need to "promote the development of curricula taught in foreign languages on all levels". Here, 'foreign languages' has replaced 'English', signalling that this document, written six years later, is now much more cautious about according privilege to English over other languages. This, together with the diachronic evolution of the documents at the institutional level noted above (from A2008 to A2020), might indicate a potential shift with respect to internationalization aims of the university and the role and position of languages, particularly a developing caution regarding English. In sum, tensions and ambiguities around the language question in higher education can be difficult to navigate for both state and institutional stakeholders, resulting in changing perspectives across time and different perspectives between bodies and organizations at the same level. We shall dig deeper into the analysis of the difficulties associated with navigating these ambiguities when we look into the media debate and the contributions by key stakeholders at the seminar to celebrate twenty years of English-taught programs in Tartu in 2013. Before that, however, let us briefly analyze the opinions of actual university members, employees, and students, in connection with the development of the university's strategic plan A2020.

3.2.2 The members of the institution – debating A2020

In 2013, UT officials began drafting a new strategic plan for the period 2015–2020, named A2020, which would replace A2015. As part of the process, discussion was opened up to the university community, and members were invited to make suggestions on what steps should be taken for the development of the university in the near future. An online platform was created in order for university members to submit their opinions, freely and openly, to be collected and shared by the Vice-Rector for Development. Table 3.2 presents an overview of this corpus of data, with the numbers of comments per language and the self-identified role of the authors of the comments. This corpus dates to the period between autumn 2013 and spring 2014.

Table 3.2: Overview of comments submitted by UT members in preparation for A2020.

Language and author	Number of comments	Number of words
In Estonian (total)	63	9864
Employees	42	7480
Students	20	2275
Other	1	109
In English (total)	20	4350
Employees	13	3210
Students	6	613
Other	1	527

From the analysis of the comments posted online by the UT community during the A2020 discussion – involving a line-by-line reading and then coding them manually – language-related issues surface more prominently in the contributions submitted in English than those submitted in Estonian. (In analysing the material, the assumption was that English-language comments were written by international scholars and students, whereas comments in Estonian were submitted by Estonian scholars and students, though there may be exceptions to this.) Indeed, out of the 20 comments in English, 11 (55%) focus to some extent at least on language issues. In the Estonian corpus, only 8 out of 63 (13%) contributors mentioned language matters. More generally, the comments in both languages tended to revolve around issues pertaining to (a) the quality of education and how to enhance it overall at the university, and (b) the salaries paid at the university and the need to raise them to more competitive levels.

Turning first to the comments in English, when language was mentioned, it was the discourse of protecting, appreciating, and promoting the Estonian language as a form of added value which was appealed to as central to the development of the university, as in the following examples:

> Preserving the use of Estonian language at PhD level should be a priority for the university in the next few years (ENG5)

> There should be better appreciation for researchers with degrees from good universities from abroad, especially if they speak Estonian too, and have worked at the University of Tartu for some years (ENG20)

In many other comments, mentions of language were situated against the background of potentially problematic issues. Some authors of comments saw the way academic language is treated by the university as structurally problematic, whether in English or in Estonian, and focused on looking for practical solutions to such problems. Others emphasized the need for the university to think more strategically when addressing opportunities for its internationalization strategy – this, some noted, would require the institution to engage more effectively with the English language, especially on the part of the Estonian-speaking staff. This more problematising discourse is exemplified in the next two extracts:

> More than 95% of academic positions advertised in the university's job web site in 2012 and first half of 2013 require functional or native knowledge of Estonian. [...] This means that more than 1000 world-class scholars need to be found from a relatively small population (ENG6)

> I would like to see a lot more internationalization (at least 50% of the academic workers hired from other universities) and better integration of the international and local faculty members. [...] Obviously, that would also require the locals to accept (occasionally) working in English (ENG14)

As for the comments in Estonian, similar issues emerged there. Some contributors focused attention on the need to safeguard Estonian as a viable language of science, noting the need to develop terminology in all fields; others emphasized the need for the university to incorporate English more effectively, recommending the introduction of more English-taught courses so that international students would have more options, or removing the requirement that all PhD dissertations in English include an extended summary in Estonian. For example:
- "Tagada eestikeelse terminoloogia jätkumine kõigil erialadel - ka neil, kus osa õpet inglisekeelne on" [Guarantee the continuation of Estonian-language terminology in all fields, including those where some of the teaching takes place in English] (EST19)
- "Enam inglisekeelseid aineid, et Erasmuse ja ka teistel välistudengitel oleks suurem valik (praegu peavad juuratudengid oma kohustuslike ainepunkte täis saamiseks näiteks inglise filoloogia ained võtma)" [More courses in English so that Erasmus exchange students and other international students would have a wider range of courses to choose from (at the moment, Law students have to take courses in, e.g., English philology to earn their required course credits)] (EST9)
- "Ülikool peab muutuma rahvusvahelisemaks ja arvestama välisõppijate eripäraga: nt miks peab inglisekeelsel doktoritööl olema eestikeelne kokkuvõte, kui välismaalane eesti keelt ei oska nagunii laseb selle tõlkebürool inglise keelest eesti keelde tõlkida?" [The university needs to become more international and take account of the distinct character of international learners: for example, why should a doctoral thesis in English have a summary in Estonian if the international student does not speak Estonian anyway, they just have a translation company translate it from English to Estonian?] (EST14)

To sum up, two main points can be taken from the online comments and discussion of A2020 among the members of the UT community (students and staff). The first is that if we take frequency as an indication of importance, we can conclude that issues of a sociolinguistic nature seem to be more relevant to international members than to local ones, who referred to such issues less often. The second point is that the tension between the nationalizing and globalizing discourses seems to be reproduced in online comments to A2020: the need to protect, promote, and develop the Estonian language in higher education settings appears together with the need for the university and its community to engage with English more. In the next section, we turn to a different site, public media, where the very same tension emerged, in this case in the context of a more heated, albeit short-lived, public debate about languages in higher education.

3.2.3 A public debate: The Pärnu Leadership Conference media discussion

From October 2012 to March 2013, a debate took place regarding the sustainability of the Estonian language in higher education, particularly for teaching purposes. The comments from the open discussion of the strategic plan, analyzed in the previous section, were collected when the presiding rector of the University of Tartu, Volli Kalm, had already been in office for a year and a half. Right at the beginning of his term of office in 2012, however, he received a rapid induction into the language question, through a debate he sparked only six weeks after being appointed rector. Kalm's claim was that the presence of Estonian in tertiary-level teaching could not be taken for granted, as it would become increasingly costly in the context of increased internationalization. The ensuing articles and commentary in the media form the data to be analyzed here. These were accessed through the media monitoring of UT's Communications Office, which compiles a record of media mentions of university-related topics and articles in the press. The debate was so intense that Kalm himself felt impelled to issue a later comment clarifying his first statement. The episode represents a rich, condensed discourse flagging key ideological tensions connected with language in higher education, with features of typical language ideological debate (Blommaert 1999). The analysis includes the different opinion pieces produced during that time and some of the online comments posted by readers.

Kalm uttered the following sentences when he was invited to speak at the Pärnu Leadership Conference, clearly placing questions of language at the center of the future of higher education in Estonia:

> The difficult questions regarding the future of Estonian higher education are tied to the competitiveness of Estonian HE compared to English HE. Master's and doctoral studies are inevitably becoming more English-based. Students will increasingly go abroad for niche disciplines [...] We are often unaware of the price of preserving Estonian-language higher education. (Kalm 2012)

This sparked a flurry of responses, both supportive and critical, many of which took the statement above out of context and continued a more general conversation about the perception of a changing balance of languages. The ensuing debate reveals the emotional resonance of the 'language question' in Estonia in postnational, globalizing times. It also becomes clear that the debate is often framed as a binary opposition between nationalizing and globalizing ideologies.

The rector of the Estonian Business School (EBS), Arno Almann, responded in an opinion piece, "[...] that studying – especially business – only in Estonian is pointless for tomorrow's students. We are moving step by step towards entirely English-language education and I believe that EBS will surely get there before

2020" (Almann 2012). EBS, a private institution founded on business principles and targeting a highly international student body, can afford to make this stance explicit, while the rector of UT is seen to have to adhere to a very different moral and political code. As an example from the other side of the public debate, Kalevi Kull, Professor of Biosemiotics at UT, made a statement in the daily newspaper *Postimees,* calling for Estonian universities to remember their duty to uphold teaching in Estonian:

> A culture is alive only if it teaches its young people in the language of that culture [...] The first duty of Estonian universities is to teach Estonian youth the values, customs, and speech of Estonian high-culture. We can justify teaching the youth of other cultures in those fields in which we are the best. (Kull 2012)

Two weeks after his initial statement, Rector Kalm responded to the high-tempered debate, specifying that his initial intention was to underline that "delivering internationally competitive higher education in Estonian is expensive, but it is the responsibility of our nation, our universities and especially the University of Tartu to do so" (Kalm 2012). Although this is a possible interpretation of Kalm's original statement, it is likely that, as rector of UT, he was advised or felt the need to articulate a more moderate view in which he more explicitly expressed support for teaching in Estonian. The discussion was particularly intensive at the end of 2012. In addition to appeals to emotional and ideological rationales, Kalm also referred to a pragmatic motivation for his statement on English-language teaching, slightly different from that of Almann. Demographic changes had led to an imminent decrease in 18-year-old high school graduates in Estonia, as in many places in Europe. Not only are there fewer potential university applicants, said Kalm, but "if all of them attend university, then who will do the jobs which do not require higher education?" He added that Estonia's immigration rules were overly strict, often obstructing even international students in Estonia from remaining after graduating.

Kalm's later pronouncements were also framed with a slightly altered logic. In addition to amending his earlier statements, emphasising the need for *both* English-medium international degrees *and* Estonian-medium education, he also appealed to Estonian patriots with a new set of claims. He noted that (a) international students studying in English sometimes learn Estonian and continue their studies in Estonian – this claim is supported mainly by Finnish students enrolled in the two-year English medical program who continue their medical studies in Estonian; and (b) former international students who leave after their studies are among Estonia's best ambassadors for promoting and introducing the language and culture in which they were immersed during their studies. Finally, Kalm also questioned why students are no longer as adept at other languages besides

English, rhetorically deflecting the criticism of English-language curricula with a nod to a different set of issues, language competence more broadly.

In a television talk show, Kalm was very careful to emphasize that Estonian must not be allowed to decline to the point where "we can use it only to buy bread and name plants and birds", justifying the requirement that dissertations contain an Estonian-language summary. He also took pains to explicitly state that Englishisation of teaching in higher education is not mercenary: "It is clear that our profit is not financial, but rather elsewhere – an open environment, communication with people who think differently, demand for teachers to restructure and rethink the way they teach." (ERR News, 22 November 2012).

Other writers shared their concerns, mostly in opinion pieces, about the risks of allowing too much English-language teaching. Students who took part in the debate expressed concern, mostly aligning themselves, perhaps more vociferous, with the nationalizing side of this debate. The chair of the Federation of Estonian Student Unions, Eimar Veldre, wrote an article claiming that the priority of Estonian higher education institutions must be to "maintain and develop thinking in Estonian", which ought to culminate in a higher diploma and achievements in research and development. He also warned that "widespread adoption of English-language teaching does not guarantee world-class education", particularly if lecturers fall short in their language skills, citing an iGraduate survey in which international students in Estonia judged their lecturers' English-language skills very critically (Veldre 2012). In a similar vein, Jane Niit, a Master's student in communication at Tallinn University, voiced concern about how the increasing use of English was affecting her generation's ability to express themselves and even think in Estonian. "Estonian and English are structurally so different", she claimed, "that these two languages cannot be fruitfully used together – they will begin to disturb each other, and to degrade the grammatical quality of written texts and speakers' language intuitions" (Niit 2012). In an anonymous comment to an article on this topic in the teachers' newspaper, *Õpetajate Leht* (Pärismaa 2013), a reader claimed:

> If we pose the question thus: 'Are we able to maintain [the language]?', then the answer rings out: Where there's A WILL, there's a way. We were able to maintain it under the pressures of Russification, but now we give way everywhere. And if we take the position that it's easier this way to go out into the world for studying, working, living, then it really will be difficult to maintain the language.

Hence, although Estonian is "among the 50 most technologically developed languages" (Zirnask 2014: 42), with Estonian-language platforms for Microsoft Word, Google, Wikipedia, and others, as well as enjoying support from the Estonian government, for example for the publication of Estonian-language textbooks and the development of language technology resources (Klaas-Lang and Metslang 2015), the society at large is wary, and neither complacency nor unanimity can be said to characterize the debate regarding the best way forward.

What the debate illustrates is, once again, the interplay between the two broadly defined discourses that have been repeatedly alluded to in this chapter and the tensions between them – the globalizing discourse, on the one hand, and the nationalizing discourse, on the other. In this case, given that the debate was played out in the public media, with different recontextualisation chains among the participants in the discussion, the confrontation between the two perspectives might have appeared to be harsher and more polarized. In any case, we see one more instance of yet another setting where views on the role and status of languages in higher education were the object of heated discussions; in this case, in the context of the public media.

3.2.4 Celebrating twenty years of English-language studies at the University of Tartu

With the memory of the media debate of late 2012 and early 2013 fresh in people's minds, the University of Tartu celebrated twenty years of English-medium teaching. As we have seen, in 1993 the university inaugurated its 'Semester in the Baltics', an effort that – given the changing times of that moment, barely two years after the country regained its independence from the Soviet Union – was a rather clear stance marker of what some scholars have termed a 'return to the Western world' (Kasekamp 2010). As mentioned above, the seminar to commemorate twenty years of English-taught programs took place just one day after another event had been organized in Tallinn to assess the implementation of the *Development strategy for the Estonian language 2011–2017*, with a round-table discussion on the role of Estonian in science and research. Intentional or otherwise, the consecutiveness of the two events adds to the sense of dialogicality that existed between them, and by extension, between the two discourses that each event came to represent (the nationalizing and the globalizing discourses).

I took part as a member in the audience in the two events, one in Tallinn and one in Tartu, and took notes in both of them. Here, however, I shall concentrate on the material from the event in Tartu, since it specifically dealt with issues of language, particularly the English language, and the internationalization of higher education in Estonia; the seminar was held entirely in English, and in addition, it was video-recorded and then posted online at www.uttv.ee. The videos are still available at the time of writing (June 2017), which has made it easier to return to the discussions held in that seminar, transcribe some of the main contributions, and analyze their content. The event in Tallinn, by contrast, was only partially dedicated to issues of language and higher education, primarily in the concluding round-table discussion, but it was not video-recorded, and it was held entirely in Estonian, which made it more challenging for me to understand all the nuances of the debate.

Many of the issues discussed during the Tartu seminar resonate with what we have seen above in the material from the media debate. Indeed, the proximity in time and the fact that one of the key actors in the media debate was also one of the main contributors to the seminar in Tartu, namely Professor Rector Volli Kalm, may significantly account for that. The rector himself opened the seminar with a short introductory address; in those opening remarks, he was quick to link the discussions of the day to issues of language and the internationalization of higher education. After the initial protocol salutations, he started with the following sentence: "Congratulations, we are celebrating twentieth anniversary of English-language studies. Universities are, or at least should be, international by nature." He then appealed to the seminar to fuel the discussion in terms of "what next?", emphasising that if anything is certain about the future, it is that the next generations are likely to live in more and more internationalized environments; consequently, the seminar presented itself as an opportunity to discuss how to tackle challenges related to this growing trend of internationalization from within the university.

The next speaker to take the podium was Professor Jaak Aaviksoo, then Estonian Minister of Education and Research, and a former rector of UT. Aaviksoo is a scholar/politician who has had an influential trajectory in Estonian politics and academia. He started his address by emphasising that rather than being a guest, he felt like a member of the institution. After a full-fledged academic introduction by the chair of the session Virve-Anneli Vihman, he remarked to the audience that he did not feel comfortable with such an introduction: "I don't think that's, that's appropriate, in a way, because somehow I'm here not as a guest, but at home", he said, which was immediately followed by the following sentence: "and I wanna start my introductory presentation..." Notice here the colloquial use of "wanna",[1] which does not correspond to the highly formal situation in which he was speaking, but served him well to highlight the stance he wanted to take:

---

[1] I would like to thank my colleague David (I must resort to using his pseudonym here, as we shall see him again as one of the key participants in my fieldwork in Tartu in the next chapter), who attended the seminar with me, for pointing out this micro-level feature of Aaviksoo's address during a later replaying of the event and for helping me think further about its potential meaning.

as one more member of the university, rather than a representative of the government. Throughout his talk, Aaviksoo fluctuated between his role as a politician and his past as an academic, having occupied key positions within the very same University of Tartu, including one and a half terms as rector, from 1998 to 2006. However, despite his efforts to align himself as a member of the institution, from the analysis of his talk it becomes apparent that he was very much talking from the point of view of a politician, as he himself made explicit references to that role at given points of the talk.

Aaviksoo's main message was clear and bold support for the country's and UT's efforts towards more internationalization initiatives. Probably aware of the debate that had unfolded in some media outlets in the country about a year before, Aaviksoo noted that the internationalization of higher education "is a sensitive issue on this country, a very sensitive issue ... and I don't know whether time is ripe and ready to discuss it in a really open, rational, academic way as we should do in this, in this university." He elaborated on the reasons why this is a sensitive issue, according to him, and explained that it is because "we are a bit afraid of losing our identity" when becoming more open and international. He framed this as a problem: "the problem is there, it's a real problem and we have to manage it one way or another, and university has been trying to do so, and I think we've been reasonably successful" (notice here the use of the inclusive 'we', once again showing his effort to be seen as another member of the university community). Aaviksoo argued that simply the fact that there was talk about the internationalization of higher education indicated in itself that there was a problem. Agreeing with the rector's opening remarks, he noted that universities are or should be international by nature, so debates around the internationalization of higher education were indicative of some embedded tension, which had to be resolved.

According to Aaviksoo, one of the key challenges for the internationalization of Estonian higher education was a lack of ambition on the part of the university community and the national society at large. He used the example of the National University of Singapore to explain that in talks with colleagues from that university, when he asked them about the biggest challenge in building such a competitive university in a relatively short period of time, his colleagues would tell him: a lack of ambition, the lack of a commitment to focus on the priorities. By extension, he noted that Estonian higher education probably suffered from the same flaw, but also by comparison, he left the door open to suggest that the University of Tartu could follow the example of the National University of Singapore and become even more competitive. As an example of this lack of ambition in Estonia, he mentioned that too few Estonian students were taking part in international exchange programs; according to him, a third of students should be studying abroad, not only for a period of exchange, but for an entire degree, "but we are complaining already when one out of twenty leaves this country," he remarked.

Naturally, Aaviksoo touched upon the language question, and here too he was clearly in favour of introducing English-taught courses and programs at the university, and even in lower levels of education. He elaborated on this in the following way:

> but now I'm asking whether, whether competitive modern education, higher education but even secondary education is all possible without English, at least in this part of the world ... A politician should avoid answering this question, but he has the privilege or the ability to ask these questions, so I leave answering these questions over to the academic community and remain, remain where I'm standing now just asking whether it's possible.

Notice here his strategic explicit positioning in the role of the politician, rather than the academic, in order to avoid having to give an explicit answer to the question, although implicitly, the answer he suggested was quite clear, if not from his refusal to give a concrete answer, from what he added afterwards:

> One way or the other we take the default position, that all our students are able read and write textbooks thesis whatever in English. And I am dreaming that one day it is possible both to study in Estonian at Tartu University but also in all programs study in English. How to achieve that I don't know, but when we think that we or the University of Tartu has already managed to do that in doctoral programs, and we really don't know how, there are no formal rules as far as I know, it is a matter of fact, we take it as natural, it is made possible by silent agreement between the academics the students and the broader community around us ...

It was certainly Aaviksoo the politician talking, especially in this fragment of the speech, with a good dose of wishful thinking rather than accurate knowledge of matters on the ground. As we shall see in the next chapter, in principle one can complete one's PhD studies in English at UT, although not without overcoming a number of language-related and administrative obstacles that, as an international student, can be difficult to beat. In sum, Aaviksoo's participation in the seminar in Tartu helped emphasize the idea that in order to become more competitive, internationally attractive, and quality education institutions, Estonian universities and UT had to show more ambition, and put more energy into internationalizing initiatives, including developing programs and courses in English.

The language question resurfaced on several occasions during the seminar, but particularly in the concluding round-table discussion. At one point during that discussion, Rector Volli Kalm and Professor Jaanus Harro, Dean of the Faculty of Social Sciences, engaged in a short dialogue on the language requirement for foreign academics, which then developed into the medium of instruction in most programs offered by the university. The exchange went as follows:

> Kalm: yea but for example, how do we ah, how do we attract ah top quality academics to our university when we have the requirement that they must know Estonian language in order to being able to teach in Estonian language?
>
> Harro: a very blunt answer would be that we won't attract top people to work here anyway, if we are speaking of the very best in the world, we need to create conditions when they are willing to sometimes come here and collaborate with us.
>
> Kalm: you didn't answer the language question.
>
> Harro: we don't require them to speak in Estonian.

In this dialogue, we see an additional nuance added by the rector, which is the idea that to require proficiency in Estonian in order to teach in the language might be counterproductive in trying to attract highly qualified scholars to the university. Harro's answer is a pragmatic one: it is difficult for UT to attract top scholars anyway, so efforts should be made to have some kind of collaboration with them, rather than to have them at UT on a permanent basis. The rector seems to want to push the language question further, but Harro denies the idea of the requirement. In short, the argument here is that requiring Estonian might turn into a problem when it comes to enhancing the university's competitiveness and international strength. Later in the discussion, however, the rector again brought up the language question, but this time to emphasize the importance of developing research in and about the Estonian language:

> Kalm: but another issue is, in our context, I don't totally agree that internationalization means quality, because we, as a national university are by law responsible for keeping Estonian language well, alive in all levels, to be a language where every science can be discussed and taught, and in that sense, however we measure the internationalization, it does not equal the quality of what the university is responsible for.

It is not all that transparent what he actually meant with this statement, but it does counterbalance the idea expressed minutes before in the sense that it may indeed be true that requiring a working knowledge of Estonian might be an obstacle for increasing UT's competitiveness, but it is also the institution's legal duty to protect, promote, and develop the language itself and research in the language. All in all, much like in the media debate, we see a certain degree of fluctuation between one pole and the other of the language question in the context of higher education, from one discourse to another, from what can be called a nationalizing to a globalizing discourse in higher education. The next section sums up the material presented in this chapter and discusses how actors position themselves in relation to these metadiscursive strategies.

3.2.5 Discursive orientations towards language in higher education: Nationalizing and globalizing tensions

The empirical evidence presented in this chapter allows us to gain more insight into the conceptual context in which the internationalization of Estonian higher education is framed. Following Hult (2015: 224), we may understand the conceptual context as "the nationally circulating language ideologies or institutionally circulating norms [that] mediate the policy action an individual takes". Briefly recalling the argument in the previous chapter, we said that Estonian higher education and its internationalization is in fact connected with other internationalizing systems of higher education and that, in that sense, it does not operate in a vacuum. In that sense, in line with previous research on the topic (e.g. Doiz et al. 2013; Haberland and Mortensen 2012; Hultgren et al. 2014), in the Estonian context too, two (conflicting) views on language in higher education clearly emerge: on the one hand, the need to protect, promote, and develop the national language in all scientific fields (the nationalizing discourse), and on the other hand, the need to incorporate and make use of foreign languages (especially English) in an increasing number of scientific fields (the globalizing discourse). As was already noted in the previous chapter, the tension in the Estonian context resonates with Bulajeva and Hogan-Brun's (2014) analysis of the Lithuanian higher education context and its internationalization policies, where the authors also detect a tension between ethnocentric and Eurocentric discourses along similar lines. Hultgren's analysis of Danish higher education also reports similar results, where 'parallel language use' seems to be interpreted as 'more Danish' by government officials and 'more English' by universities. Needless to say, different discursive orientations towards language policy issues are not exclusive to European higher education institutions, and tensions along similar lines have also been documented elsewhere, for example in Colombia (Miranda et al. 2016), China (Han et al. 2016), and the South Pacific (Willans 2016).

What is more interesting about the Estonian case, and indeed, something that might make it unique, is that the tension between the nationalizing and the globalizing discourses can be observed as emerging from 'same-level' stakeholders; that is, different documents and different individuals from the same organization (e.g. the Ministry of Education and Research, or the University of Tartu itself) can espouse different, sometimes opposed, views on the topic of language and the internationalization of higher education (although see Hultgren 2014, with similar results in her analysis of the Danish case). If we start by looking at university and public officials – that is, the authors (usually anonymous) of the policy documents we have analyzed above – they could to be described as being the most caught between the two discourses, the nationalizing and the globalizing. This is particularly visible in the contrast between the *Development strategy for the Estonian language 2011–2017* and the *Strategy for the internationalization of Estonian higher education 2006–2015*, and particularly in the use of the label 'foreign language(s)' in the latter as a way to avoid referring to English more explicitly. This is indicative of the ambiguity which public officials are aware that they need to handle, and indeed, in the *Internationalization strategy* itself there are traces of both discourses, the globalizing one (which I have argued, takes precedence in the document) and the nationalizing one (which is more backgrounded).

Turning to the university officials more specifically, the institution for which they bear responsibility is legally bound to protect, promote, and develop Estonian language and culture (University of Tartu Act 1995). However, in order to position the university as a key player among global universities, UT needs to be, among other things, a powerful attractor for international students and staff, and this requires and reinforces the increasing presence and use of foreign languages (English in particular), in all spheres of university life. The balancing act between these two mandates is not an easy one to steer, as we have seen in the contrast between the official policy documents, on the one hand, and the public media debate, on the other. In A2008, drafted in 2003, the globalizing strand is explicitly visible and incorporated in the document, with specific references to the need to develop courses and programs taught in English. Six years later, in 2009, A2015 and the *Language principles* reformulated this need, saying that the university should develop courses and curricula taught in foreign languages. Another five years later, A2020, drafted in 2014, has a much-lowered tone when it comes to globalizing efforts, perhaps due to the fact that internationalization was much more under way and visible in the university by this point. A2020 does contain traces of the globalizing discourse, but they are framed much more implicitly, elevating the need to "ensure the continuity of Estonian intellectuals and language and culture" to a global scale, as seen above.

These changes in orientation regarding language issues within the university by its public officials can be read as each administration's way of marking their stance towards the two main discourses mentioned above. At the same time, the changes in content and wording also need to be read in connection with the changing environment within the whole university. In 2003, there were very few English-taught programs offered at UT, while in 2014 their proportion had increased significantly, with a corresponding increase in international (non-domestic) students enrolled in them, and a better understanding in most faculties of the associated challenges. In addition, in 2003, the globalizing discourse had barely penetrated the university sphere: engaging with it overtly and explicitly represented a lower risk to public officials. By 2009, internationalization and the concomitant debate had changed to the extent that officials may have seen it necessary to temper that discourse; by 2014, this cautiousness has solidified. It may be that A2020 resists explicit mention of either 'English or 'foreign languages' because they deem these activities to already be strongly present, or the need for increased globalisation to be self-evident by this stage, but considering the public debate preceding the publication of A2020, it is more likely that they were acutely aware of the potential divisiveness of these words, and hence aimed to reduce controversy. This may have resulted from the rector himself being caught up in a public debate where arguments for and against the nationalizing and globalizing discourses were launched in different media outlets, as we have seen in the analysis of the media discussion. In the public debate, the university rector had to navigate back and forth between the two discourses in several media appearances. This highlights the difficult position in which university officials find themselves and the complexity of striking a balance between the dominant discourses.

In this chapter, we have also looked at university members and their orientation towards language issues within higher education. From the analysis of the online comments provided during the preparation of A2020 we can see that, first of all, it was mainly international members of staff who showed an awareness of and a concern around specifically language-related issues at the university, whereas local Estonian scholars generally did not prioritize linguistic matters among the main strategic issues for the university. Although the nationalizing and globalizing discourses are present in both groups – with references for example to the need to develop Estonian terminology by means of extended PhD dissertation summaries – a more instrumental view towards language issues at the university emerges as more relevant in these comments (cf. Hultgren 2015); in fact, the absence of any significant discussion of the role of language at the university in the set of comments in Estonian is indicative of a more pragmatic orientation. Indeed, such an orientation might reveal an inclination by university members towards the globalizing rather than the nationalizing discourse, or at least a more neutral view on language issues in higher education, a position that emanates partly from the fact that they are engaged daily in conducting various, complementary activities at the university in different languages, from coffee breaks with colleagues in their department, to teaching and collaborating with colleagues abroad.

The public discussion on language issues at universities in late 2012 and early 2013 allows us to grasp the orientation held on such matters by members who are not strictly related to UT. Although the debate was sparked by the rector of

UT commenting on the cost of maintaining higher education in Estonian at all levels of education, many from within and outside the university felt prompted to engage in the discussion. What emerges from the series of articles and comments published during that short-lived but high-tempered debate is an apparently stronger orientation towards the nationalizing over the globalizing discourse, although proponents for both were present during the discussion. In framing the nationalizing discourse, resistance to domination from a foreign language is apparent in many comments and opinions. In a country where arguments based on language resistance have been at the core of prominent discourses about the nation for generations – ever since the earliest conceptions of nationhood – this is not surprising. Indeed, some of the commentators noted an often-voiced idea that for many decades, Estonians had managed to resist Russification, while now they apparently embrace Englishisation willingly and without strong opposition. In short, there is concern for the future of the Estonian language and culture in the field of higher education, a concern that in this public discussion relates to a generalized worry regarding the sustainability of Estonian globally (Ehala 2014).

In contrast to this, and as a kind of response to the nationalizing discourse that appeared to be emphasized in the public media debate, some of the key contributions at the seminar held at UT to commemorate twenty years of English-language studies in October 2013 remarked on the necessity for the institution, indeed for the entire higher education system in the country, to push decidedly towards more internationalization initiatives and goals. Both Rector Kalm and Minister Aaviksoo noted that, while it is true that Estonian higher education needs to ensure the sustainability of Estonian in scientific research, more needs to be done in order for the country to avail itself of a high-quality and internationally competitive higher education system, one that is attractive to both students and researchers from other parts of the world. In any case, the media discussion and the key contributions to the seminar in Tartu highlight the fact that the language question in the context of the internationalization of Estonian higher education reaches deeper than the arrangements that a university needs to undertake in order to situate itself internationally. The overall message from the analysis of all the diverse materials presented in the chapter is that this is a question of national importance, one that is fraught with issues that, obviously, transcend purely linguistic matters, and that relate to educational and economic stakes.

3.3 Conclusion

In this chapter, we have seen how different stakeholders with a close interest in language issues at the university orient themselves towards and engage with different discourses around language in higher education. In so doing, these different groups recreate and shape both the nationalizing and the globalizing discourses currently present in the field of higher education by strategically mobilising a set of semiotic resources available to them in the socio-historical moment (Blommaert 2005). In this mobilisation of semiotic resources, the language ideological component seems to be of central importance, and so in any analysis of language policy and language planning processes, linguistic ideologies and discourse analysis necessarily merit consideration (Ricento 2000; Spolsky 2009); indeed, language ideologies constantly reshape the social ground in which particular orientations towards language can emerge (Ruiz 1984). Mapping linguistic ideologies, however, is usually not an easy task and one needs to avail oneself of an eclectic methodology to draw them from different sources (Ajsic and McGroarty 2015), as we have done here. Although the analysis in the chapter has not departed from a single specific policy document (cf. Johnson 2009), the evidence provided shows how different agents engage the circulating discourses about language in higher education, and in so doing recreate, challenge, or sustain them, providing the background to enable what is sayable or thinkable in connection with the topic at hand in the specific Estonian context. Estonian is one of the smallest official European languages in terms of speaker population, and hence recurring linguistic ideological issues are particularly acute in the country. The material presented in this chapter will gain fuller meaning and more significance once we delve into the analysis of the actual opinions and view of speakers ('regular' members of the university) on the issue of language in the internationalization of higher education, something that we have already touched on in this chapter (particularly in discussing contributions to the A2020 online forum) and which we shall examine at length in the next chapter.

4 Language ideologies and the internationalization of higher education in Estonia

4.1 Introduction

Extending the argument presented in the previous chapter, we turn here to speakers' ideas and beliefs about languages in the context of an Estonian higher education institution and its internationalization process, with a particular focus on how the tension between the two broadly identified discourses (nationalizing and globalizing ones) are felt by speakers 'on the ground'. The chapter presents the results of fieldwork conducted in 2013–2014, when a series of in-depth interviews and focus-group discussions were conducted in Tartu in order to find out more about individual speakers' reactions and knowledge of the university's formal language policy and of the institutional approaches to language issues. We shall focus on the discourses and opinions expressed by two main groups: Estonian scholars, on the one hand, and transnational academics, on the other. This categorisation, of course, is arbitrary and is not unproblematic: how should one classify, for example, an Estonian scholar who has spent extended periods of his or her career abroad, including possibly all their education and training period? And might it not be questionable to classify a scholar from abroad who has lived and worked in Estonia for a long time simply as foreign? These open questions aside, the focus here will be on individual speakers' opinions, analytically tracing possible connections between the ideas they express and their life trajectories; for the sake of presenting the results in a way that is manageable, we shall focus first on the views of transnational scholars, followed by the opinions of local Estonian researchers. The starting point for all interviews was a conversation on the speakers' linguistic trajectories – their language biographies – followed by a discussion of how they perceived their sociolinguistic environment – what languages they used on a daily basis, in what ways they saw the university adapting sociolinguistically to its current challenges, and so on. In a context of rapid transformations and changes in a short period of time, how do speakers perceive the situation at hand? What role do languages play in their daily activities and realities?

4.2 Transnational scholars' views on the internationalization of Estonian higher education

As seen in the previous chapter, especially with the online forum contributions to the development strategy of the University of Tartu A2020, one group that can be particularly sensitive to the effects of the tension between the different discourses circulating about the language question in higher education is that of transnational scholars: academics who have moved to the country in recent years precisely as a result of the internationalization efforts of higher education institutions and education authorities in Estonia. The number of exchange students and staff coming to Estonia, particularly through the Erasmus program, has continuously increased over the past few years. This is especially the case for students, but the number of exchange staff has also risen considerably, going from 58 visiting teachers in 2000–2001 to 655 in 2013–2014 (see Figure 4.1). Nevertheless, until recently, little if any attention has been paid to the role of transnational scholars in the overall make-up of the international university. As we have seen in previous chapters, research has tended to focus on the multilayered dimension of language policy creation and implementation (Hult and Källkvist 2016; Soler-Carbonell et al. 2017). International students and their practices and ideologies have certainly been analyzed (e.g. Mortensen and Fabricius 2014), but the linguistic practices and needs of academics remain less investigated. A notable exception is, however, Jürna's (2014) study of the language practices of a group of transnational scholars in Denmark. In her study,

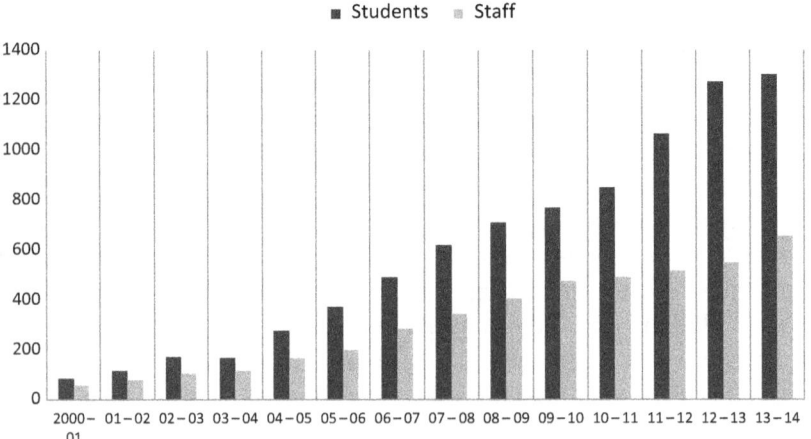

Figure 4.1: Erasmus mobility in Estonia – Incoming students and staff 2000–2014.
Source: Erasmus Statistics – European Commission (http://ec.europa.eu/education/tools/statistics_en.htm).

the author finds that knowing Danish is highly valued in general by her informants, but this positive evaluation is not always met with an equivalent degree of engagement with the language. Instead, opinions such as "Danish is often helpful, but not required" (p. 229) or the idea that "everybody speaks English" (p. 233) are commonly expressed by the participants in her study. Scholars who do indicate having incorporated Danish more actively in their repertoire state reasons such as the prospect of staying longer in the country, having children, or being part of wider social networks including Danes. As we shall see below, strong parallelisms will be detected between the results reported by Jürna (2014) and those of the present study.

During the academic year 2013–2014, I conducted fieldwork at the University of Tartu. The study was designed as an ethnographic research to investigate the role and the status of different languages in Estonian higher education, with the aim of observing the different discourses underpinning that context. In the spring semester, a series of in-depth interviews (Hoffman 2013) and focus-group discussions were conducted among scholars at the university with different profiles, from PhD students to professors in a range of disciplines within the institution. Twenty-two of the participants were transnational scholars. They represent different nationalities; most of them were of European origin, but also Asian and Latin American. Their time of residence in the country varied, from less than a year to up to seven years. A 'criterion sampling' strategy (Dörnyei 2007: 128) was used to gather the participants of the study, the criterion being that informants should be researchers at the time of interview with a scholarly status (from PhD students above). Table 4.1 summarizes some basic features of the participants who were interviewed in the study.

Table 4.1: Features of the transnational scholars interviewed at UT.

Pseudonym	L1	L-interview	Time in Estonia at the time of interview	Faculty
Annette	Norwegian	English	18 months	Humanities
David	Dutch	English	5 years	Humanities
Tania	Russian	English	4 years	Humanities
Jekaterina	Russian	English	18 months	Humanities
Carmelo	Spanish	Spanish	10 months	Social Sciences
Emma	Russian	Spanish	1 year	Social Sciences
Laura	Spanish/Catalan	Catalan	2 years	Medicine
Lisa	German	English	4 years	Science & Technology
Martin	Spanish	Spanish	6 years	Science & Technology
Qiu	Chinese	English	3 years	Science & Technology
Serge	German	English	9 years	Science & Technology
Nolan	Urdu	English	10 months	Science & Technology

In addition to these in-depth interviews, one focus-group discussion was conducted with ten scholars from the Computer Science Department. The ten faculty members came from mixed backgrounds and academic ranks, from PhD students to professors. Only two of them were Estonian nationals (not included as part of the study); the rest were international members who had been living in the country for at least one year. The group discussion lasted an hour, it took place in English, and it was held on university premises. Table 4.2 summarizes some basic features of the participants in the focus-group discussion.

Table 4.2: Features of the transnational scholars interviewed at UT (focus-group discussion).

Pseudonym	L1	L-interview	Time in Estonia at the time of interview	Faculty
Antonio	Spanish	English	4.5 years	Science & Technology
Mario	Spanish		6 years	
Oscar	Spanish		5 years	
Naaim	Urdu		4 years	
Pak	Persian		4.5 years	
Teo	German		1 year	
Sasha	Russian		4.5 years	
Fabio	Italian		1 year	

The conversations during the interviews and focus-group discussions revolved around a number of different topics. Much like Jürna's (2014) study examining the stance of transnational scholars towards Danish in Denmark, here too a relevant question was to find out about transnational scholars' attitudes towards Estonian and their motivations towards learning and acquiring it or not. As we have seen in the previous chapter, one of the tenets of the 'nationalizing' discourse is the promotion of the Estonian language among international students and staff. From that perspective, it would seem all the more relevant to find out how those at whom this promotion is explicitly directed feel about it. As we shall see, and to foreshadow the argument, participants noted, almost invariably, that Estonian is the language that they encounter most regularly in their workplace. They might use more English, but Estonian is the language that has more presence in their respective departments. Yet their stance towards the language varies: from more supportive of it and actively engaged in trying to learn and use it, to more neutral or resisting positions. Several characteristics of these two broad ideological stances can be identified among the speakers, to which we turn in the following paragraphs.

Those more favourable towards Estonian emphasized their motivation to acquire the language in different ways. Carmelo and David, for example, saw it as their 'duty' or 'obligation' to engage with the language professionally (even though they were both at an early stage of their learning process). David explained that in work meetings, he is still afraid to use his "broken Estonian"; but recently (at the time of the interview) he had been at a meeting where he was the only person who did not speak Estonian, so he said it would be fine to have the meeting in Estonian – "I'd rather it be me who is a little uncomfortable than them". Carmelo saw it as a way of "giving back" to the country and to the institution: "if you're doing a PhD here, in addition to it being of help for your career and for yourself as a person, this needs to help our country too", thus embodying the position that someone from Estonia would take, in his view.

Sometimes, however, participants felt that their goal of learning and using Estonian frequently needed to be emphasized, to the extent that these transnational scholars felt they needed to struggle for that. Lisa was a clear example of this. As a PhD student in biology, her studies are mostly in English, but the day-to-day activities in her department are in Estonian, so she felt she really wanted to engage with the language from an early stage. However, many times she felt she had to try quite hard to take a stance as a learner of the language, particularly in more informal, small-talk situations:

> Lisa: It was such a weird feeling, I was thinking well now I'm really nice and I try but it feels rather that you have to fight and that you disturb someone, you're so slow, and the others want to be polite and talk English to you, and still I can't speak Estonian if I'm not comfortable, if there are people who I see can't wait, then I say well if you want to speak English then let's speak English. But my supervisor is really encouraging this, it's really like it's nice.

As Lisa's case illustrates, the route towards Estonian, even for those who are most motivated to learn it and use it regularly, is filled with the particular circumstances and events of one's own life trajectory that crucially shape one's lived experience with the language (Busch 2015). In fact, it was often the case that those who had managed to attain a good knowledge of Estonian had done so because of factors in their extra-professional lives, which included finding an Estonian partner, having children, and having reasonable prospects of staying in the country for a longer period of time (as was the case in Jürna's 2014 analysis of the similar Danish data). In the case of Serge, for instance, it was after meeting his future wife that he decided he would learn Estonian and engage actively with the language:

> Serge: actually in 2000, I learned Estonian, I started to learn Estonian, because I got acquainted to a girl
>
> Josep: mhm
>
> Serge: we met in France at a choir festival, we fell in love, and of course I was very engaged to learn Estonian

Having children is another frequent route towards needing to engage with the language more frequently. Even if this does not lead to actual acquisition from the parents, children bring Estonian to the home and they do acquire the language at school. In the case of Martin, he explains that moving from the city center to a residential neighborhood in the outskirts of the city, coupled with having children, made a difference in his activation of Estonian:

> Martin: también ayudó el vivir en este lugar donde vivimos, porque en el centro no sé, era todo mucho más impersonal y aquí sí tenemos vida de vecinos, te preguntan cosas, les hablas y tal, también tener un niño te pone en contacto con la gente del lugar, entonces empiezas ya a hablarlo y hablarlo pues da un salto, no?, en tu conocimiento también, empiezas a escuchar las frases correctamente de la gente y no las que tú dices y empiezas a decir uy, esto se dice así, cosas así. Entonces empecé a hablarlo yo diría vamos, no sé, si me pusiera una nota no sabría muy bien cuánto poner, por ejemplo yo he escrito en el currículum que lo hablo de manera moderada

> [Martin: it also helped that we moved to the place we live now, because in the center I don't know, everything was more impersonal, and here we have neighbours, they ask you things, you talk to them, also having a child puts you in contact with other people from the place, and then you begin speaking more and more, so you improve in your knowledge, right?, you begin hearing sentences correctly from people, and not the way you utter them, and you begin to realize ok, this goes like that, and so on. So I began speaking it I would say, I don't know, if I were to grade myself I don't know how much I would award myself, for example I've written in my CV that I speak it moderately]

Turning now to those who expressed more neutral or negative opinions about the need to acquire and use Estonian, we can note some trends here too. Almost invariably, they emphasize that in their contexts, on a daily basis, they do not need the language, that everyone around can easily accommodate to English or other languages they may know (e.g. Russian). Sasha, a participant in the focus-group discussion at the Computer Science Department, presented the argument in the following terms:

> Sasha: Actually there is no need to know Estonian, I think. Because all the people know, for me, all the people know Russian or English. The young people they know English and Estonian, and the older people, from Soviet Union, they know Russian or Estonian as well, so for me it's kind of easy to manage with two languages, Russian and English.

In the case of Russian speakers, it was interesting that some expressed that they would prefer to use English, instead of Russian, to communicate in public. This emerged in the conversation with Jekaterina, who, much like Sasha, indicated that depending on the generation of her interlocutor, she would choose whether to address them in Russian (with older people) or English (with younger ones).

Jekaterina explains her experience as a process of adaptation, as in her first year she would try to use more Russian, but later decided she would rather use English instead, or try to use some Estonian at first, before switching to Russian, for example with members of older generations:

> Jekaterina: it depends on some, to whom I address. With younger generation, I usually address in English
>
> Josep: English, yea
>
> Jekaterina: I, as my Estonian is still small, I rarely practice my Estonian, for example at the café I can speak and tell some phrases in Estonian, but I communicate usually in English because it's comfortable and they understand, it's practice for me again
>
> Josep: have you tried to speak to them in Russian sometimes?
>
> Jekaterina: yea it was in the first year after my coming maybe some first month I tried to speak Russian, but mostly I saw reaction "I'm sorry I don't speak Russian" that's why I switched to English
>
> Josep: and because sometimes in these cafeterias you can also find Russian-speaking, ah
>
> Jekaterina: maybe, but right now I don't do that I don't practice that
>
> Josep: you go to English yea
>
> Jekaterina: yea at once, just English, with older generation of course first, currently first I try to speak some Estonian, some just primitive phrases, but after this phrase I just say in Estonian sorry my Estonian is too poor may I speak in Russian, they usually switch to Russian

Particularly in the case of those who had been in the country for a shorter time (from one to two years), there seemed to be an ideological construction of the perception that one can get by easily without Estonian. Annette, a lecturer in the Scandinavian department, explained that

> Annette: most people speak English. Of course, if I go to Narva then it's not so easy
>
> Josep: Mhm
>
> Annette: But then I don't go there so very often
>
> Josep: Mhm
>
> Annette: But in Tartu and in Tallinn it's okay, and now I even get by, because sometimes if you go to the shop, the people, the cashiers, they don't speak English that well
>
> Josep: Mhm mhm
>
> Annette: So, but I think I can get by now somehow

The key seems to be Annette's last point, the idea that she thinks she can get by somehow with her limited knowledge of Estonian and with English. Nolan shared this feeling, and while he was taking Estonian language lessons at the time, he felt English could be used generally everywhere: "and I'm trying to learn slowly but you know I almost never had to ah how to say it like English is always you can use it pretty much everywhere here so it has been very smooth". This feeling of not needing Estonian and therefore not being motivated to make a more decided effort to acquire it might come about for two reasons: the likelihood that they will not stay in the country for an extended period of time, combined with a prioritisation of issues other than learning the language. Emma, a postdoctoral scholar, expressed it in the following terms:

> Emma: No creo en las capacidades de estudiar estoniano. Mi marido que lleva aquí ya tres años empezó a estudiar estoniano. Él tiene talento para las lenguas extranjeras, pero el resultado es, no es tan bonito, porque a veces seguimos con problemas hablando estoniano. A veces hasta el marido que ha estudiado estoniano tres años, visitando los cursos, sabe leer el menú en el restaurante [...] Y yo de verdad no creo que vamos a vivir muchos años aquí

> [I don't believe in my own ability to learn Estonian; my husband, who has already been here for three years, started learning Estonian. He has a talent for foreign languages but the result is not so good because sometimes we still have trouble talking in Estonian; sometimes my husband, who has studied the language for three years taking courses and so on, he is able to read the menu in the restaurant [...] And the truth is, I don't think we'll live here for many years.]

Pak, a PhD student in the focus-group discussion, also explained:

> Pak: I receive emails that arrive regularly about free courses for teachers and staff to learn about Estonian and Estonian culture. I haven't taken any of them, I usually delete them, but I know it's there at least.

Different attitudes towards Estonian and towards language learning in general might also be affected by the participants' disciplines. IT scientists, for instance, might be less concerned with issues of a sociolinguistic or language policy nature; Mario, again from the group discussion, presented this idea as follows:

> Mario: I think, in our field, we are pragmatists. If we were not pragmatists, we wouldn't be here ((laugh)) so all these discussions you're having sound to me like people are having in that other building there ((refers to the university's main building)) ((laugh)) but we do not have that kind of discussions, we haven't even asked it ourselves.

The "here" that Mario refers to in the extract needs to be read as a grey day in the Estonian early spring, after a long winter of many grey and dark days; and the "discussions you're having" refers to the conversation that was taking place, and my questions about the university's language policy document and the tension around the need to protect, promote, and develop the Estonian language in the context of increased internationalization of higher education.

Importantly, in addition to differences between the disciplines, there are certain key moments in scholars' trajectories at the university, particularly in the case of PhD students and postdoctoral researchers, when the need for Estonian is heightened and can generate more tension and problems for such researchers. Laura, a postdoctoral scholar in the area of biosciences, explained that she needed to take a certain course to conduct some experiments, but that at that point, the university was offering that course only in Estonian; although there were plans to offer it in English in the near future, it was unclear whether this would be soon enough for her to get the necessary course certificate. Along similar lines, she explained the case of two PhD students from abroad in her laboratory, who needed to pass certain obligatory courses to continue their studies, but those were only offered in Estonian at that particular moment, which generated complaints from the students.

Laura: si els entrevistes suposo que ja t'ho diran, però sí que es queixen bastant, perquè ells per exemple tenen assignatures de doctorat obligatòries

Josep: aha aha

Laura: que necessiten fer per passar els crèdits de doctorat i són en estonià. I clar és, sí que han demanat, i bueno, no es farà en anglès? I sí, l'any que ve, segurament, però bueno, aquest any, que és quan ho han de fer, és en estonià

Josep: aha. És curiós perquè a nivell de doctorat normalment la universitat fa publicitat dient 'tots els doctorats en anglès'

Laura: sí, per això també es queixen

Josep: clar

Laura: és que si m'han acceptat al curs de doctorat i ho venen com una cosa internacional

Josep: sí

Laura: després que em facin fer els cursos en estonià sí no, no té molt sentit, saps?

Josep: té poc sentit, sí

Laura: si ho està venent com per gent de fora i

Josep: sí sí sí sí

Laura: és clar, llavors, ells van a classe i van pràcticament a dormir

[Laura: if you interview them, they'll be able to tell you, but yes, they complain quite a lot, because they, for example, they have obligatory PhD subjects

> Josep: aha aha
>
> Laura: That they need to pass, they need the credits for the PhD, but these are in Estonian. And of course, they have asked, and are they not going to be in English? And yes, next year, probably, but well, this year, which is when they need to pass them, they are in Estonian.
>
> Josep: aha, that's interesting, because at the PhD level, the university always advertises itself as saying 'all doctoral studies are in English'
>
> Laura: yes, this is also why they are complaining
>
> Josep: sure
>
> Laura: because, if they've accepted me to a PhD course and they sell it as an international thing
>
> Josep: yes
>
> Laura: then for them to make me take the courses in Estonian, it doesn't make a lot of sense, you know?
>
> Josep: it doesn't make much sense, yes
>
> Laura: if they're selling this for people from abroad and
>
> Josep: yes yes yes
>
> Laura: of course, then, they go and sleep in those classes]

A typical key moment for PhD students is the preparation of the final manuscript for the defence of their dissertation. Naturally, the stakes are very high at this last stage of the PhD project, when funding might be running out, and students need to complete and defend their thesis so that they can be considered for job positions afterwards. There is a requirement that PhD dissertations written in a language other than Estonian must be accompanied by an extended summary in Estonian. However, institutional support for those who do not write Estonian is very limited, and so the preparation of this summary can be challenging. This was certainly the case with Martin, a recent PhD graduate in the field of life sciences, who found himself precisely in the situation described here, needing to defend his dissertation as soon as possible since the funding for his project had already finished.

> Martin: O sea me parece muy bien que haya un resumen, eso me parece muy bien, pero en mi caso el apoyo fue, o sea no, no encontré problemas en tener apoyo para ello pero sí que fue algo que no se pagaba extra a nadie y fue totalmente gente que me ayudó
>
> Josep: mhm mhm
>
> Martin: por nada, por un vino que le di a una y unos chocolates y tal
>
> Josep: mhm claro claro
>
> [...]

Martin: así que eso fue

Josep: claro claro

Martin: y además si le sumas el hecho de que son meses o semanas o incluso días muy importantes no?

Josep: sí!!

Martin: porque si estás sin financiación, tienes que saber qué pasa con tu vida, un momento así tan delicado que estás ahí culminando un trabajo de tanto tiempo, sobre todo además que una vez que lo entregas todavía tienes que esperar un mes y pico, mes y medio algo así en recibir una respuesta para hacer unos cambios y tal luego imprimirla

Josep: sí sí

Martin: son un par de semanas o tal

Josep: ya ya ya

Martin: todo eso son cosas que no dependen de ti

[Martin: I mean, I'm very much in favour of the idea of adding a summary, I think that's a very good idea, but in my case, the support was, I mean, no, I didn't have any problems in getting the support I needed, but yes, this was something that no one got any extra payment for, it was simply just people who would help me

Josep: mhm mhm

Martin: for nothing, for just a bottle of wine that I gave to someone and some chocolate and so on

Josep: mhm yes of course

[...]

Martin: and that was it

Josep: of course, I see

Martin: and on top of it, if you add to it that these are months, or weeks, or even days, which are very important, right?

Josep: yes!!

Martin: because you are without funding, you need to know what's going to happen with your life, such a delicate moment there, in which you are completing the work of so much time, because also once you hand in the document you need to wait for another extra month or so, month and a half, to receive the answer to then make some changes and get it to print

Josep: yes yes

Martin: it's a couple of weeks or so

Josep: yea yea

Martin: and these are things that do not depend on you]

At the time of the interview, Martin was working as a postdoctoral scholar in the same department where he had graduated a few months before, and he was getting ready to move with his family to another country in Europe where he had won a permanent position for himself. So, even though he was talking from a position of security, he recalled the weeks and months prior to his graduation as quite stressful. The requirement to add an Estonian-language summary to his thesis certainly added to that stress, particularly since he had to rely on his own network of specialist-friends in his area to prepare that summary, that is, he had to get by without much institutional support for preparing the extended summary in Estonian. Martin's case, and that of Laura and her PhD colleagues, reflect quite well the push-and-pull forces that transnational scholars may feel in connection to the Estonian language in Estonian universities. These push-and-pull forces may generate different paths towards positions of either adaptation or resistance towards Estonian. In either case, the path is not always clear-cut. Being more inclined to learning and using the language or not can depend on a number of different factors, including one's personal stance towards language learning, one's willingness to spend time and effort on it, the length of the time one has stayed in the country, and one's future prospects of remaining there for a longer period, as well as one's own discipline and the ideological stance that emanates from within that discipline.

The point to take from the above discussion is that different life trajectories will be reflected in different stances towards Estonian, and that whether one acquires the language or does not acquire it is the product of a complex set of variables intersecting in unpredictable ways. From the institutional perspective, and returning to the 'nationalizing' discourse that rests at the basis of much of its official discourse, we might argue that the 'protection, promotion, and development' of the Estonian language is a double-edged sword for transnational scholars: on the one hand, they might be happy to be given the chance to learn the language and immerse themselves in the local culture in a more in-depth way, but when this turns from an option into a requirement and a necessity, then more tension and frictions may arise. In that respect, it is probably not a coincidence that the promotional flyers and information brochures that the university prepares for newly arrived scholars from abroad portray the Estonian language in ways that present the learning of it as an option and, beyond that, they construct an exotic and colourful image of the language that may have unexpected consequences: attracting the attention of foreign visitors initially, but dissuading them from making any serious efforts to actually learn and acquire the language during their stay.

During fieldwork in 2013–2014, I collected a number of brochures and other material prepared by the university to welcome its newly arrived members. This included a booklet called "Welcome guide for international staff 2013/2014" (a document that can be found online and that has been published every year since at least that time, with only minor changes in content from year to year). The main purpose of the booklet is to offer a general overview of the university, the city of Tartu, and Estonia more generally, with practical information on a number of issues. Naturally, the guide touches on language, but it does so mainly to inform new staff members of the possibilities for learning both Estonian and English. In the one page dedicated to information on "Language courses for international staff" (p. 15), we read that international staff and their family members "are invited to join Estonian language courses on various levels", with courses that should provide them with the basics "for getting by in Tartu"; international members are also "welcome to attend a course about Estonian culture".

These are all free courses that the university offers to its international community. We can see here an attempt to narrow down the policy objective of promoting the Estonian language among those who do not have it as their L1 – foreign staff members – an objective which all policy documents analyzed in the previous chapter explicitly noted as an important goal for Estonian universities. At the same time, however, on the very same page of the 'Welcome guide' which discusses Estonian language courses we read about classes offered by the university on English for academic purposes. While it may not be written in such an inviting way as with the Estonian language courses, the guide does make the point that UT employees have the option of attending courses on English for academic purposes, also free of charge. Once again, this is in line with objectives of the *Language principles* and other policy documents of providing the university community with good language skills in English, but inevitably, this leaves the door open to transnational scholars like Emma, who decide to concentrate on improving their English, rather than investing their time (or spending it) trying to learn what they view as the exotic and limiting Estonian. In fact, the idea that Estonian might actually be too exotic for transnational scholars to seriously consider learning appears also in the Welcome Guide, albeit indirectly so. Page 10 of the guide includes a list of Estonian tongue-twisters (see Figure 4.2), which might be considered double-edged: amusing and funny, on the one hand, but highlighting the exoticism and awkwardness (and by extension, the unreachable nature) of the Estonian language.

Needless to say, as with all tongue-twisters, the words and phrases in this list are highly symbolic and not particularly practical in terms of everyday language use (certainly not for transnational scholars). The purpose of this list in the Welcome Guide can be understood as showing the uniqueness of the language; indeed, these are highly iconic (Irvine and Gal 2000) features of Estonian (particularly the rhyme of vowel sounds, as highlighted in two of the examples in the list). At the same time, however, the list can also be read as highlighting the

Try these Estonian tongue twisters!	
Kuuuurija	Moon explorer/researcher
Jäääär	Ice edge
Töööö	Work night
Kõueööaimdus (7 vowels in a row)	Anticipation of a thunder night
Hauaööõudused (7 vowels in a row)	Terrors of the night in the grave
Pagari piparkook	Baker's gingerbread
Kummikutes kummitus kummitas kummutis.	A ghost with rainboots haunted the chest of drawers.
Vanapagana rahatagavara	The Devil's money reserve
Ulata õlu üle Ülo õela õe õla.	Pass the beer over Ülo's mean sister's shoulder.
Võib võid võtta või ei või võid võtta?	May I take some butter or may I not take some butter?

Figure 4.2: List of tongue-twisters in Estonian included in the Welcome Guide (p. 10).

inherent difficulty of the language, a stereotypical idea that is not infrequently discussed both by foreigners who try to learn the language and by Estonians themselves. The latter implicit interpretation can make transnational scholars refrain from trying harder to engage with the language and simply keep it at a minimal communicative level, a consequence of the transient nature (Fabricius and Mortensen 2014) of their communities, seeing that they might be gone in just two or three years to a different country. Indeed, the last page of the Welcome Guide includes a glossary (*sõnavara*) of some basic Estonian terms and phrases translated into English (see Figure 4.3), another way of implicitly telling the international community of the university that this, in fact, is what they will need to know in Estonian.

In short, the way the university presents language issues to its international community might, inadvertently or otherwise, create the ideological space for a disengaged stance towards the Estonian language by the very same community to which the university wishes instead to promote the language. Next, we turn to look at how Estonian scholars themselves see the language question in the context of increased internationalization of the higher education system in the country, and how they feel about the balance between the need to protect, promote, and develop the Estonian language and the urgency of becoming more internationally attractive and competitive.

Sõnavara. Glossary

Tartu Ülikool, TÜ	University of Tartu, UT
peahoone (ph)	Main Building
TÜ aula	UT assembly hall
ruum, auditoorium	classroom
õppeinfosüsteem, ÕIS	Study Information System, SIS

Tere/Tervist	Hi/Hello
Head aega/Nägemist	Good bye
Tšau (ciao)	Hello, Good bye (informal, between friends)
Aitäh/Tänan	Thank you, Thanks
Palun	Here you are, Here it is, You're welcome, Please
Terviseks	Cheers, Bless you (literally: to/for health)
Jaa, Jah	Yes
Ei	No
Vabandust	Excuse me, I'm sorry
Kuidas läheb? Hästi	How are you? Fine.

üks, kaks, kolm, neli, viis, kuus, seitse, kaheksa, üheksa, kümme, üksteist, kakskümmend, kolmsada, neli tuhat – 1, 2, 3, 4, 5, 6, 7, 8, 9, 10, 11, 20, 300, 4000

E, T, K, N, R, L, P (first letters of weekdays, often used in opening hours)
esmaspäev, teisipäev, kolmapäev, neljapäev, reede, laupäev, pühapäev – Monday, Tuesday, Wednesday, Thursday, Friday, Saturday, Sunday

Mis su nimi on?	What is your name? (informal, between friends)
Mis te nimi on?	What is your name? (formal, polite, between strangers)
Minu nimi on …	My name is …
Palun üks kohv	A coffee, please
Palun üks õlu	A beer, please
Kui palju see maksab?	How much is it?
Ma ei saa (eesti keelest) aru	I do not understand (Estonian)
Ma ei räägi eesti keelt	I do not speak Estonian
Palun aeglasemalt	Slower, please

Avatud & Suletud	Open & Closed
Lahti & Kinni	Open & Closed / Occupied
WC	▲▼
Mehed & Naised	Men & Women
Sissepääs & Väljapääs	Entrance / Admission & Exit
Tasumine sularahas!	Paying in cash
Tasuta	For free

Figure 4.3: Glossary of terms included in the Welcome Guide (p. 38).

4.3 Local scholars' views on the internationalization of Estonian higher education

A number of participants that I was able to interview during my fieldwork in Tartu could be classified as 'local' scholars, researchers who have been involved with UT and Estonian research and higher education for a significant number of years (despite the problematic nature of classifying someone as 'local' in the modern world, discussed at the start of the chapter). A total of twenty such scholars were recruited in a convenience sampling fashion, and through a snowball technique, particularly relevant for recruiting those from the faculties of Medicine, Social Sciences, and Science and Technology. Several of those from the Faculty of Humanities belonged to my own network of scholars at the university, which explains the slight overrepresentation of scholars from this faculty in my sample; those from other faculties, however, were contacted through an instructor of courses on English for academic purposes, which not infrequently had an impact in terms of how I was seen as arriving at the interview and my goals in carrying it out – very often, at the start of the interview, participants would bring to my attention that their English was not 'perfect', or they asked me to pay no attention to their English skills, indicating they had an image of me as a scholar interested in English language issues. As seen in Table 4.3, all the informants reported knowledge of several languages, most of the interviews were conducted in English, and many of the informants had been at UT for many years, in one case as far back as the 1970s.

Table 4.3: Features of the local scholars interviewed at UT.

Pseudonym	Reported languages beyond Estonian	L-interview	Years at UT	Faculty
Tauno	German, Russian, English	English	Since 1989	Medicine
Piret	English, German, Finnish, Russian, some Japanese	English	Since 1997	Medicine
Lena	Russian, English	English	Since 1989	Medicine
Jaanika	English, Russian	English	Since 1992	Medicine
Katrin	English, Russian, Finnish, some French	English	Since 1992	Medicine
Ülle	Russian, English	English/Estonian	Since 1976	Science & Technology
Henno	English, Russian, German	English	Since 1997	Social Sciences
Kätlin	English, Russian	English	Since 1994	Social Sciences

Table 4.3 (continued)

Pseudonym	Reported languages beyond Estonian	L-interview	Years at UT	Faculty
Marco	English, German	English	Since 2003	Humanities
Kadri	Finnish, English, Russian	English	Since 1989	Humanities
Merje	Hungarian, Finnish, English	English	Since 1992	Humanities
Lisa	Russian, German, English	English	Since 1982	Humanities
Mihkel	English, Russian	Estonian	Since 2008	Humanities
Karin	English, Russian	Estonian	Since 1991	Humanities
Kristel	English, Finnish, German	Estonian	Since 1996	Humanities
Toomas	Russian, English	English	Since 1995	Humanities
Tiit	Russian, English	Estonian	Since 1984	Humanities
Pille	Finnish, Russian, English	Estonian	Since 1987	Humanities
Viktoria	English	English	Since 2004	Humanities
Aet	Russian, German, English	Estonian	Since 1984	Humanities

As seen in the previous chapter, when I analyzed the online comments to UT's new strategy A2020, the topic of 'language' was not immediately recognized as an important one for the university's agenda by local scholars, judging from the less frequent references to this topic in the online forum the university set up to comment on those issues its members felt should be dealt with in its new strategic plan. However, when prompted to discuss this in more detail, the interviewees did provide their different views and opinions on the subject at hand, reflecting on the different opinions around the language question at the university at the time of the interview, discussing what they saw as the challenges ahead, the developments over recent years, and the public discussion that had taken place around language in higher education. In this section, I present a summary of the relevant themes that emerged from the interviews with the twenty local scholars that participated in the study, supported by extracts from the conversations to illustrate the different points made in them.

One first idea that emerged as a common thread across several interviews with scholars from different faculties was the notion of 'normal' at the university. For scholars in the medical sciences, it seemed only natural that the university and its members had to engage more and more with the English language, whereas for scholars in the humanities, particularly those in history, 'normal' meant the capacity to work in different languages, including German and Russian, two key languages for accessing their sources and the material they work with. Talking about the different reasons for introducing English-medium programs in the Faculty of Medicine, Tauno, a key scholar in that faculty, explained that this was just a necessary development in his mind, something needed if UT wanted to be considered a normal university, if it was to be able to offer exchange opportunities for students from abroad. According to Tauno, the increased presence of English and the need to engage with it more and more might require a change of attitude, as we see in the extract below, hinting here at some resistance to English that he had observed in the faculty, something to which we shall return later.

> Tauno: but I think it is some kind of change in mindset we also understand the mind in the future I hope it's very nice for students and also teachers can free can freely feel yea [inaudible] in this English-language course I saw in other universities it's quite normal
>
> Josep: mhm mhm
>
> Tauno: if you want to be the normal university
>
> Josep: mhm mhm
>
> Tauno: normal faculty of medicine it means that we can communicate in Estonian but also in English
>
> Josep: mhm mhm
>
> Tauno: it's the normal

In the department of history, however, 'normal' seems to be interpreted differently. Lisa and Aet, the two historians I interviewed, both agreed that it should be seen as 'normal' that historians in Estonia had to master several languages, in particular German and Russian, the two key languages for accessing the sources they normally work with. Lisa put this in the following way:

> Lisa: yea I think we have to realize it differently in that all these cultural studies and history and philology it's very normal that we should know more languages than only one it's really important

Lisa explained why it can be a problem that young scholars cannot easily engage with historical sources in their original language:

> Lisa: I think this is among historians, this is very big problem for example; here in social department that's not too big problem because they have contemporary sources and so English is very ok, but for historians that's very big problem with younger generations not able read sources and then they choose topics where they can manage everything in Estonian but this is, well, this is so narrow so small world then

Aet has been trying to address the issue by helping students realize the importance of knowing German and Russian well as early as possible in their studies. According to her, once they realize they really need these languages, students are too far advanced in their Master's degrees, and they have already lost too much time trying to figure out the topic of their dissertation. She was certainly emphatic about the need for students of history to know several languages in order to do their work properly, and while she did welcome the opening up of the university and its becoming more international, receiving more and more students from abroad, she was consistent with Lisa in pointing out the lack of linguistic preparation of young historians as a potential problem for the discipline.

> Aet: kõik meie allikad on ju kirjas saksa keeles, vene keeles, rootsi keeles, isegi ladina keeles, me ei saa ainult hakkama eesti ja inglise keelega, me ei saa, ja seda kui ma enda õppeajaga võrdlen, kõik õppisime keeli, me saime veel siis vene keelt, inglise keelt, saksa keelt, ja ladina keelt. Ajaloos meil on vaja seda, ikkagi nagu vana baasi, põhja sinna alla, ja keeli nagu võrrelda, ladina keel kui sa oskad siis, kui sa õpid inglise ja saksa keelt siis sa oskad juba noh mingeid nagu seoseid mida, vene keel on teist moodi, aga mis praegu on häda on just see, keele tase on nii kohutavalt langenud, ja mida me õpetame kui meie tudeng ei oska lugeda materjale
>
> [All our sources are written in German, in Russian, in Swedish, even in Latin, we cannot get by with only English, we can't, and if I compare with myself, we all studied languages, we studied Russian, English, German, and Latin. In history we need this, indeed it forms a solid base, fundamental, and it's useful to compare languages, if you know some Latin, when you study English and German you can already make some connections, Russian is a bit different, but it's a shame now that the level of language knowledge has decreased so drastically, and what are we supposed to teach if our students cannot read the materials]

The idea of 'normal', then, is interpreted differently in different departments and faculties, as a result of disciplinary differences in terms of the role of language in the production of knowledge (Kuteeva and Airey 2014). Returning to the Faculty of Medicine, there is strong support for an increased presence of English at the university, so much so that some of the participants from that faculty who were interviewed imagined a near future where English had a more substantial presence in their department. This was the case with Lena, who explained that such a growing role of English would be welcome in the faculty, allowing them to receive more foreign students and visiting professors, even if that meant a decreased role for the Estonian language.

> Lena: I think that step by step the importance of English increases and it's good and we have more foreign students and I think here will be more visiting professors and invited speakers and it will be good, it would be good to speak in our seminars and workshops in English not in Estonian

The above should not be interpreted as a sign of a completely unproblematic relationship with and uncritical view of English in the Faculty of Medicine. Jaanika, Katrin, and Tauno all remarked that the motivation for introducing English-taught programs in the faculty was essentially economic. Indeed, according to the rules and regulations, students going through the English-language track in medicine need to pay the full fee for their studies, 11,000 euros per year. From 1996 to 2013, English-taught courses in the Faculty of Medicine were available for the first two years only, and after that, students would join the regular track in Estonian. As noted above, this option attracted mostly Finnish students, who in two years were able to acquire the necessary Estonian language skills to continue their education in Estonian. In 2013, a full six-year program in English became available, which was intended to attract a more heterogeneous pool of international students. This may create new challenges for those in the faculty when it comes to the English language.

True, Tauno says that "the English language is not a problem in medical field", and Katrin explained that "I'm not afraid of English". Indeed, the publication record of scholars in the field of medicine is overwhelmingly in English, and it has been so for a number of decades (we shall look into this in more detail in the next chapter); so the idea of working in English and publishing in English is not as troublesome in medicine as it may be in other fields. However, teaching requires a different set of attributes, preparation of seminars and lectures, oral skills during sessions with students, and so on, and this may well be something for which not all members in the faculty are as ready as they could be. The new cohorts of foreign students will likely come with heterogeneous levels of competence in English as well, and will come from more heterogeneous cultural backgrounds (as opposed to the largely Finnish population of students received thus far), and the six-year program will mean that more teachers will be involved in the English-language track for longer periods. In that sense, still referring to the need to incorporate English in order to become a 'normal' university, Tauno explained that there might be resistance from teachers in the faculty to engage with the language more actively for two main reasons: language skills and mindset.

> Tauno: I know that nobody want to make English because it's not easy, it needs knowledge of English, it's a different, you have a change in your mind, but if you want to be the normal faculty, the normal program, we have to do this one, it's some kind, it's very stupid to close

When asked about the support they receive from the university, all agreed that they do receive support and there are a number of courses and options available. However, those in the Faculty of Medicine in particular noticed that not everyone takes part in courses offered by the Language Centre, and several noted that those who perhaps need these courses most are the ones that seem less ready to take them.

This was confirmed by the course instructor who is responsible for these courses at the Language Centre, David, whom we will hear more about in the next section.

> David: so it's a... anybody can attend nobody's forced to attend it's a free for all, so the ones who attend are the ones who just like to follow courses, may have some time or just like to improve their language and a maybe they see it as a need, but they're quite eager participants. So the ones who might actually need it, they're not being, I think they're not being encouraged to go

According to David, the university's approach in making English more widely available to its community members has been rather limiting, in the sense that it sees English as only a skill at which researchers and teachers need to be proficient. Following negative reports from student evaluations in English-taught courses, David explained that the university management decided to run a test among those teaching in English in the Faculty of Medicine. David expressed his disagreement with the testing approach, and was of the opinion that to motivate those who might need more support in English, other alternatives would need to be sought (e.g. individual, one-on-one tutorials), but nothing materialized institutionally along those lines.

At the same time, teachers and researchers in the Faculty of Medicine are very much aware that they first and foremost train local doctors, so knowledge of Estonian is inescapable, and not everything can be delivered in English. Tauno explained that it is highly probable that patients are not comfortable with a trainee doctor who is not proficient in Estonian taking care of them. Jaanika referred to this in her interview.

> Jaanika: and another thing, we can teach in English but the patients from the south Estonia or old ladies or men they don't know English. If the students go on the fourth year to the hospital, they can't manage if they don't know Estonian at all

In fact, the university acknowledges that Estonian will be inescapable for students of medicine in Tartu, whichever the main language of study that they follow. In the information for prospective students on the website (https://www.ut.ee/en/prospective-students/medicine-studies), the following is mentioned in connection to the language of instruction within the English-taught program:

> Language: English. However, to be able to communicate with local patients, some knowledge of Estonian language is required as well. A limited number of Estonian courses are a compulsory part of the curriculum, but the students should also put additional effort into learning Estonian (passing the compulsory courses alone might not be sufficient).

In addition, some scholars in the Faculty of Medicine are reluctant to implement two full parallel programs, one in English and one in Estonian. Teaching all courses in two languages would seem to go against university policy. However, at the moment, it seems to be the way that the medical faculty operates, where teachers might be delivering a course in Estonian one day of the week, and another day they impart the same lecture in English. This is why Lena, as we saw above, was reluctant to have too much of a balance, and Katrin too was wary of it, adding that Estonian is still the preferred language of many in the faculty.

> Katrin: it also seems silly that a really good professor has to speak exactly the same thing twice, only once in Estonian and then in English, but I think the rules say that we can't make everything in English and of course in Estonian it's a little bit sometimes it's still easier to make jokes, so I think everybody enjoys speaking in Estonian

Other critical voices were heard from scholars and researchers in the Faculty of Medicine. Piret, for example, noted several clear mismatches between officially stated policies and de facto practices, some of which affected her own PhD students. Piret supervises foreign PhD students who were attracted by the possibility of completing their degrees in English at Tartu; however, once they had started their studies, it appeared that some compulsory courses were only available in Estonian (much like Laura's experience, discussed above with the transnational scholars).

> Piret: so this is kind of ah, they, they will come to the university to make the PhD here, so the university takes them as students, and should also provide the needs for graduation, in this field, the medical faculty or the university generally, I don't know from which level to blame somebody, so they haven't kind of found any good solution

Piret was clearly not happy with the current arrangements for her students, who would have to wait until the compulsory courses they needed to pass were made available in English. Piret had a general feeling of frustration with the mismatch between policy and practice. She belonged to one of the units within the faculty that is most highly internationalized, but in her experience, not enough institutional support is given to their unit; she felt there was a lack of recognition given to the principal investigator of her group, a prominent Estonian scientist who had decided to return to the country after a period of successful stays abroad. This lack of institutional support was visible to Piret in other examples, maybe more mundane ones. During the interview, she explained that on the occasion of an international choir festival which she helped organize in Tartu, they asked the university if they could prepare some brochures to deliver during the festival, advertising the possibility of studying in Tartu. According to her, the university didn't seem very interested in collaborating in that initiative.

> Piret: they didn't come up with anything fancy, it was really surprising for us, their solution was or their argument was that Finland and Sweden and Norway they have a lot of good universities by themselves so the students just do not want to come, so it was kind of, it was, so let us be here very small very tiny not doing very big things and let's be happy with it, I don't know it was kind of frustrating

Other voices critical of the internationalization agenda came from two scholars from other faculties, Ülle, from Science and Technology, and Kätlin, from Social Sciences. The latter was milder in her critical view than the former, expressing her reservations about the internationalizing trends in a more philosophical way, and asking herself simply when it would be enough, at what point would the university and its members think that they have reached a sufficient level of internationalization. Ülle, however, expressed stronger reservations around the development of more courses and programs taught in English, explaining that she was not sure whether Estonia should pay for the higher education of students from other countries – English-taught programs do carry a fee that students need to pay, but it is unlikely that this fee is enough to cover all the expenses associated with the degree, so some Estonian taxpayers' money is dedicated to sustaining English-taught programs. Instead, she stated, more attention should be paid to local students.

> Josep: *mis sa tunned et oleks vaja, või see ülikool nagu, ülevalt alla aitaks selle protsessiga?*
>
> Ülle: this is a very good question, because I am not sure that our university our government must pay for this that we prepare such students for other countries, *ma ei ole kindel, et me peaksime kinni maksma hindude, hiinlaste ja jaapanlaste haridust pigem võib-olla nad tahavad jääda, nad on põgenikud, aga samas esimesel võimalusel nad tahaksid siiski minna Euroopasse, ma ei ole selles kindel, et me peaksime selle kinni maksma*
>
> Josep: *see on suur küsimus, jah*
>
> Ülle: *sest meil väikese rahvana püsima jäämiseks, me peaksime eelistama oma inimesi ja oma üliõpilasi, see ei ole populaarne seisukoht*
>
> [Josep: What do you think should be needed, or the university like, from above, in order to help in this process
>
> Ülle: *this is a very good question, because I am not sure that our university our government must pay for this that we prepare such students for other countries* I am not sure whether we should pay for the education of Indians, Chinese, or Japanese, rather, maybe they do want to stay, they are refugees, but at the same time, maybe as soon as it is possible for them, they would like to leave and go to Europe, I'm not sure we should pay for that

Josep: this is a big question, yes

Ülle: because we, as a small nation, in order to survive we should prioritize our own people and our own students, this is not a widely held point of view]

Returning to the idea of 'normal' in higher education, Ülle was certainly of the opinion that teaching should be in the national language, but that research, particularly in her faculty, should be in English, in contrast to the situation in other faculties, more nationally oriented.

Ülle: but of course, how to explain this, this is of course good if we do textbooks in Estonian and popularisation of our disciplines in Estonian, but I afraid that quite difficult is write doctoral theses in Estonian in other disciplines that are international disciplines and all these articles you must have in English so and so and so. I think it's normal if we write PhD thesis in Estonian if we are talking about Estonian history, then it's normal, but if you want to do in these disciplines where all scientific work is international, not national sciences, then we want to be, that will be in English, of course, but for teaching, we must use Estonian language, I agree with this, and develop of course specific language for all these disciplines. In higher education, of course I respect that scientific language is English, of course, I am very agree with this, but we must teach our local students with normal local termins (terms), local language

With this national orientation, it was probably not a coincidence that Ülle was the only interviewee to refer to a problem that, until then, I had not asked about in any of my previous interviews: the question of Estonian-Russian students, whose Estonian language skills might not be sufficiently good to properly follow their courses at the university (an idea that was largely absent in the majority of policy documents analyzed in previous chapters, except for the national-level *Lifelong learning strategy*). Having concentrated so heavily on the question of the balance between English and Estonian, previous interviews had completely skipped this question, and this is something I shall briefly return to in the final chapter.

Ülle: *ja meil on mudugi see, väga palju üliõpilasi on venekeelsed, ja siis sellega on meil küll probleemi keele kasutusega, et nad ei saa aru eesti keelest korralikult*

Josep: *kas nad on eesti-venelased?*

Ülle: *eesti-venelased jah*

Josep: *aha*

Ülle: *ja ja paljud isegi võib-olla selle pärast langevad välja, et nad ei suuda eesti keelest [aru saada] ja ometi nad on teinud eesti keele eksami väga hea hindega, et sisse saada. Et noh, nii et probleem on, väga suur probleem, eesti keele oskus vene üliõpilaste hulgas*

[Ülle: and of course we have very many students who are Russian speakers, and with that we do have a problem with the language use, that they do not understand Estonian correctly

> Josep: are they Estonian-Russians?
>
> Ülle: Estonian-Russians, yes
>
> Josep: aha
>
> Ülle: and and many maybe that's why they drop out, because they can't handle Estonian, even if they have passed the Estonian language exam with a good grade in order to be accepted. So yes, this is a problem, a very big problem, the Estonian language skills among Russian university students]

As might be anticipated, the realities of different faculties did show up in the different opinions of the interview participants, as well as in their explanations of the motivations behind developing English-taught courses and programs in their departments. Henno, speaking from a key position in the Faculty of Social Sciences, explained that in the case of his department, English-taught programs were developed to attract international students, and in this way make up for the diminishing number of local students, whose quality had also decreased in the recent years.

> Henno: the primary push was demographic. The number of Estonian students is decreasing and we already couple of last years, we've seen that the quality of incoming students is getting poorer and poorer, then we decided that 2015 we open all Master programs in English hoping that this will bring bigger pool or at least provide this bigger pool to recruit student

Henno was openly in favour of developing English-taught programs, regardless of the resistance that these programs could encounter both from below (from other students in the department) and from above (from higher-level faculty staff and at the level of university management).

> Henno: and of course we had this discussion, there have been several attempts to move some of the Master programs into English and there has been resistance among the students, probably those students who were against this were the loudest, I wouldn't say there was a big number of students who were against this decision, probably for most of the students they don't care because there are quite many courses anyway which are already offered in English, our international colleagues, so that they anyway have to study in English. In many of the courses in Estonian, majority of reading is in English, so that they anyway have to handle, but of course there's some this kind of very emotional statements, oh if you teach everything in English then the Estonian language remains only as a spoken language and it totally and so on and so forth, this is this this kind of issue that we face

Henno acknowledged that, when it came to higher-level staff, they mostly supported developing English-taught programs, but also that his department had been alerted to the fact that they should tread carefully when it came to major changes.

In the context of the Master's program in philosophy having become an officially English-taught program, the university management was aware of the potential for a debate on language-and-identity issues to spread to different faculties.

> Henno: when we came out with this idea, in study office they said, oh maybe we should, because just before us there was philosophy that switched to English and this created this kind of emotional outburst among some of not our institute[1] [departmental] colleagues, but actually our Faculty of Social Sciences, so there were some people who were very outspoken in this matter, um, and then yea they said, oh if you want to move on with this idea, first get confirmation from your own colleagues from other institutes because they were the most, most vocal on this matter, so that this was this was rather this kind of not to say be careful, but it was more prepare the ground for this proposal

One particular initiative that Henno welcomed was the recent move by the university management to enable international students to live together with local students in the same student residences; until then, international and local students had been segregated, but recently they had been allowed to stay in the same dormitories. This, according to Henno, was a sign of the normalisation of the presence of foreign students in the university and in the town, which he evaluated as a positive move.

Pille, from a key position in the Faculty of Humanities, agreed with Henno in seeing the need to develop English-medium programs in order to attract more foreign students. This, according to her, is a completely normal process, seeing the direction that higher education is taking around the world, although her position is more cautious than that of Henno, hinting more at the establishment of parallel language use in teaching.

> Pille: *aga just viimastel aastatel on tehtud juurde ingliskeelne baka õppekava näiteks business administration, just, ja meditsiin. Eelmisest aastast on kaks väga olulist muutust, on ka arstiõpe ka võimalik õppida inglise keeles, siis tegelikult on kõikides eestikeelsetes õppekavades osa, on ju igas eestikeelses õppekavas on ka kirjandus, mida loetakse võõrkeeles, seda öelda, et eesti kava 100%, seda kindlasti ei saa nii öelda, on kirjandus mida antakse võõrkeeles, mis on normaalne, et loetakse võõrkeeles, on külalisõppejõude, et see on selline igati normaalne protsess, minu arvates*

> [but yes, just in the last few years English-taught BA programs have been developed, for example business administration, yes, and medicine. From last year there have been two important changes in medical studies, it is possible to study in English as well, in fact in all programs there is an Estonian-language component, and in Estonian-medium programs there is literature that to read in foreign languages, so that a one hundred per cent Estonian program, it is not possible, there is literature in foreign languages, and it's normal that it's in a foreign language, there are foreign teachers, this is sort of a normal process, in my view]

---

1 At Estonian universities, "Institute" is equivalent to "Department".

In the extract above, Pille uses the term 'foreign languages' several times, a label that, as we saw in the previous chapter, is frequently used in Estonian language policy documents connected to the internationalization of higher education. The use of this label in policy documents was discussed in several interviews, and invariably, all informants agreed that this was in fact a euphemism to avoid referring to English explicitly. This was a topic I talked about in more detail with Pille, since she had had a key role in developing the official language policy document of the University of Tartu. She explained that it is true that the policy document emphasizes the idea that programs need to be developed in foreign languages, in general, but that the idea is to develop English-taught programs.

> Pille: *aga samas rõhutatakse seda, et ka rahvusvahelise õppe arendamise jaoks on vaja pakkuda ingliskeelseid õppekavasid, noh muidugi räägitakse üldiselt võõrkeelsetest õppekavadest, noh, selline eufemism natukene, tegelikult mõeldakse inglise õppekavasid*
>
> [but at the same time it is emphasized that, to develop international studies it is necessary to offer English-language programs, well of course there is mention of foreign-language programs in general, but well, this is a bit of a euphemism, in fact the idea is to think about English-medium programs]

Pille, however, was explicitly in favour of a multilingual higher education. Even though it might be expensive to offer programs in more languages, other than Estonian and English, she saw this as an important goal. There should be, according to Pille, a feeling of reciprocity: if Estonian is to have a place in foreign universities, then other languages should also be awarded some space in Estonian higher education: "*et kui me tahame, et ka eesti keel oleks nähtav ka maailmas, et ka teistes ülikoolides oleks, me peame ise samamoodi käituma*" [so, if we want Estonian to be present in the rest of the world, so that it features in other universities, we have to act in the same way].

Another informant who had been closely involved in the production of the university's language policy document was Viktoria, who worked as a university administrator from 2004 until 2013. She explained that in the development of the policy document, the use of the 'foreign languages' label was "definitely a deliberate decision", but something that at first was intended to truly capture a multilingual goal of many within the university management.

> Viktoria: I don't remember when but I think that was something that was definitely discussed and in fact there was already an internationalization strategy at the university level that we wrote in 2005 or something like that, and I think even there, there were people who were involved with the English-language program development who really didn't want at that point yet, they weren't ready to say it's all about English, who were saying, but maybe we want to develop some Russian-language curricula or something else

Viktoria, however, acknowledged that with the passage of time, it became more and more apparent that in fact, the discussion was about English alone. Even if part of the target was potential international students from Russia, those students would want to come to Estonia to study in English, not in Russian.

> Viktoria: by now, I think there's enough experience with marketing and student recruitment in Russian, as well as discussion within Estonian-Russian students, where the marketers are international marketing teams that say no, Russian students who want to come to the European Union for studies don't want to study in Russian, so that's kind of how things have developed in that way, but also I think by now it's just that you know the times have changed, the university experience has changed, so now it's sort of like obviously we're talking about English-language curricula

According to Viktoria, the university has made huge improvements in developing towards a more internationally friendly institution in a relatively short period of time, from adapting and improving its website, to making general information more available in English to the international community in Tartu. With this in mind, now would probably be a good time to rethink and rewrite the language policy document of the university, in Viktoria's mind, but this does not seem to correspond to the opinion of the university management, who apparently decided it was not necessary to revise the *Language principles* that had been in place as part of the university's development strategy for 2009–2015, A2015. The new strategy plan A2020, as we saw in Chapter 3, has not explicitly addressed matters of language in any direct way, so it remains an open question whether this laissez-faire strategy will have any impact on the university's functioning in terms of the development of programs and curricula, and in terms of the situated practices of its members.

4.4 Conclusion

The analysis presented in this chapter reveals important results and nuances in speakers' language ideologies in a context of growing internationalizing initiatives at the university. For both transnational and local scholars, the different realities they live in are largely influenced by the different disciplinary fields in which they work. Regardless of background, scholars in medicine face a different reality, with different challenges, compared with scholars in the humanities and social sciences, mostly due to the different ways in which different disciplines operate with and through language. In addition, it is also possible to say that transnational scholars may face an added set of challenges, particularly in connection to how they are affected by the balance between Estonian, English, and other languages. Their motivation for and their path towards learning and using Estonian seems to be shaped by a number of factors which are generally non-work related – it is life outside work that might push speakers towards Estonian more decidedly. In fact, transnational scholars seem to be comfortable with the implicit stance offered by the university that, in the end, the chances are they will not need the language to carry out the relevant activities that form part of their work. However, when the language does become important in professional or academic situations (for example in having to obtain credits for PhD courses that are only offered in Estonian, or when preparing the summary of a PhD dissertation), the situation of transnational scholars tends to become more vulnerable. For local scholars, on the other hand, the linguistic ambivalence at work is something they are aware of, and, whether for economic or demographic reasons, many see the trend towards offering more English-taught programs as an inevitable development. Perhaps the humanities are still an exception, but the language policy implications of and the ambiguities associated with having to combine teaching in Estonian and in English are increasingly clear to scholars from all disciplines, with potentially important consequences for all of them and their everyday activities at work.

5 A historical perspective on language choice and attitudes in academia and higher education in Estonia

5.1 Introduction

This chapter aims at situating historically the evolution of the different language regimes within academia and higher education in Estonia, a necessary exercise if we wish to understand the present-day sociolinguistic configuration of Estonian universities. As we shall see, different historical periods have been associated with different language regimes, not surprisingly; so, one needs to understand every historical moment as a product of number of contingencies, and the present moment is no exception to that. The question that the chapter then turns to is how, in contemporary times, do teachers and students adapt to and react to the current language regime in place at the university. By contrast to the direct opinions from scholars that we have seen in the previous chapter, here we will turn to more indirect evaluations, not prompted explicitly by me as a researcher, with an analysis of participant-observation fieldwork conducted with two groups in two courses of academic English in Tartu. The observations yielded important information with respect to how speakers feel about academic English and their ideas associated with it as an abstract concept. Afterwards, the chapter presents the results of a separate study of the language attitudes and experiences of a group of undergraduate students in social sciences studying in English-medium courses at Tallinn University. The overarching goal with these two sets of data is to understand current attitudes and ideologies in Estonian higher education in light of the historical evolution of the different sociolinguistic changes that have unfolded in the Estonian context. We will thus dig deeper into the issues we have already seen in previous chapters, this time historicising our object of study and illuminating the topic with new sets of data that should help give us a fuller picture of the language question in Estonian higher education.

5.2 A historical perspective on languages in academia and higher education in Estonia

In order to better understand the current situation in academia and higher education in Estonia, we need to situate it in its historical context. In Chapter 3, we saw the recent developments in Estonian higher education in terms of the

https://doi.org/10.1515/9781501505898-005

languages of instruction over the past twenty years or so, and we have noted the tensions and ambiguities that the growth of English-medium courses and programs has generated in the country. It is important, however, to look even further back in time and to see how, over the past centuries, different language regimes have been in place in the Estonian scientific and higher education context, reflecting the changing sociolinguistic regimes that have shaped the country's history (a preliminary analysis of part of the data we shall look at below has already been presented in Soler-Carbonell 2014a, although here the scrutiny is taken further, with significant additional sets of data and information).

A source of inspiration in this first part of the chapter is Mortensen and Haberland (2012), whose analysis looks into whether English can be rightly called "the new Latin" of academia. Taking the University of Copenhagen as their case study, the authors suggest that the use of English today cannot be compared to that of Latin in earlier periods of Danish academia, emphasising that the motivations for using English nowadays (more commercially oriented) are radically different from the ones driving the use of Latin in pre-modern times, and Danish in modern and more recent times (Mortensen and Haberland 2012: 175). Drawing on Bull's (2004) model, Mortensen and Haberland propose that the history of modern European universities can be divided into three phases: (1) the Kantian university, during the seventeenth and eighteenth centuries, functioning mostly in Latin; (2) the Humboldtian university, spanning the eighteenth to the twentieth centuries, working mostly in national languages (e.g. Danish); and (3) the postnational university, since the end of the twentieth century, incorporating a much more active use of English. In each phase, a different legitimising principle was in place: 'ratio' ('reason') in the Kantian university, 'nation' in the Humboldtian, and 'bureaucracy' in the postnational.

Still following Mortensen and Haberland (2012: 177) and Bull (2004), the key point here is that changes in the local language regimes of universities should not be seen in isolation, but they should be read in connection to other societal and larger scale, supranational and global, changes. The Estonian context is not an exception to this, and here too we see the emergence and decline of different languages used for scientific and higher education purposes, closely following the changes experienced by the country at large. In this respect, however, the three-phase model proposed by Bull (2004) and Mortensen and Haberland (2012) does not fit entirely the Estonian context, due to its historical particularities. If we look at the history of the University of Tartu since its establishment in 1632, we can see how different periods have gone hand-in-hand with different language regimes in the country and at the university. Table 5.1 (based on Tamul n.d.) summarises them in chronological order.

Table 5.1: Historical chronology of the University of Tartu.

Years	Historical period	University name	Language(s)
1632–1710	Swedish Empire	Academia Gustaviana (1632–1665) Academia Gustavo-Carolina (1690–1710)	Latin
1802–1918	Russian Empire	Kaiserliche Universität zu Dorpat (1802–1892) Imperatorskij Jur'evski Universitet (1893–1918)	Latin, German, Russian
1919–1940	Estonia's first independence	Tartu Ülikool (University of Tartu)	Estonian
1940–1941	Soviet occupation	Tartu Riiklik Ülikool (Tartu State University)	Estonian, Russian
1942–1944	German occupation	Ostland Universität zu Dorpat	Estonian, German
1944–1989	Soviet occupation	Tartu Riiklik Ülikool (Tartu State University)	Estonian, Russian
Since 1989	Estonia's re-independence	Tartu Ülikool (University of Tartu)	Estonian, English

Source: adapted from Tamul, n.d. (http://www.ut.ee/en/university/general/history)

In the first period, during the seventeenth and early eighteenth centuries under Swedish rule, Latin would have been the default language at the university, although that does not mean that other languages, including Estonian, were completely absent from the educated world (the first Bible in Estonian was published in 1637). The university then remained closed for almost the entire eighteenth century, and reopened its doors in 1802, under the Russian Empire. Although German was declared the language of instruction at the university, other languages had some space as well. If we look at both Master's and doctoral theses produced during this period across the four faculties (Theology, Law, History and Philology, and Physics and Mathematics), we can see that German had a dominant position in all of them during the entire nineteenth century (see Figures 5.1 to 5.4), particularly during the second half of the century, when scientific production was most intense. (There were three Master's theses in French defended in the period 1802–1850 at the Faculty of History and Philology, and one Master's thesis also in French in the period 1851–1895 at the Faculty of Physics and Mathematics; these are not reflected in the graphs below, given these very low numbers.)

Interestingly, we see that Latin was used more frequently in the first half of the century than in the second half, when it faded away somewhat. In 1895, Russian was declared the language of instruction at the university, following a number of reforms in line with the general Russification trends of the time.

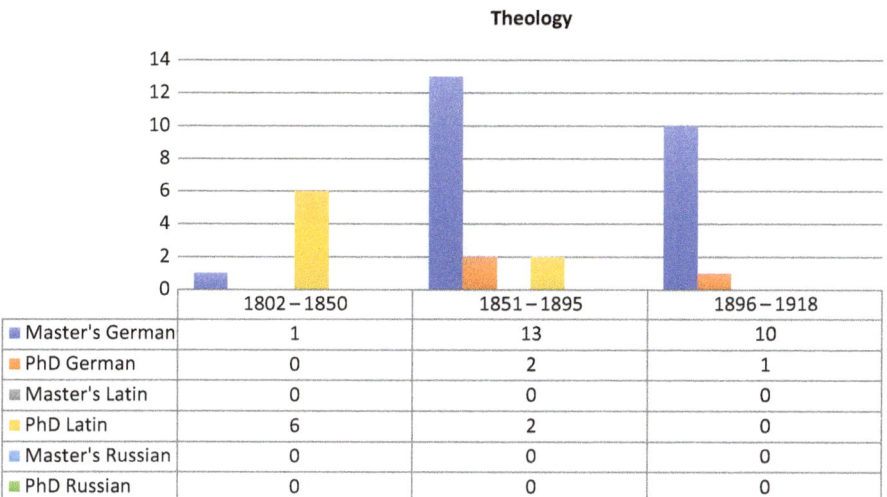

Figure 5.1: Theses defended at the Faculty of Theology 1802–1918.
Source: Based on data from Oisaar (1973).

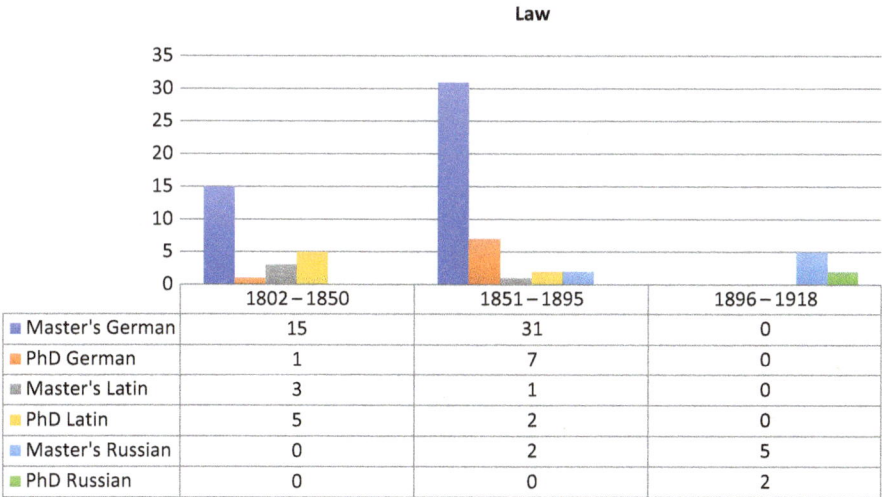

Figure 5.2: Theses defended at the Faculty of Law 1802–1918.
Source: Based on data from Oisaar (1973).

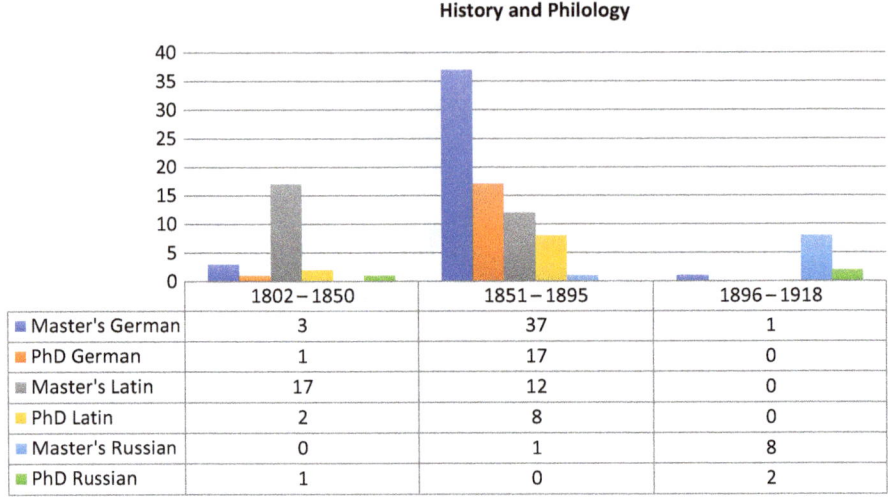

Figure 5.3: Theses defended at the Faculty of History and Philology 1802–1918.
Source: Based on data from Oisaar (1973).

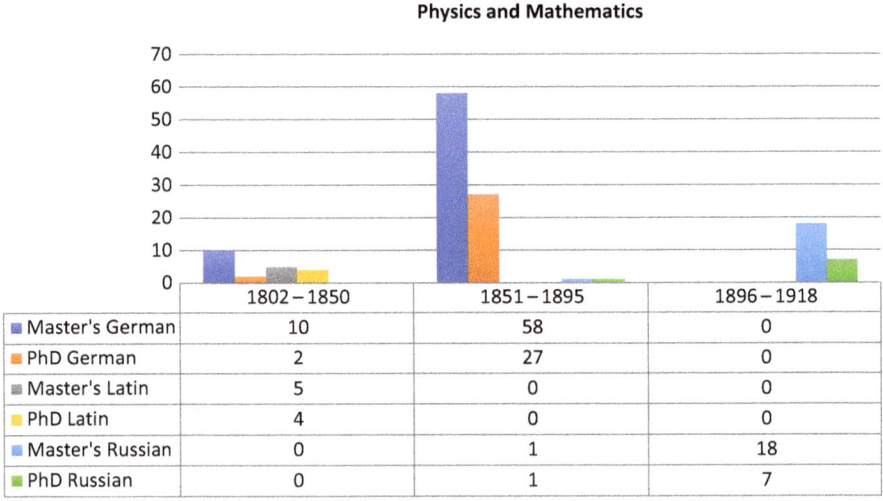

Figure 5.4: Theses defended at the Faculty of Physics and Mathematics 1802–1918.
Source: Based on data from Oisaar (1973).

With the exception of the Faculty of Theology, the theses produced during the period 1896–1918 reflect this changed policy. Notably, the number of theses in this latter phase declined significantly, likely as a consequence of the tumultuous nature of those years. (Those who read Estonian and Russian can expand on the details of the theses defended at the University of Tartu during 1802–1918 in Oisaar 1973.)

The interwar period and the World War II years brought more changes into the societal and university landscapes. In line with the nationalist agenda of the time, Estonian was declared the language of instruction of Tartu University in 1919; building on landmark events of the previous decades (e.g. the first scientific conference on the Estonian language held in 1908), the 1920s were a period of stabilization and development for Estonian, with key contributions by renowned linguists, and the establishment of an Estonian language professorship at Tartu University (Kasik 2011: 17). With the first Soviet occupation of the country in 1940–1941, the university curriculum was brought in line with that of the Soviet Union; subsequently, during the German occupation (1941–1944), German was declared the institution's language of instruction, but with little effect. The university was still in fact under the regulations of the University Act of 1938, which indicated Estonian as the medium of instruction (Tamul n.d.). The impact of World War II on the university was significant, with the loss of twenty-two of its buildings, including accommodation for staff and libraries (Tamul n.d.). Another important outcome of the war was the exile of a large number of academics, including all active linguists with the exception of Paul Ariste (Kasik 2011: 18).

Russian gained progressively in importance during the years of the Soviet occupation of the country (1944–1991), especially starting in the second half of the 1970s, however Estonian still maintained a prominent position within the university. Generally speaking, in the first decades the university made relatively few efforts at Russification, beyond symbolic gestures, including the removal of a statue of Gustav II Adolf in the 1950s. The reality is that up to the 1960s, key professors in many fields had already been active during the Estonian Republic of the interwar period. Maybe this explains why up until the early 1970s, it was viable for scholars to choose to write their dissertations in Estonian, as attested by the number of theses in this language defended both at the University of Tartu and at the Estonian Academy of Sciences from the late 1940s until the early 1970s (see Figures 5.5, 5.6, and 5.7).

From the start of the 1970s, both candidate theses and doctoral theses had to be written in the Russian language, as awarding the degrees had to be approved by the attestation commission in Moscow (Kasik 2011: 134). Data for theses published in the late 1970s and 1980s has not been found, but it appears that those were years of rather low scientific productivity, in the context of a

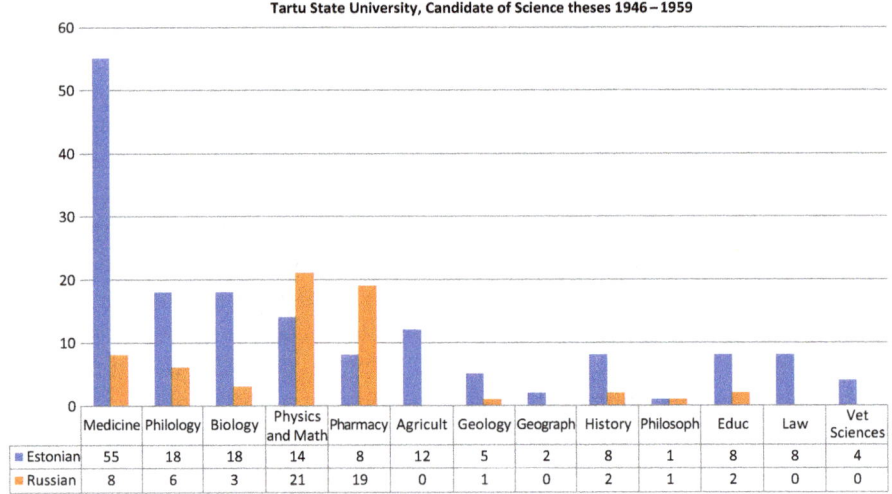

Figure 5.5: Candidate of Science theses (*kandidat nauk*) at Tartu State University, 1946–1959.
Source: Based on data from Tiik (1961).

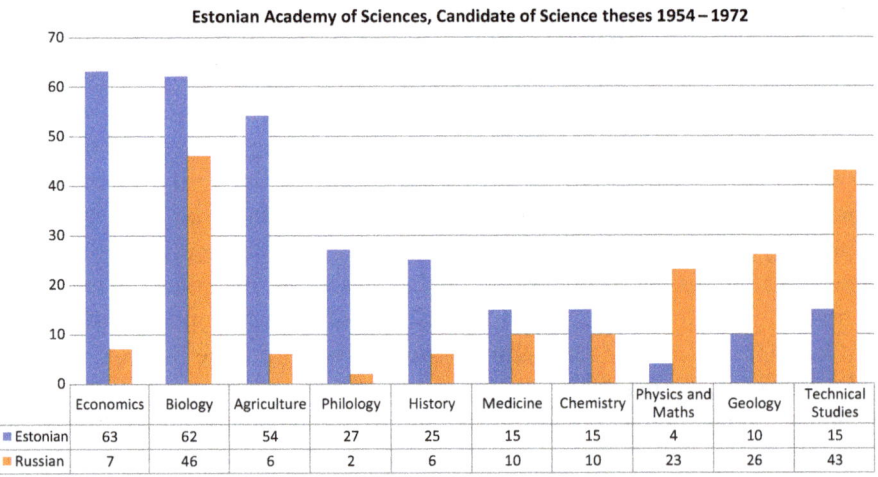

Figure 5.6: Candidate of Science theses (*kandidat nauk*) defended at the Estonian Academy of Sciences, 1954–1972.
Source: Based on data from Liblik (1973).

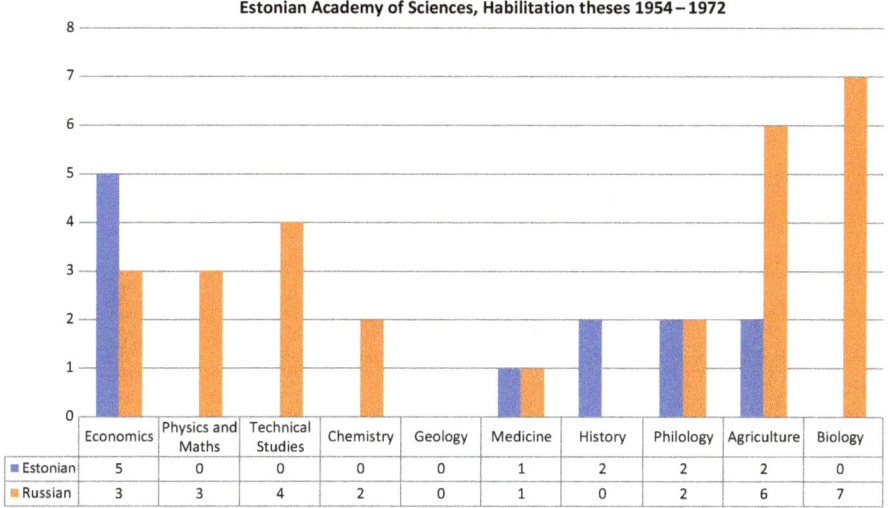

Figure 5.7: Habilitation theses (*doktor nauk*) defended at the Estonian Academy of Sciences.
Source: Based on data from Liblik (1973).

Soviet Union increasingly in crisis, and within a broader economic recession in the 1970s. However, one possible way to overcome the lack of information on the languages used in doctoral dissertations during the last period of the Soviet Union is to look instead at the languages which members of the Estonian Academy of Sciences used in writing articles. Granted, scientific articles and doctoral theses are different genres, written for different purposes and with different audiences in mind; nonetheless, looking at the evolution of the output of academy members and the languages they used for publication purposes throughout the decades can give us important information about developments and changes in the language regime of academia in Estonia. In that respect, looking at the languages in which members of the Estonian Academy of Sciences have published since the 1950s onwards, one gets the impression that a change towards publishing increasingly in English was already well in place in the 1980s. In Figures 5.8, 5.9, 5.10, and 5.11, we can observe a representation of the production of a sample of scholars who are current members of the Estonian Academy of Sciences, divided into four divisions: Astronomy and Physics (Division 1); Informatics and Engineering (Division 2); Biology, Geology, and Chemistry (Division 3); and Humanities and Social Sciences (Division 4). Data for these figures have been obtained from a representative sample of academicians in each division (8 out of 24 in Division 1; 8 out of 23 in Division 2; 10 out of 29 in Division 3; and 9 out of 21 in Division 4).

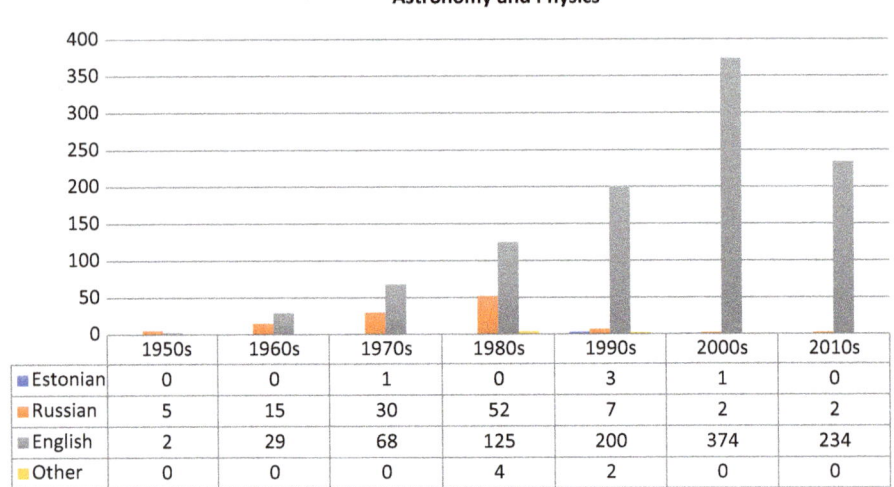

Figure 5.8: Publications of members of the Estonian Academy of Sciences – Astronomy and Physics.

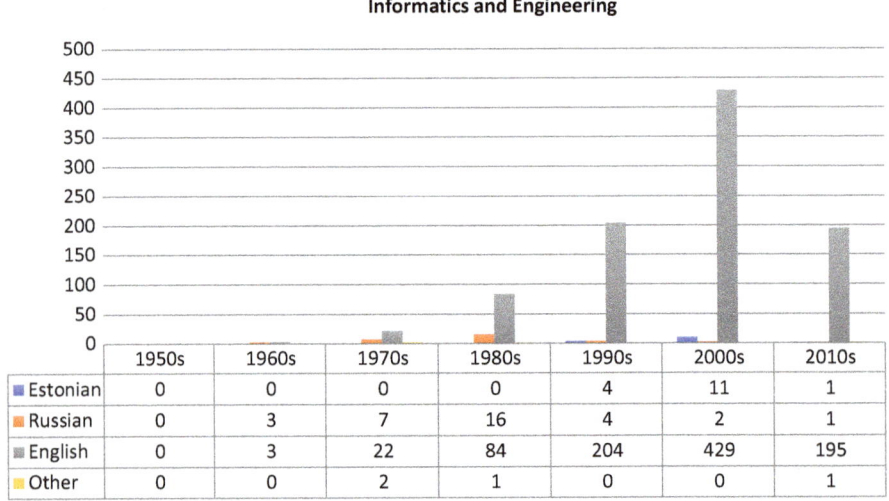

Figure 5.9: Publications of members of the Estonian Academy of Sciences – Informatics and Engineering.

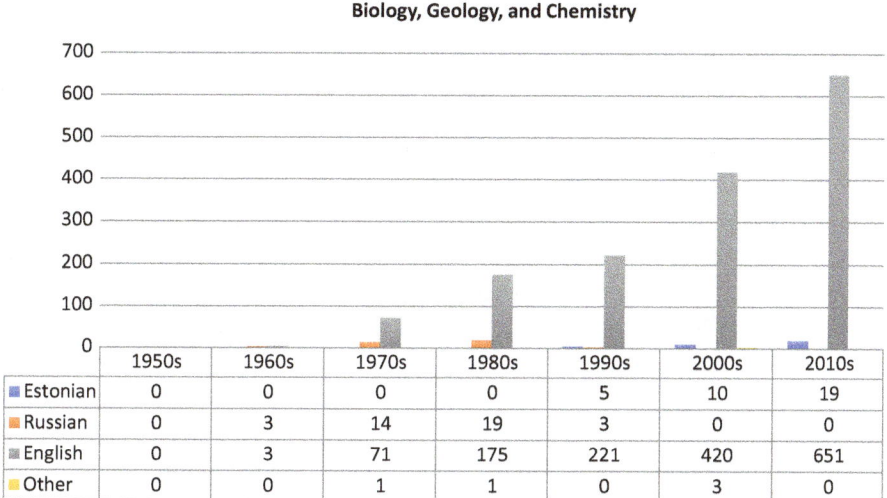

Figure 5.10: Publications of members of the Estonian Academy of Sciences – Biology, Geology, and Chemistry.

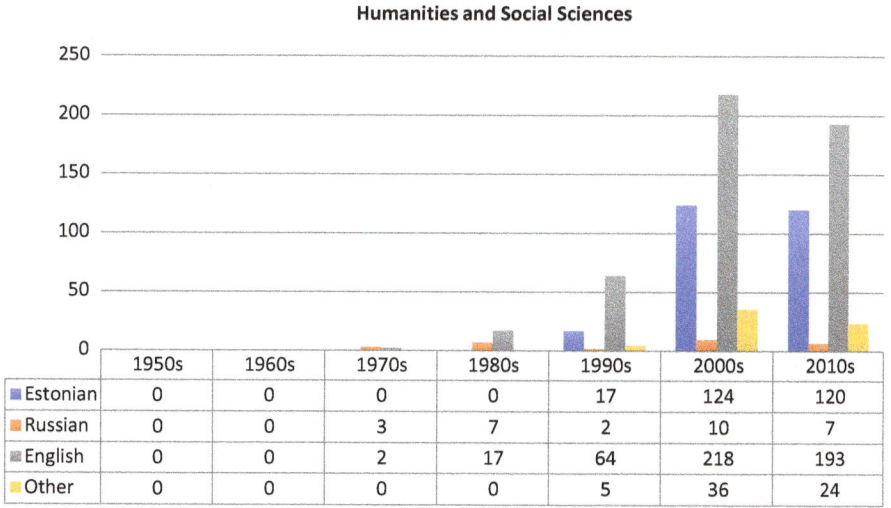

Figure 5.11: Publications of members of the Estonian Academy of Science – Humanities and Social Sciences.

The CVs of the selected academicians were consulted online on their Estonian Science Information Portal (etis.ee) sites, where information on all of their publications is available, including the language in which each item was published. Only publications such as journal articles, monographs, and book chapters were included in the count; popular science works, by contrast, were excluded. This may have biased the results somewhat, given that the vast majority of popular science works are written in Estonian, but in reality, these publications constitute only a small fraction of the overall scientific production of all the academicians.

In Figures 5.8 to 5.11 we see a rather clear and distinguishable pattern: even before the 1980s, English was already the default language in which current members of the Academy were publishing their work, something that has increased and solidified over the years, particularly in the first three divisions. In Astronomy and Physics, Russian was a less frequent but viable option until the 1980s, but quickly faded away in the 1990s. By way of contrast, the current academicians in the Humanities and Social Sciences became active publishers only later, primarily from the 1990s. They show a more multilingual portfolio of publications, and not surprisingly, it is the only division where Estonian-language items represent a significant share of the overall scholarly production; but even in this division, English-language publications outnumber the rest.

This pattern is in line with what we see in the theses published at the University of Tartu since the 1990s, given in Figures 5.12, 5.13, 5.14, and 5.15.

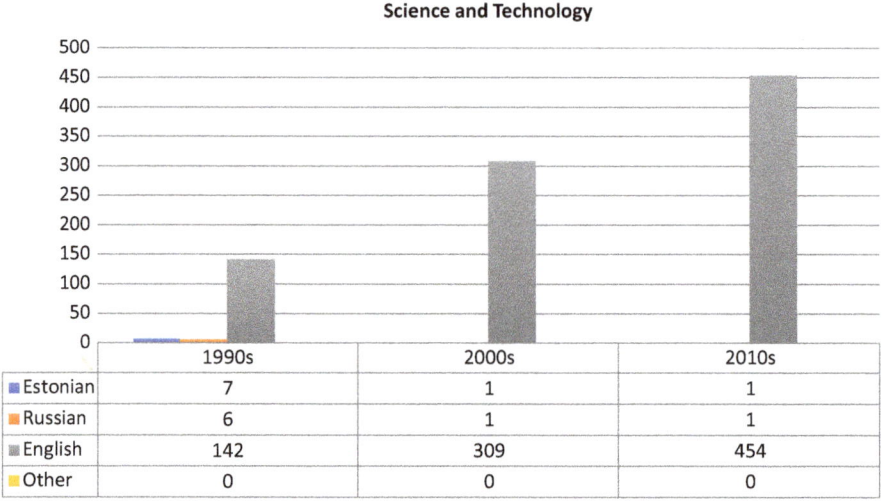

Figure 5.12: PhD theses defended at UT, 1991–2017: Faculty of Science and Technology.

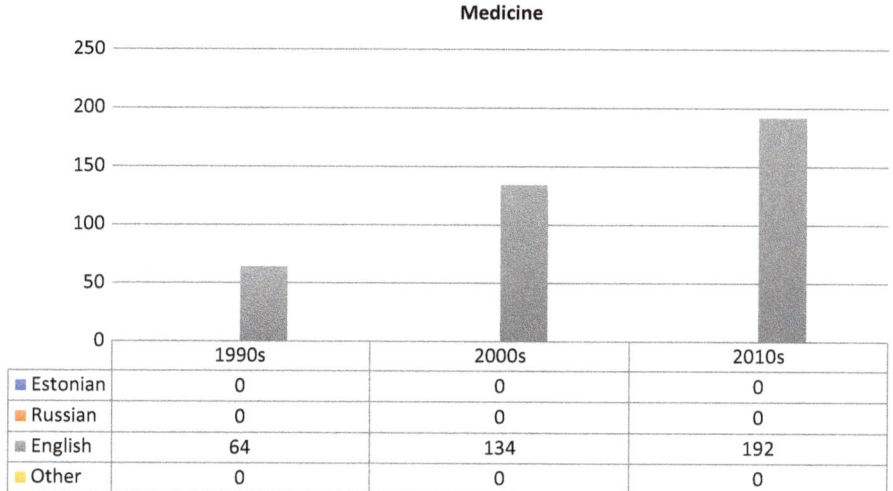

Figure 5.13: PhD theses defended at UT, 1991–2017: Faculty of Medicine.

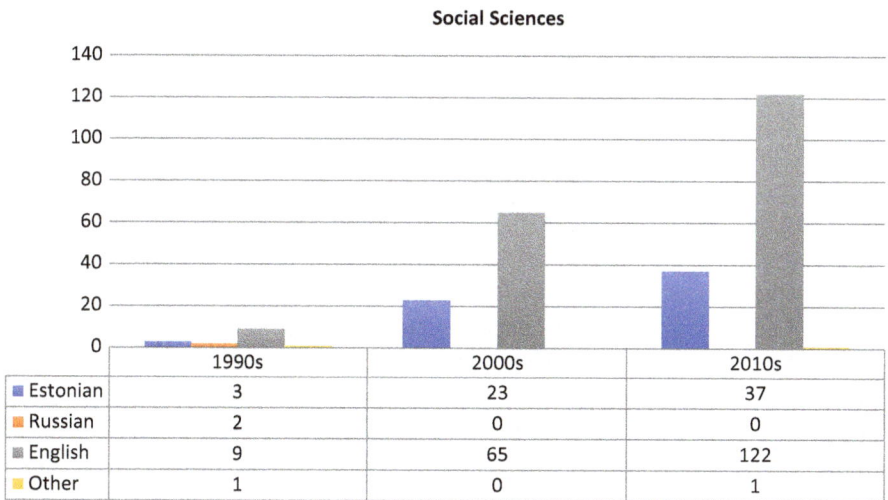

Figure 5.14: PhD theses defended at UT, 1991–2017: Faculty of Social Sciences.

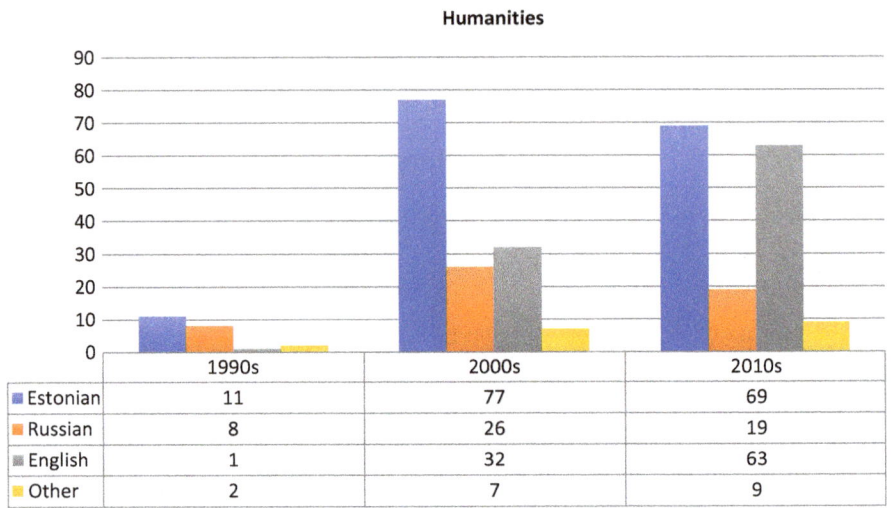

Figure 5.15: PhD theses defended at UT, 1991–2017: Faculty of Humanities.

Here the same pattern is repeated, with only the Faculty of Arts and Humanities showing a significant number of theses published in Estonian, although even in this faculty, English-language theses are clearly on the rise, while theses in other languages are declining. The dominance of English in the hard sciences and medicine, and the more frequent presence of Estonian in the arts and humanities, is in line with more general disciplinary patterns of variation and the role that language plays in scientific production and dissemination in each field (Kuteeva and Airey 2014). We shall return to this idea below. For now, the point that needs to be emphasized is that the shift towards English as a language for scientific publication is not an isolated factor, but as stressed above, it needs to be read against the background of broader and larger societal transformations. Not only had the English language already established itself in a dominant position as an international language for scientific communication in the 1980s, but the turn from the 1980s to the 1990s was also a highly consequential political and social moment for Estonia. The regaining of the country's independence did not just mark a change in the political landscape, it also signalled the end of an era where the Estonian majority felt the country had been held back from the sphere it belonged to, that is, with other countries in Western Europe. Many, then, saw re-independence as a 'return to the Western world' (Kasekamp 2010). So, much like societal changes in the turn from the nineteenth to the twentieth century marked a shift from German to Russian as a language of scientific production, so too in the 1980s societal changes (nationally and globally) marked a shift towards English, albeit to a much greater and more sustained level.

To sum up, this first half of the chapter has provided a historical overview of the different language regimes that have been in place in the context of academia and higher education in Estonia over the past centuries. In line with Mortensen and Haberland (2012), drawing on Bull (2004), changes in the language regimes at universities have to be analyzed jointly with broader societal changes, not in isolation. The long-term perspective provided here allows us to see that sociolinguistic configurations are not fixed and permanent, but in constant change, albeit large-scale changes rarely happen overnight. In the nineteenth century, it was German, not Estonian, that functioned as the 'national' language at the university, as opposed to the cases of Denmark or Norway explored by Mortensen and Haberland, and Bull, respectively. This is in line with the fact that higher education was mostly attained by the Baltic-German elite of the time, precisely the group that would carry the ideas of Enlightenment and Romanticism to Estonia. The Russification wave of the last period of the Russian Empire at the turn of the century enhanced the presence of Russian in Estonian academia, albeit with a low level of impact. The first independence period in the second quarter of the twentieth century brought Estonian to center stage in the country's science and higher education, and the language still managed somehow to maintain its presence throughout the Soviet occupation of the country. The last major change in Estonian scientific production has been the more active use of English, since around the 1980s. A general political will to turn to Western powers combined with the firm establishment of English as a language of international scientific communication have resulted in current Estonian scholars mainly writing their work in English. Only in disciplines in the arts and humanities and, to some extent, in the social sciences do scholars seem to be able to keep a multilingual portfolio of publications. In other fields, for example in science and technology and medicine, the language of publication does not seem to be a question, but it looks 'natural' that English is chosen (see also Ljosland 2007 and 2011 for similar results in the Norwegian context).

This picture of most scientific texts being published in English should not obscure the fact that in the different stages of scientific production, other languages may play significant roles, even though the end product is increasingly presented in English (see also Bretxa et al. 2016; Salö 2016). However, the disciplinary divide that we can observe seems clear and is consistent with how different areas of knowledge operate and use language. Kuteeva and Airey (2014), drawing on Bernstein (1999), propose that these disciplinary differences can be explained by the fact that in the more technical fields, language plays a less relevant role in the construction of knowledge. Contrarily, in the humanities, language is a central element in discussing and negotiating meaning and developing arguments. Kuteeva and Airey's analysis suggests that language policy documents would benefit from explicitly acknowledging this complex and multifaceted reality in the context of higher education. This would help the relevant authorities in being able to better diagnose the language needs and requirements of speakers, and offer them more effective language support.

It is true that in the data presented above, we have focused substantially on the language of PhD theses. However, this seems to be an important issue for language policy-makers in the country; some argue that if PhD theses shift entirely to English, this will add to the feeling that Estonian is not properly fit for scientific discussions. In line with that, the idea of the need to protect, promote, and develop the Estonian language appears in almost all policy documents in connection to the internationalization of higher education in the country, as we have seen in Chapter 3. More specifically, the *Development plan of the Estonian language 2011–2017* states that PhD theses written in a language other than Estonian should include an extended summary in Estonian, precisely with the aim of enhancing the development of specialized terminology in the language. The *Development plan* notes that in 2010, 80% of dissertations written in a language other than Estonian included an Estonian-language summary, and set the goal for 2017 that 95% of those theses would include such a summary. However, if it is left entirely up to the student to develop the summary in Estonian, without much guidance or systematic support, this can be problematic, not only for those who do not speak/write Estonian (as we saw in the previous chapter with the example of Martin), but also for Estonians who are L1 speakers of the language, who might not be all that used to writing in academic Estonian.

Although there are scientific journals of high quality where Estonian scientists could in principle publish their work in Estonian, even the journals published by the Estonian Academy of Sciences operate mostly as English-medium journals. So, beyond those in the humanities, there is little incentive for Estonian researchers to publish in Estonian, caught in a system that offers little rewards to publish scientific texts in a language other than English. It is certainly true that when it comes to popular science texts, Estonian scholars seem happy enough to write those in Estonian; it must be recognized, however, that those texts are written more sporadically, since they carry less value for career development, and they include a more simplified jargon, less loaded with specialized terminology. So, attempts by policy-makers to enhance scientific publication in Estonian, increase the scientific output in the language, and strengthen its terminological pool need to be carefully thought out in order to avoid the trap of the policy–practice disconnect, a disconnect has been observed and documented in the context of higher education in the Nordic European countries (Hultgren and Thøgersen 2014).

The above data and discussion have focused on the shifting preferences in language choices made by Estonian scholars for scientific publication, that is, for knowledge dissemination. This has been taken as a symptom, an index, of the changing sociolinguistic regimes operating in the field of Estonian higher education in different periods of time. Certainly, one should be careful not to equate the dominant position of a language in scientific dissemination with a dominant position within the entire field; at present, while English does enjoy a dominant position in that respect in a great number of higher education systems in the world, this does not mean that science is produced exclusively in that language (cf. Bretxa et al. 2016; Salö 2016). In any case, in combination with what has been presented and discussed in previous chapters, it seems undeniable that English now occupies an increasingly relevant position in Estonian higher education, as a result of a concatenation of a number of socio-historical factors. Building up from the interviews presented in the previous chapter, what remains to be answered is how those who find themselves engaged on a daily basis within Estonian higher education adapt to, react, and feel about the increased relevance of English. This is the question that the next two sections attempt to illuminate in more detail, starting with implicit views of what 'academic English' actually is for teachers at the University of Tartu, and moving next to the analysis of the attitudes of students towards learning through the medium of English in Tallinn.

5.3 Ideas about academic English among teachers and researchers in Tartu

During the autumn term in 2013, from September to November, I took part in two courses at the University of Tartu designed to support its community of researchers in developing their skills and fluency in academic English. Both courses were relatively well attended, with 10–12 participants, who were researchers and scholars from different faculties across the university, but mostly from the Faculty of Humanities and Social Sciences. One of the courses was designed as a general course on academic communication (I shall call it Course A), the other specifically targeted oral presentations in academic settings (I shall refer to it as Course B). Participants came from different departments and faculties of the university, and were of different ages and levels of seniority, from professors and associate professors to PhD students. The vast majority were local Estonian scholars, although some international researchers were also present: a social scientist from Russia and a chemist from Ukraine in Course A, and two Chinese scholars (one biologist and one literature scholar) in Course B. The instructor of the two courses was the same person, an experienced scholar in academic language, whom I shall refer to as David. David played a major role in allowing me access to both courses and helped me greatly in obtaining participants' consent for me to observe them and for our sessions to be audio-recorded.

During the sessions that I observed, my role as a researcher merged with that of a course participant, that is, I conducted participant observation throughout the two courses. Once consent was gained from all participants, I was able to turn on the audio-recorder so that I could later transcribe the key passages that were relevant for my research and in this way, recover the details of the important instances that I had observed and noted down as field notes. In total, I recorded approximately 18 hours of classroom interaction in the two courses together, and the expanded transcribed notes amount to approximately 14,000 words.

My essential goal with the observation of those sessions was to gain access to an insider's perspective of what 'academic English' represented for a group of scholars at the university, to uncover the kinds of ideas and representations they held around 'academic English' in an indirect manner, without explicit elicitation through a direct interview question. In a context where the need, or indeed, the pressure, to engage more and more with the English language is on the rise, especially orally (for teaching) but also in written form, the question of what researchers think about academic English, what notion of it they have, was an important one in the frame of my project. This was the question that I sought to answer with my participant observations in the two courses that I attended and observed. In what follows, I present my analysis of what transpired to be the most relevant ideas about academic English, as reflected in the discussions held during the two courses.

Naturally, one of the key actors in shaping an idea of academic English in both courses was David, the instructor, who had his own predefined idea of academic English, which he naturally intended to convey to the course participants. Since the two courses were framed slightly differently, David emphasized a similar idea of academic English in slightly different ways. Course A was framed as a course on academic communication, focusing mostly on pragmatic aspects of the use of English in international settings; Course B was designed to enable participants to reflect on and practise their oral skills in academic English, particularly for conference presentations. In both courses, David attempted to find a difficult balance between the idea that one has to pay attention to the context first, rather than proficiency or language correctness, and his perception and observation that students attend his courses to either 'brush up' their English or to work on their grammar and vocabulary.

In one of the seminars, the discussion revolved around the use of the form 'wanna' in a formal setting; the instance discussed in the seminar corresponds to the actual 'wanna' that we have already commented on in Chapter 3, uttered by

Jaak Aaviksoo during the opening conference of the seminar to celebrate twenty years of English studies at Tartu University. David presented this as an instance in which linguistic form and context did not match, an instance that he found surprising: in such a formal setting, this 'wanna' seemed to be off, not appropriate for the context.

> D: there's this fine line between, I think he feels at home, but he's delivering a very formal speech, especially in that context, and also in this 'wanna' I think you can see his personality coming out, and I think it's great, but it was very conflicting for me somehow, and it's very comfortable to say this, if you start using it a lot, it becomes part of your language, and I think if you think about the academic context, you really have to watch out for this, these 'wannas' and 'gonnas', and I think he mentioned that he was in the States, he studied in the States, or?

This sparked a lengthy discussion between David and one of the course participants in terms of how formal and informal you can be in your language depending on the context, and what constitutes correct versus incorrect language, and how important it is to be expressive emotionally while at the same time making sure that you are linguistically correct so that the message can be appropriately transmitted. In the concluding part of the discussion, another participant intervened to say that according to her, this was simply an expression of how Aaviksoo is, of his personality, someone who, beyond controlling certain forms, is more interested in getting his message across. This was an opportunity that David took in order to introduce (once again) his idea of how important it is to look at context first, look at the actual message, and only later on judge the correctness or appropriateness of the actual linguistic formulation. We see this in the extract that follows, which also includes David's idea of what Estonians think of English language learning.

> D: one thing I want to clarify, I didn't say it was a mistake, the fact that he used 'wanna' is not a mistake
>
> P1: is a vocabulary
>
> P2: colloquial
>
> D: but it's not a mistake
>
> P1: not a mistake
>
> D: it just conveys a specific type of, well, how he felt, and of course the reason why, I will have to explain it again, the reason why I brought it up is because of the context
>
> P1: style, it's not the same style what you think
>
> D: and it's actually well it's not his first language as well, and therefore well it's actually ok that he does it, but then your question if you were to have that kind of speech in the UK,

then of course it would just ring, or raise some eyebrows, not because it's wrong, but just because, it's just within that context, it's unexpected, whereas for example if you were to do that in the States, then everybody would be like oh, aha, normal, but the reason why I pointed that out is because I never expected it, because I think when Estonians want to learn English, they want to learn perfect English, and I don't think there is such a thing, and that's something I think that you have to try and get rid of, you don't want to learn perfect English, yea, I think what you want to be is much more aware of how you are communicating and what you are communicating and then build from this, because unless you live in an English-speaking country, unless you breathe it and use it on a daily basis, will you learn to speak it like natives do, and then again I use inverted commas in natives, but if you live in this environment, and you are using it only on a sporadic basis, not on a daily basis, then there's only so much you can do, and you also wouldn't want to achieve that, in that sense, you maybe can't.

From the very first session, David had clearly aligned himself with a critical view of 'native speakers', which he viewed as rather unhelpful and difficult to deal with. Instead, he time and again tried to highlight the idea that speakers should be aware of their context first and foremost, to understand the context in which they find themselves and to be able to use language to their advantage in order to successfully communicate their ideas. This argument against native speakerism and in favour of mastering the context first is reflected in the following extract.

> D: but there's something to be said I think about native speakers and we'll come back to this later, I think it's a very interesting concept that we have about native speakers and maybe something that's not always right, somehow we hold them quite high in our, in the way we perceive them for example about their fluency, something that we consider to be the epitome, that they are the custodians of the language, they're the ones who speak it so well or know it so well, because it's their native tongue, but in terms of the context that you are in, so again that context, for teaching and presenting, maybe they are the ones who are, you know, which actually don't speak very good English, so something to discuss, and we'll discuss it later on. Because like you said it's better to communicate when there are non-native speakers

However, time and again David also found himself trapped in discussions of language correctness, rather than context appropriateness. Participants raised questions about the correctness of their suggestions, which David tried to steer into discussions of the appropriateness of the language. One of the central discussions in Course A was dedicated to email reading and writing. Here, David tried to emphasize the notion that it is important to read between the lines and see how questions and requests can be formulated in email writing, and how we should respond to them. One of the course participants, however, kept insisting on her need to know whether a particular formulation was actually correctly formulated or not, to which David refused to reply directly with a yes or no answer.

P2: finally, I understood correctly, after 'Dear Martin', I put 'I hope you are doing well', is it correctly, not familiar?

D: ah, there is of course familiarity, so you are at a level where you know each other professionally, I wouldn't really say personally, professionally, because if you know each other personally, then the question 'how are you' is much better because then you leave the other person the choice to answer.

Not surprisingly, when discussing matters of proficiency and fluency, David would again try to emphasize the importance of context, and the importance of how to operate in different kinds of settings and under different circumstances. Some participants did indeed see his point; in the following extract, one of the course participants (P5) mentioned she might in fact be more proficient in English than in Estonian to talk about certain work-related topics. At the same time, however, others (e.g. P8 in the extract) kept clinging to the idea that proficiency and fluency is about vocabulary knowledge.

D: yea so, I think this fluency in speaking is something, because we have to speak in so many different contexts and about so many different topics quite often, ah, this communication as speaking to becomes very complicated, I think this fluency is about being able to find the glue that is going to connect all the things that we want to say, ahm, like for example, the example I gave last week, the question how are you doing, because we actually don't encounter this question very often, intuitively we don't know how to answer, intuitively we see ok it's a question, a question requires yes–no answers, so I notice that it's a question, just to be polite I will answer yes, but of course it's the wrong answer in that case, so how do we build up fluency, when we think about fluency very often we look at it in terms of our language proficiency, fluency is related to language proficiency, which means that in Estonian you should be quite fluent, but you might be less fluent in Estonian when you have to talk about a topic you actually don't know

P5: but not only, even in our own topics, because we don't have the Estonian terms very often

D: ok, so then you have the conflict of the English language creeping in

P5: yea, it's easier to say it in English

D: right, so you would even say within certain topics you are much more fluent in English

P5: there are no agreements about certain terms yet, and then it's easier for students who are writing their papers to use the English term because then you can be sure

D: yea exactly, so for me in Estonian, I'm quite fluent in coffee breaks, small talk, but when it comes down to topic-specific meetings, then I'm lost, so how about you in English, would you say you are fluent in academic English, no, why not?

P8: I think I lack the active words, sometimes when I speak I need to think what was that word? I just stop in this case

Similar issues emerged during the seminars in Course B, oriented towards developing participants' skills in academic oral presentations in English. Because of the structure of the course and the different activities in it, in contrast to Course A, David was more able to comment on participants' linguistic production in a more detailed way, focusing on issues of linguistic correctness, particularly in connection to pronunciation matters. This was an issue that repeatedly emerged several times during the course, in spontaneous questions from participants or in more detailed and focused feedback from David. It was especially clear on two occasions when giving feedback to one course participant who decided to deliver her presentation by reading from a written script. In both cases, her performance was good, but her spoken English was not as well rounded as possible. In view of that, David had to balance his feedback between on the one hand commenting on her language correctness and accuracy, and on the other hand having still delivered a good enough presentation.

> D: you should see your papers as helping you but not as a necessity for your presentation, because I think you could do without them as well, I'm sure you could, but you just have to flip a switch, ahm, because really, also the problem with reading is pronunciation, because the words look so different in English, so that also means that if you are unsecure about a number of words, then you just have to look them up in a dictionary, go to dictionary dot com or the Oxford student reference and there will be the pronunciation of words, and this will help you to find comfort as well

Much like in Course A, some course participants often seemed to want to focus on issues of linguistic correctness, rather than adaptability to the context, again particularly with regard to the pronunciation of certain words. This was the case, for instance, after the discussion of the presentation of one of the participants, where she had focused on an ethical dilemma. At the end of the exchange, one of the participants directly addresses David to ask him to clarify the pronunciation of 'dilemma'.

> P2: but also dilemma, actually, is it really a dilemma?
>
> P3: depends on
>
> P2: because you have to be considerate, it's not dilemma, you just can't put yourself on that place, that's all, it's not dilemma, I would say
>
> P3: I think that this is dilemma
>
> P2: you think it still is dilemma, ok
>
> D: you want to say something?
>
> T: no, no, I don't have anything with this problem
>
> P2 ((turning to D)): it is 'dilemma' or 'dailemma'?
>
> D: 'dailemma'

This was, once again, despite David's explicit stance that participants should see the course as an opportunity for them to develop as presenters and to experiment with different tools for their presentations during the course so as to eventually become more effective presenters. David articulated this stance in the following terms during the third seminar of the course.

> D: but before we start, how are you in that becoming a presenter process? Do you see a transition, or do you see that it's very easy to fall back into old tactics? Yea, because of course well my ultimate aim is for you to really take you out of your comfort zone and I hope that you will try different things and do different things, specifically if you really focus on that preparational aspect of your presentation, because I think that we never spend enough time on this, even I, you know, I know that I never spend enough time on this, as much as I would like to, because time is a commodity that we can't, well, seem to have enough of, but I would like for you to really take that opportunity to grab the time that you have here to experiment, so I hope that you are in transition? Yea?

Whenever the opportunity presented itself, David did deliver feedback to participants about their performance as presenters, and the way he saw they were developing or had developed as more effective speakers during the course. In the following exchange with one of the course participants who had shown greater difficulties with linguistic correctness and fluency, David expressed his satisfaction at seeing how, despite her linguistic struggles, she had become more fluent and more effective as a speaker over the course of the past seminars.

> D: are you content with the result?
>
> P1: it worked only if I am not nervous, that mean in a relaxed situation, but now, we are practised here maybe two months, maybe approximately, it gives maybe some courage to practise
>
> D: and I can see you did, I'm really glad you mention that, if you just used your notes and not read, you yourself become so much more expressive
>
> P1: yea
>
> D: so you use your non-verbal communication so much more, but you're also so much more aware of your audience, whether they are understanding you or not
>
> P1: yea yea, I have time to control the audience
>
> D: yea yea, and I think that you can also in this way feed off from your audience and see how they are reacting, how you are performing, and you can take some energy from that as well
>
> P1: exactly, it's very important to notice, some smile, some question mark, or, yea
>
> D: so, I mean, bravo, is my reply, yea

All in all, what emerges from the observed sessions in the two courses is a double-sided image of academic English. On the one hand, course participants often seemed to place emphasis and importance on issues of proficiency: vocabulary and pronunciation. On the other hand, David, while not infrequently giving feedback along proficiency lines, explicitly attempted to put more emphasis on aspects of pragmatic competence, efficiency, and adaptability to the context, rather than on language correctness and accuracy. This discrepancy might have developed from the participants' own experiences of language learning, heavily geared towards gaining linguistic competence and proficiency, and also from a corresponding lesser amount of exposure to discussions and debates around issues of pragmatic skills in academic contexts. In any case, it seems that when it comes to thinking about academic English, scholars at university (at least those who took part in the courses I observed) would tend to think first and foremost about linguistic issues, and they would think of themselves as in need of gaining linguistic fluency and proficiency – a stance that might be helpful to some extent, but which might not be fully suitable when thinking about interacting in academic settings in English, both at the university (when teaching courses, for example) and abroad (when delivering papers in English at conferences).

5.4 Students' language attitudes towards English-medium instruction: A view from Tallinn

So far, the bulk of the book has mostly concentrated on the data collected from the University of Tartu and from scholars of the level of PhD students and above. In this final part of the present chapter and of the volume more generally, however, I would like to incorporate into the analysis another higher education institution in the country, Tallinn University, and another group of stakeholders, Bachelor's and Master's students. While achieving a balance in terms of quantity of data from the different institutions, the University of Tartu and Tallinn University, would be unachievable and unrealistic at this point, adding the views from students in Tallinn provides a complementary view on the language question in the context of higher education in the country, allowing for a more complete picture of the situation in Estonia, particularly in relation to the question of how those who find themselves immersed in the field of Estonian higher education feel about the growing presence of English in that field. An analysis of Tallinn University (TLU) and its internationalization efforts merits attention for several reasons. TLU is one of the largest public universities in the country, the third after the University of Tartu and Tallinn University of Technology in terms of number of students. After a recent university-wide reform, TLU is composed of six schools (large units that have resulted from the subsuming of smaller departments); the university also houses five centers of excellence and eight academic unit centers. Although it currently offers studies in most fields of knowledge, its strengths lie in the humanities and the social sciences (four of the six schools are within these areas). It has approximately 800 employees (400 of whom are academics) and 7,500 students (as of 1 September 2017). Foreign degree students comprise 9.5% of the total student population (at 1 November 2017), and foreign lecturers and research fellows amount to 11.5% (tlu.ee/en/university/About-Us/ TU-in-Numbers, accessed 8 December 2017).

Compared to the University of Tartu, Tallinn University is certainly a younger institution, whose origins can be traced back to 1919, when the Tallinn Teachers' Seminar was established. In 2005, Tallinn University was given its current name and structure, after several universities and academic institutions in the city merged and were consolidated within the new TLU. Since then, the university has continued to grow both physically, incorporating newly constructed buildings and infrastructure, and in the number of students and academic outputs. Compared to other universities in the country, Tallinn University has a fairly substantial provision of programs in English: 7 Bachelor's degrees, 7 Master's, and 14 PhD programs. The desire to internationalize was clear by the second half of the 2000s and the early 2010s. To that end, the university drafted two strategy documents: *Tallinn University development plan until the year 2014* and *Tallinn University's internationalization strategy 2008–2015*. The latter document in particular provides the basis and strategic guidelines for the institution to become more internationally competitive. The development of English-taught programs and subjects appears explicitly in the two documents, more prominently in the latter, although little is said about English-medium instruction (EMI) from a strictly pedagogical point of view.

From 2012 to 2014, I was employed part-time at Tallinn University, mainly developing and delivering Master's and Bachelor's English-medium courses in intercultural communication at the then Institute of Communication. I saw this as an excellent opportunity to find out about students' perspectives on EMI, and their experiences with this kind of learning. As mentioned above, the majority of my fieldwork was conducted in Tartu, but including the perspective of students in Tallinn would bring some important nuances to the study and potentially add relevant insights to it. With this in mind, a small-scale study was conducted in order to dig deeper into three questions: (1) the proportion of EMI courses reported by students, and their variation according to level of study and field of specialisation; (2) students' attitudes towards English in higher education and academic research; and (3) students' assessment of the perceived degree of difficulty when studying in English as compared to their L1. The questions and methodology were inspired by previous studies (Bolton and Kuteeva 2012; Hellekjaer 2010) that had developed similar kinds of analyzes in Scandinavian countries (Sweden and Norway, respectively). In order to obtain the data, an online questionnaire was delivered to the student population of the university during the first half of the autumn semester 2013–2014. The questionnaire was prepared using an online template and was spread via key contact points (through departmental administrative staff). Prior to that, a pilot survey had been conducted with a more reduced group of students in spring 2013 to check the validity and reliability of the survey. Both questionnaires, the pilot and the subsequent full survey, were delivered in English. Because of limited resources, preparing an Estonian version of the survey was not possible.

The survey included 60 items with multiple-choice questions and Likert-scale statements. Additionally, a series of focus-group discussions and in-depth interviews were conducted with a small number of students studying social sciences (N=12) to find out more about the three guiding questions of the study. Interviews and discussions followed a semi-structured design. For this aspect of the study, the participants were restricted to those students taking an English-taught course at the university, and the discussions and interviews were conducted in English – participants were given the opportunity to express themselves in Estonian instead, if they felt they would be able to make their points more clearly that way, but English was their preferred choice throughout the interviews and group discussions. The approximate length of each group discussion was one hour, and the in-depth interviews lasted for around half an hour.

A total of 185 responses were collected from the online questionnaire, from both Estonian students (70%) and students from abroad (30%). For the purposes of this study, however, the focus will be only on those respondents who declared that they had Estonian nationality (N=129). The majority were female (n=94, or 72.86%), mostly BA students (n=79, or 61%) and from the field of social sciences (n=60, 46.5%). There were 30 (23%) respondents from the arts and humanities area, 13 (10%) from pedagogical studies, and 24 (18.6%) from natural and health sciences. Their L1 is overwhelmingly Estonian (n=121, 93.7%) and the vast majority of them are under 25 years old (n=93, 72%). As for the participants in the focus-group discussions and in-depth interviews, the distribution is very similar: they were mostly female (n=9, n=3 males), BA students (N=10) from the area of social sciences, and all of them (n=12) were under the age of 25.

Turning now to the first question about EMI, which is about the percentage of their university coursework that the students reported as EMI, we can see in Figure 5.16 that the percentage of EMI courses reported in 2013–2014 was rather low.
As can be seen, the majority of the respondents indicated that the number of courses in English in their area is rather limited. Moreover, from the whole sample

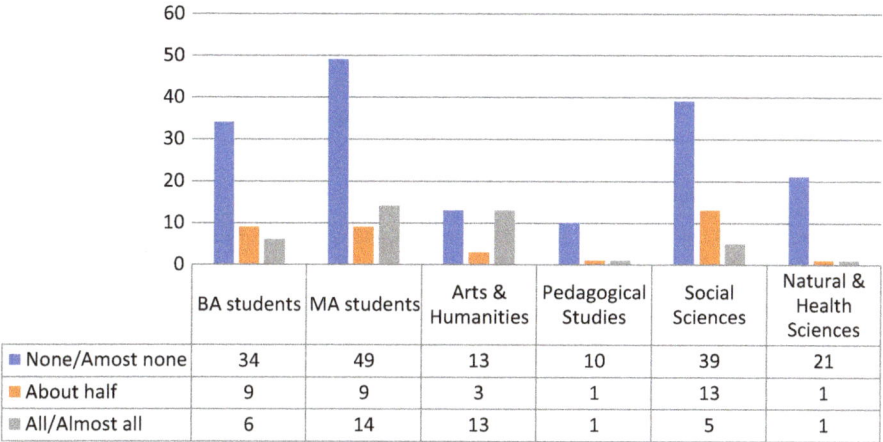

Figure 5.16: Students' reported percentage of EMI courses.
Question 20: Indicate in percent how much of the lectures in your studies are held in English

of Estonian students, N=65 indicated that they had never taken an EMI course before this semester, which is even more indicative of the low provision of English-taught subjects. In percentage terms, there appear to be more EMI courses at MA level than at BA level, although the difference is small. In terms of academic field, EMI courses dominate in the arts and humanities. The explanation for this lies in the fact that, as noted above, this is indeed one of the stronger academic areas at the university. In any case, the picture obtained from these results is that the provision of courses in English in 2013–2014 was somewhat limited and concentrated in the humanities. These results are partly in line with previous studies (e.g. Bolton and Kuteeva 2012), which show that students report having more EMI courses at Master's level than at Bachelor's level. However, in contrast to Bolton and Kuteeva's (2012) findings, the discipline area that shows the largest proportion of EMI courses at TLU is the arts and humanities. In their study at a Swedish university, Bolton and Kuteeva (2012) found that it is students in the disciplines of science and technology that report having a larger share of EMI courses. In the case of Estonia, however, this is in line with the country's offerings of EMI programs overall; at least in 2013–2014, more EMI programs were offered in the humanities and social sciences than in other disciplines (Soler-Carbonell 2015).

When it comes to students' attitudes towards EMI studies and academic English in general, Table 5.2 summarizes the most relevant findings from the survey. The results show that there was strong support and demand for English-taught courses (Q42), and that the question of terminology is perceived as a challenge among my sample (Q43) (we shall return to issues of terminology below in

Table 5.2: Students' attitudes towards EMI courses and English as an academic language.

Q42: the university should offer more courses taught in English

	Totally Agree/Agree	Neutral	Disagree/Totally Disagree
Humanities & Social Sciences	66%	27.5%	6.5%
Natural & Health Sciences	79%	17%	4%

Q43: the most difficult challenge about academic English is to translate the specific vocabulary into my L1

	Totally Agree/Agree	Neutral	Disagree/Totally Disagree
Humanities & Social Sciences	64%	17%	19%
Natural & Health Sciences	75%	12.5%	12.5%

Q46: the emphasis on using English as an academic language at our university is a threat to the use of Estonian as an academic language

	Totally Agree/Agree	Neutral	Disagree/Totally Disagree
Humanities & Social Sciences	21%	28.5%	50.5%
Natural & Health Sciences	33.5%	21%	45.5%

Q48: the dominance of English in international academia gives an unfair advantage to native speakers of English

	Totally Agree/Agree	Neutral	Disagree/Totally Disagree
Humanities & Social Sciences	23%	40%	37%
Natural & Health Sciences	21%	41.5%	37.5%

the discussion of the focus-group and interview data). In addition, the respondents did not perceive Estonian academic language to be threatened by academic English (Q46) and they generally did not feel at a disadvantage vis-à-vis native speakers of English in academic contexts (Q48). In presenting the results, the sample is divided into two groups: those studying in the humanities and social sciences on the one hand and those in the natural and health sciences on the other. There is significant overlap between the areas of arts and humanities, pedagogical studies, and social sciences, and considering the sample size, it seemed reasonable to treat those students as one group, in opposition to those in the natural and health sciences.

Finally, in relation to the students' perceptions of the difficulty of studying subjects in English as compared with their L1, Table 5.3 summarizes the most relevant results. It was found that in some cases there does indeed appear to be a perceived difference when studying EMI subjects. Importantly, however, the language of instruction did not seem to produce any significant differences in the attitudes

Table 5.3: Students' perceptions of the degree of difficulty/easiness in studying their subjects in English as compared to their L1.

Q22: To what extent do you find words and expressions in the English language/L1 lectures unfamiliar?

	All words/Most words unfamiliar		All words/Most words familiar	
	EngIndex	L1Index	EngIndex	L1Index
Humanities & Social Sciences	3%	9.5%	97%	90.5%
Natural & Health Sciences	4%	4%	96%	96%

Q24: How often do you want to ask about unfamiliar words and expressions during lectures in English/L1?

	All the time/Usually		Sometimes/Never want to ask	
	EngIndex	L1Index	EngIndex	L1Index
Humanities & Social Sciences	4%	4%	96%	96%
Natural & Health Sciences	0%	0%	100%	100%

Q25: To what extent can you follow the lecturer's line of thought during lectures in English/L1?

	Difficult/Sometimes difficult to follow		Usually easy/easy to follow	
	EngIndex	L1Index	EngIndex	L1Index
Humanities & Social Sciences	18%	3%	82%	97%
Natural & Health Sciences	16.5%	8.5%	83.5%	91.5%

Q27: How often do you want to ask about unclear content during lectures in English/L1?

	All the time/Usually		Sometimes/Never want to ask	
	EngIndex	L1Index	EngIndex	L1Index
Humanities & Social Sciences	5%	4%	95%	96%
Natural & Health Sciences	0%	4%	100%	96%

Q28: How important are the lecturers' transparencies/PowerPoint slides or other visual aids for your understanding of the lectures in English/L1?

	Very important/Important		Not very important/Not important at all	
	EngIndex	L1Index	EngIndex	L1Index
Humanities & Social Sciences	61%	52.5%	39%	47.5%
Natural & Health Sciences	54%	58.5%	46%	41.5%

Q29: How difficult do you find taking notes during lectures in English/L1?

	Impossible/Sometimes hard		Usually easy/easy to take notes	
	EngIndex	L1Index	EngIndex	L1Index
Humanities & Social Sciences	19%	4%	81%	96%
Natural & Health Sciences	21%	4%	79%	96%

reported by the students. For example, when wanting to ask for clarification about unfamiliar words or unclear content during lectures (Q22, Q24, and Q27), the language of instruction in a course does not seem to lead to significant differences. That is to say that students report they do not want to ask questions during lectures, regardless of the language of instruction, and find as many difficult words in their L1 as they would in English. This view was supported by the focus-group discussions as well, a point we shall return to in more detail below.

As noted already, there were indeed some items where the degree of perceived difficulty in studying through the medium of English can be higher, including following the lecturer's line of thought (Q25), for instance. PowerPoint slides and other visual aids were perceived as important resources for understanding lectures when these are in English, more so than when lectures are in the L1 (Q28), although the difference does not seem too large. Finally, taking notes is also considered more difficult in English as opposed to doing so in the first language (Q29).

In sum, responses to the first two EMI-related questions analyzed in this small-scale study regarding students' attitudes towards EMI at Tallinn University, students reported having only a few courses taught in English, and these were more abundant in the fields of arts and humanities than in natural sciences and technology. The further results indicate that students had a positive opinion of these courses and that they demanded more of them; in addition, they did not see the use of English at university as problematic in nature, certainly not a threat to Estonian as an academic language. Finally, EMI courses were perceived to entail more difficulties than studying in the L1, although not across the board, that is, not in all way nor for all learning activities in class. It may be argued that there are context-specific features that shape students' perceived level of difficulty, regardless of the language of instruction. To find out more about such specific features, a number of in-depth interviews and group discussions were conducted with a sample of students in social sciences. In the next section, we turn to the analysis of some key passages of these interviews, which shine additional light on the questions of the perceived difficulty of EMI and the students' experiences with this type of course.

5.4.1 Focus-group discussions and in-depth interviews

During the in-depth interviews and focus-group sessions, the discussions revolved mainly around students' experiences with learning subject-specific courses through the medium of English. Not infrequently, discussions revolved around the perceived difficulties in connection to studying in English; often, the first reaction was to answer affirmatively, to say yes, it is indeed more difficult to study one's subjects in English. However, upon further reflection, some participants contended that in fact, the question of the language may not be that relevant, since academic subjects are difficult per se, whether one studies them in one's L1 or not (cf. Kuteeva and Björkman 2012). The following example, extracted from the first focus-group discussion, illustrates the point:

> Extract 1: Academic language is complicated
>
> Q: How do you feel when you are studying in English? A subject that is not English language, of course. Is it OK for you?
>
> S1: Now it's OK. At the beginning it was, 'what?' too much to read!
>
> S2: I think it's OK, yes, because even if I had to study it in Estonian, it would be hard. I had several texts in Estonian. It's always complicated to read academic language. It doesn't make a real difference whether it's Estonian or English.

In this above example, the two students narrowed the discussion down to the reading they did for their subjects. S1 conceded that studying in English was more difficult "at the beginning" since she felt she had "too much to read". However, S2 goes on to suggest that it might have been just as difficult to handle the course readings in Estonian. In another group discussion (Extract 2 below), the focus on speaking rather than reading, that is, on the active production of the language. Two participants in that focus-group discussion engaged in an exchange that seemed to point to both sides of the coin: are the perceived difficulties a matter of a language barrier or a disciplinary (context-specific) issue? For S6, it seems that it is a context-specific problem (although he did not structure his argument in these specific terms), whereas for S1, it would seem to be more of a language-related problem:

> Extract 2: The problem of "getting to the discussion"
>
> S6: In my opinion, the talking part is difficult. If you have courses in English, Estonians don't want to answer, they don't want to discuss different topics, that's why…
>
> S1: Yeah, because when we have these discussions, then I am afraid that I am talking wrong, so or like I don't understand the question like the others understand, or whatever. So that's why I think a lot of students don't want to discuss.
>
> Q: It inhibits…
>
> S6: I think everybody understands what the topics are about, but they don't want to get to the discussion.

Estonians are in general quiet, implies S6, not encouraged to debate, and they will not easily volunteer to participate and give their opinions in classroom discussions. S1, by contrast, argues that it is a question of not understanding properly what is being debated and therefore being afraid of making mistakes, and thus not sounding authoritative enough. However, S6 concludes his argumentation by saying that he thinks that everybody understands the topic, but people "don't want to get to the discussion". Given the way in which S1 and S6 construct their argument, it is not clear whether not participating in classroom discussions is a language-related problem or a context-specific issue. It would be reasonable, in fact, to assume that it is a question of both elements at the same time, interacting in a complex manner.

Whether there are context-specific issues or problems of a linguistic nature, discussions kept coming back to the idea of learning subject-specific vocabulary and terminology as something particularly challenging; this has been mentioned already in discussing the results of the general survey above. Indeed, this appeared to be one of the main reasons why studying in English might be more demanding than studying in Estonian. Much like in the discussion we saw among the participants in Extract 1 above, a key concern expressed in another group discussion was centerd on the fact that, regardless of the medium of instruction in a given course, most of the specialized literature is in English. So, overcoming the mismatch between reading the specialized literature in English and then engaging in an academic discussion in Estonian was seen as potentially problematic.

> Extract 3: The struggle with specific vocabulary
>
> S1: And a lot of the academic vocabulary, you can't put it into Estonian. One of our lecturers, [name of the lecturer], who gave us [name of a subject] and a lot of other subjects, he was always talking about 'basic assumptions' and he said there is no way to translate it directly to Estonian, there aren't any particular Estonian words to describe this concept, 'basic assumptions'.
>
> Q: 'põhilised alused' or something.
>
> S1: 'oletused', so that makes it, as you said, to read in English and then to produce something in Estonian is even more difficult. A lot of PR vocabulary comes from English but you don't have them in Estonian. Yeah, that makes things more difficult.

The issue of specialist terminology and field-specific vocabulary was also a major concern in one of the in-depth interviews conducted in Tallinn, in this case with Jaana, a student undertaking a Master's degree in communication sciences who had spent an extended period of time in the UK, where she obtained a Bachelor's degree in social sciences. In addition, she had spent long periods in countries such as Australia, the United States, and Spain. With that personal background, one would have imagined that her advanced knowledge of English should have placed her in a very comfortable position to tackle her studies, enabling her to read the specialized literature without significant problems and engaging in classroom discussions having mastered the content of the readings.

However, she instead encountered a number of difficulties during her advanced-level studies in Estonia, not because of problems with language proficiency, but because she felt she had to become integrated into a new academic community, a new discourse system (Scollon et al. 2012), and this demanded some effort, something she did not anticipate. So, even though she had an excellent command of the English language, which she initially considered a very useful asset, it turned out to be more complicated than that. In most of her subjects, much like in the discussion in Extract 3 above, the vast majority of the course reading was in English, but she was asked to write and produce essays in Estonian. Again, this produced a mismatch that she found difficult to overcome, as she explained during the interview:

> Extract 4: "My academic language is English"
>
> Jaana: Right now I can switch from English to Estonian as quickly as possible, I don't even have to think about it. However, my academic language is English, and that made it so much harder for me to write in academic Estonian, because I am not familiar with the concepts. So that's really hard for me.

By acknowledging that her academic language is English, she was saying that this is the language that she most commonly uses to learn and study her subjects, the language she uses to be a university student. Having to deal with "academic Estonian" made it problematic for her to use her academic tools at her best. In short, she had to background the language in which she had been academically trained to that point (English), and while still passively using it (for the purposes of reading the specialist literature), she was required to actively use a different language (Estonian), in which she had not received formal academic training at an advanced level, even though it was her first language. Importantly, in addition to that, not only did she not receive any formal training or support to develop her academic skills in Estonian, but she realized that she was being penalized for inappropriate translation of theoretical concepts from English into Estonian. This became apparent later on in the interview, as we can see in Extract 5. Her complaint about a lack of "training as to how to translate" should be read as a complaint about missing formal and explicit academic support, not so much related to learning how to 'translate' but rather about receiving help to communicate effectively and to be able to produce the required assignments optimally in Estonian.

> Extract 5: The "problem" with translation
>
> Jaana: My problem is, my biggest problem is, how can I, if I have to argue and summarize other people's thoughts and ideas and then put it into Estonian, how can I do that if I don't have any training as to how to translate? Lost in translation is a big problem, because the

words can mean a lot of different things, and if you are not an expert in the content, then there can be big misunderstandings, especially in philosophy, political theory... so, I understand it, but I can't put it into Estonian because I don't know these words and structures. So that's my problem.

In this final extract, we may infer that Jaana is indeed struggling to adapt to this new academic context, with the language question becoming more vivid and problematic for her. During her Bachelor's studies, she had to invest a lot of effort, at the beginning, in understanding how to become a full-fledged undergraduate student in the context of the UK. Now, she found herself having to overcome similar obstacles, but paradoxically, the fact that she was studying her degree mostly in her first language added an extra layer of complexity for her, because she had been trained academically in English. Jaana's case is perhaps rarely found, but given the increasing intensity of academic mobility at both graduate and undergraduate levels, her case can be revealing of the kinds of obstacles facing more and more students today. Moreover, she may very well be more acutely aware of the language problem since in the humanities and social sciences, as she argues herself, language does seem to play a bigger role in the creation and dissemination of knowledge, as opposed to its role in science and technology (Kuteeva and Airey 2014). However, her experience raises important and fundamental questions in relation to language and higher education. For instance, we may wonder what type of language(s) we expect from university graduates and the level they should attain in them; how students can best develop both their L1 and other languages for different functions and purposes, including academic ones; or what is considered and expected to be good and appropriate 'academic' language, both in English and in their L1.

To summarize, the results from the questionnaire showed that among the surveyed student population at Tallinn University, there is strong support and demand for English-taught courses. Students did not feel that English poses a threat to academic Estonian, and they did not feel disadvantaged by the fact that they are not native speakers of English. They were more concerned about the challenges of learning and using subject-specific terminology. This connects with the level of difficulty students perceive in studying in English. The survey showed that there are some areas where studying in English can be perceived as more difficult, but it is the data from the focus-group discussions and the in-depth interviews that are more revealing about that. Students generally expressed greater concern about terminological issues. Arguably, this is a complex topic with no clear-cut interpretation; students agreed that, regardless of the language of instruction, studying their subjects is a difficult task. Nevertheless, one of the most difficult tasks that they were confronted with was the adaptation of specialized terminology into Estonian. This was clearly exemplified in the case of

Jaana, but it also appeared as a theme in the focus-group discussions. What is most problematic here seems to be a lack of institutional and structural support for students, pointing to the fact that they were left on their own when it comes to important tasks in their degrees, including writing academic essays. Indeed, writing in academic Estonian seemed to be especially difficult for some of them, particularly because most of the relevant literature they read and the concepts they work with are in English.

5.5 Conclusion

This chapter has presented a historical overview of the different language regimes in academia and higher education in Estonia, followed by a portrayal of the language attitudes of a group of students towards English-medium instruction in the current context. An important point that the historical overview has tried to develop is that changes in language regimes in higher education are linked to broader societal and global changes, in line with Bull (2004) and Mortensen and Haberland (2012). Historically, Estonian higher education has seen a number of languages occupy different spaces and niches in that field; in the area of languages for publication, scientists in Estonia have gone from publishing mostly in German in the nineteenth century to doing so in English in the late twentieth and early twenty-first centuries. These are not incidental changes, but modifications that are very much linked to the changing position of the country within Europe and the changing patterns of writing for publication more globally.

In previous chapters, we have seen that the language question in present-day Estonian higher education is normally framed against a context of the need to protect, promote, and develop the Estonian language. In parallel with that, there is also a strong awareness of the need to incorporate other languages, most notably English, for internationalization purposes. When it comes to the views speakers have of academic English, based on the sessions with teachers and researchers I observed in Tartu, that there is a tension between two ideas: linguistic proficiency and pragmatic competence. Many of those attending the courses seemed to come with the motivation of improving their English-language competence, while the courses were designed primarily to help speakers reflect on their pragmatic skills, give them space to practice them, and eventually allow them to strengthen their belief that they are effective, indeed legitimate, speakers of English in international academic contexts. This is a relevant mismatch (linguistic versus pragmatic competence) that might have important consequences for the professional and academic development of speakers, and it is an important point to which we shall return in the general discussion in the next chapter.

The language attitudes of the group of students investigated in the chapter also indicate the potential existence of discrepancies and mismatches. While these students show support for the development and implementation of EMI courses, pedagogical challenges can emerge, leading to potentially problematic issues for those students involved in such courses. This is particularly the case if little focused support is supplied from within institutions. Given the nature of the data (attitudes reported in a survey and in group discussions or in-depth interviews), the learning challenges expressed by the students (e.g. in connection to terminological issues) may or may not coincide with the real challenges that they experience. However, one does have the impression that, at present, the question of the internationalization of Estonian higher education has been tackled mainly from the marketing and branding perspective, paying more attention to the needs of the institution rather than those of teachers and students. Here, once again, the point emphasized by Mortensen and Haberland (2012) becomes salient: changes in the language regimes of universities, in any context, are not innocent, but respond to specific drivers, and it seems that in the Estonian context, socio-economic rather than pedagogical reasons may have prevailed thus far (whether to increase economic revenue or to counteract dwindling student populations in specific departments). To put it briefly, English is not the present-day Latin of academia for many reasons (Mortensen and Haberland 2012), most importantly because the incorporation of English is motivated by factors radically different from those that underpinned the use of Latin in past centuries; this might not seem all that surprising, given the differences between contemporary and past societies, but it does signal the importance of understanding why particular languages occupy certain spaces and fulfil certain functions in any given context, what motivations have led to that specific sociolinguistic state of affairs, and who benefits more or who loses more as a result of such arrangements.

6 Language policy discourses at the internationalizing university: Estonian perspectives on a global issue

6.1 Introduction

In this concluding chapter, I take stock of the different issues and themes that have been presented in the previous chapters and read them in light of current debates on the role of language in the context of the internationalization of higher education and academic research. In doing so, I revisit the themes and questions proposed at the beginning of the book, in the introductory chapter, and return to some of the key theoretical points that deserve further comment and exploration, taking into account the material presented in the volume. Specifically, I concentrate on discursive and ethnographic approaches to the study of language policy, with nexus analysis as a potentially useful framework to employ in such approaches, and I further emphasize the role of language ideologies as a powerful engine both mediating and recreating particular frameworks for social action and the interpretation of reality. The chapter concludes by mentioning some related themes and questions that fall outside the scope of the book, but that deserve further and more adequate treatment in future studies.

6.2 Applying discourse approaches to language policy

This book has attempted to analyze in some detail the present-day situation of Estonian universities through the lens of a discourse analytic approach. In what follows, I shall delve deeper into the benefits and limitations of such a framework, with specific reference to nexus analysis (Scollon and Scollon 2004) as applied to the study of language policy situations (following Hult 2015). I will also attempt to summarize and underline the specific features of the internationalization of higher education in the Estonian context, thus signalling the potential theoretical contributions to current discussions in the field from this particular empirical site.

We noted at the start of the volume, in the first chapter, that universities are particularly rich sites for exploring tensions and ambiguities around language policy matters from a language ideological and discourse perspective. The reason for this is that universities constitute social spaces that are shot through with a number of discourses – two of these are the ones that have been broadly defined in the volume as 'nationalizing' and 'globalizing' discourses. Each of them carries its own accompanying ideological assumptions, which can make universities particularly vulnerable to certain paradoxes and anxieties, and language is a particularly noteworthy site where such tensions and anxieties are played out. This is not exclusive to universities, naturally, and we have noted in the introduction that tourism and global businesses have been analyzed sociolinguistically along similar lines (Heller et al. 2014). In the context of becoming internationally leading global companies, universities are expected to achieve a set of goals, for which plans are designed and actions undertaken; the fulfilment of these plans and the development of these actions is increasingly tied to a growing use of English within institutions of higher education. In parallel with that, universities continue to be viewed as essentially state institutions, embodying as such a set of national values and features that, not surprisingly, are connected to a discourse of protection, promotion, and development of the national language, which is to be preserved in the domain of higher education. In the context of these two broadly defined discursive and ideological constructs (the globalizing and the nationalizing ones), the questions that I set out to investigate at the start of the volume were: How are these two discourses encompassed? How is English constructed at present as simultaneously a necessity and a potential poison in the context of a growing number of universities? How is the protectionist discourse presented? What is at stake for the relevant stakeholders in these debates? How do they position themselves vis-à-vis the two broad discourses mentioned above? These are some of the broad questions that have guided the exploration and inquiry presented in this book.

Although combined in a rather eclectic fashion, in the book we have seen elements of the three main components of a nexus analysis: discourses in place, historical bodies, and the interaction order. We shall delve deeper into the issues touched upon in connection to the three discourses, but first of all, in this paragraph I shall briefly summarize the material covered in the preceding four chapters, by way of recapitulation. In Chapter 2, we saw the conceptual/ideational discourses in place – the sets of ideological standpoints – emerging from a number of policy documents from different countries (Finland, Estonia, and Latvia) and at different scales (institutional, national, and supranational). Material discourses in place were also presented and analyzed in the chapter, in this case considering the physical and online presence of different languages in one university in each of Estonia, Latvia, and Lithuania. Moving on, in Chapter 3 we delved deeper into the construction of discourses in place and the circulating discourses in Estonian higher education, with an analysis combining policy documents (including an online discussion of one such document by members at the University of Tartu), a public media debate on language issues in higher education, and the speeches and interventions of two key figures in Estonian higher education (Professor Jaak Aaviksoo and Professor Rector Volli Kalm) during the celebration of twenty years of English-taught courses at the University of Tartu, a seminar held in October 2013 in Tartu. The latter part of Chapter 3 served to introduce a relevant feature in the framework of nexus analysis: the historical body. Indeed, individual speakers, with their specific personal and biographical characteristics, contribute importantly to the particular configuration of a given policy action. Speakers' individual trajectories may lead to particular ideological stances in relations to a language policy situation. With that in mind, Chapter 4 aimed to present the range of opinions by the widest possible group of scholars immersed in Estonian higher education, and in so doing, delve deeper into the different sets of beliefs and attitudes held around the internationalization of higher education and the role of language in that context. Finally, Chapter 5 first attempted to historicize the object of study, tracing the different language regimes in place across different historical periods in Estonian higher education; following that, the chapter looked at the different views and attitudes towards academic English held by two other important sets of stakeholders: teachers and researchers, on the one hand, and students, on the other. The chapter incorporated the final component of nexus analysis in order to complement the investigation of the previous elements. It added an analysis of the interaction order, with the results from a participant-observation study conducted during 2013–2014. This component contributes to a more nuanced analysis, in partiuclar by considering the view(s) emerging from classroom interactions on the notion of 'academic English'.

The policy action around which the above discourses circulate is the internationalization of Estonian higher education and the role of language in this process. In Chapter 2, we saw that Estonian universities, unsurprisingly, do not operate in a vacuum, and they are not immune to changes in higher education systems in the diverse neighbouring countries of Nordic Europe and the Baltic states. We delved deeper into the configuration and circulation of discourses in place in Estonian higher education in Chapter 3, analysing different materials and the language ideological stances that emerge from them. The social spaces that constitute Estonian higher education are of course filled with real people with different backgrounds and different personal trajectories. We saw a variety of them in Chapters 4 and 5, where we delved deeper into the various opinions and ideological positions emerging from interview and interactional data. All in all, following the framework provided by nexus analysis (Scollon and Scollon 2004; Hult 2015), the approach taken here is also related to the ethnography of language policy (ELP) (Johnson 2009) and its attempts to break a priori dichotomies of 'macro' and 'micro' and of policy 'creation' and 'implementation', and to foreground the agentive capacity of social actors in a given policy situation (Johnson 2013b).

Conceptual problems aside – for example, with its insistence on 'structure' versus 'agency' that does not quite break with pre-established dichotomies (cf. Pérez-Milans 2018) – what can be highlighted, in my view, from the ELP framework is the genuine adoption of ethnography in the study of language policy situations (Blommaert 2013b), its attempts at carefully tracing how resources are organized, given value, and distributed in a given social setting connected to a policy action, and how ideological spaces for the promotion and development of certain languages are either fostered or hindered (Johnson 2009). It seems, then, that language ideology is key in understanding how different social actors are positioned within a social milieu; language policy and language ideology, then, are firmly interrelated, so much so that Spolsky (2004) considers ideology (the beliefs and attitudes of speakers) as one of the key components of any language policy analysis. The study of language ideologies has a long and well-established tradition within anthropological linguistics (Kroskrity 2000; Schiefelin et al. 1998). If the study of language policy is to become more anchored in ethnography, a focus on language ideology and an explicit engagement with the well-seated discussions in the literature from that field of inquiry (cf. Woolard 1998) is not just to be expected, but also to be actively sought. Here, I can only present some sketchy desiderata in that vein, but it is hoped that they will suffice in providing the seeds for further theoretical and methodological elaborations of ethnographic approaches to the study of language policy situations.

In that respect, many scholars working today with discursive and ethnographic methods in language policy and planning analyzes would most probably not be uncomfortable with several ideas that have emerged from and have solidified within the study of language ideologies, including the insistence upon the examination of 'the cultural and the historical specificity of construals of language' and 'the unavoidable significance of the ideological dimension [of language]' (Woolard 1998: 4). This is not to say that ELP scholars are not aware of the significance of ideology in language policy and planning contexts, nor am I calling for a terminological refining in our theoretical discussions ('let's talk more about ideology'). The latter would not, in fact, be that productive anyway, given the conceptual fuzziness of the very term 'ideology', which Woolard emphasizes in her essay. Instead, the point is rather that if we, as language policy scholars, are to make a significant contribution to social theory and to a critical examination of the contexts we examine that might lead to actual social change, then an explicit alignment with linguistic anthropological work and with critical sociolinguistic studies (cf. Heller 2011) should be more actively explored. I have no doubt of the critically minded nature of many of the studies framed under ethnographic and discursive approaches to the study of language policy that of late have become increasingly fashionable. The point, simply, is to front more emphatically the idea that different agents have different discursive resources at their disposal, and in the study of social situations, including language policy actions, it is crucial to identify who has access to what resources, how these resources are being used, and to what effect.

Once again, this kind of approach is probably not too different from the one proposed by scholars within the ethnography of language policy (cf. Hornberger and Johnson 2007). Where critical sociolinguistics and ELP would seem to depart, though, is in their understanding and conceptualisation of social agents and their situated positions within a hierarchically organized field, for it would seem that within ELP studies, agents are presupposed to have a given position and a given set of discursive resources, whereas critical sociolinguistic approaches try to step away from these predefined notions and conditions. Importantly, then, following Heller (2011: 193), 'even in the most hierarchical of spaces, different perspectives can clash, and new things come up for which discursive frames are not yet ready and must be fashioned'. Indeed, critical sociolinguistics and the ethnography of language policy share an emphasis on ethnography as a means of uncovering where different discourses may clash and how that clash can impact on the configuration of particular ideological frameworks that can open up or hinder social spaces, to the benefit or detriment of particular languages and groups of speakers. However, more can be done in the exercise of aligning anthropological and critical sociolinguistic studies more closely with ethnographic approaches to the study of language policy (see also Pérez-Milans 2018 for a detailed treatment of this particular alignment).

6.3 Language ideology and language policy: The case of Estonian higher education

In this alignment of ELP and critical sociolinguistics, an emphasis on the study of language ideologies seems of crucial importance when it comes to uncovering potential clashes, contradictions, dilemmas, and paradoxes. Wodak (2006: 188) also refers to such 'ideological dilemmas' as important in understanding how different arguments are recontextualized and meanings are co-constructed in different public spaces and in discussions of language policy situations. Indeed, it is in points of confrontation of different arguments, whether in explicit language policy debates (cf. Blommaert 1999) or in more implicit formulation of themes and ideas in policy documents, that we need to turn our attention in order to fine-tune our understanding of the stakes at play in the context of a language policy action. In the context of the internationalization of Estonian higher education, we have certainly seen and analyzed contradictions and dilemmas throughout this book. In Chapter 2 we saw how agents across different layers of policy-making (supranational, state, and institutional) make strategic choices in positioning themselves more in line with nationalizing or globalizing trends and discourses on the language question in higher education. These choices, however, are not always straightforward, and they can sometimes be unexpected. While attending to the nationalizing pressures, it would seem that conceptually (i.e. in the ideas expressed in their policy documents), universities in Finland, Estonia, and Latvia align with globalizing discourses and the need to push their institution more decidedly in the international direction and to become a global key player. Materially, however, institutions in Estonia, Latvia, and Lithuania would seem to be more in line with the nationalizing discourses, favouring as they do the presence of their respective national languages in their linguistic landscape, while leaving the material presence of other languages (namely English) to the online spaces of the university and to individual actors in shaping the appearance of university corridors.

Chapter 3 delved deeper into the organization and circulation of different discourses in Estonian higher education. We saw in that chapter a much-needed complement to the previous chapter, with an analysis of a more extensive number of policy documents in the country by a wider range of policy-making actors. This allowed us to see that the potential contradictions uncovered in the previous chapter (between nationalizing and globalizing discourses) are also present between same-level actors at the same time (e.g. between different actors within the Ministry of Education and Research) and in the selfsame actor at different periods of time (e.g. within university policies of one single institution produced at different times). Indeed, the *Estonian higher education internationalization strategy 2006–2015* seems to foster a globalizing stance in connection to issues of language in higher education, whereas the *Development plan of the Estonian language 2011–2017* is more in line with a nationalizing stance; in fact, the latter cites the former as opening the possibility for entire disciplines to turn to English-only instruction, noting this as a potential danger for the sustainability of Estonian across all areas of higher education. Both documents are authored by the Ministry of Education and Research, although importantly, the *Development plan* was written in conjunction with the Estonian Language Council, which might explain this different orientation. In a similar way, the strategic plans developed by the University of Tartu from 2003 to 2014 also show a reorientation of the institutional stance towards issues of language in the context of the university's internationalization efforts. In 2003, a globalizing orientation was more explicitly noticeable in the university's policy documents, emphasising an explicit need to create and develop English-taught programs to attract more international students and staff; by 2009, the explicit mentions of English had been replaced by the more ambiguous 'foreign language'; and by 2014, any mention of English or 'foreign languages' had disappeared from the policy frameworks of the university.

Indeed, in Chapter 3 we saw evidence that in recent years, questions about language in the field of higher education have become increasingly fraught, with more intense public debates. As always, public discussions of this type, such as the one sparked by Professor Rector Volli Kalm when he mused publicly about the cost of maintaining Estonian-language higher education, serve to flesh out a number of related issues that are not necessarily linked to language alone, but to questions that range from more abstract notions of identity to more concrete economic and practical interests. The public speeches of Aaviksoo and the very same Kalm in the context of the twentieth anniversary of English-taught courses in Tartu, shortly after the public debate had taken place, serve to highlight even further the overlapping nature of language issues with more wide-ranging questions about the exact meaning of the internationalization of higher education for Estonian universities and the practical consequences of this process. Aaviksoo's speech was especially remarkable in that sense, in particular his attempt to balance his role as professor and former rector of the university (and thus, just another member of the academic community) with his role at that time as politician and Minister of Education and Research; listening to and analysing his speech, it would seem that he cleverly managed to find that balance, being in the convenient position of not having to give clear and definite answers and arguments to the questions he was posing to the audience, while simultaneously leaving his stance clear, between the lines of his speech, indicating that he was very much in favour of the push towards a globalizing position, strengthening the discursive assumptions behind that perspective. In any case, the tension between opening up the country's higher education system while keeping a safe place for Estonian in it seemed to be the underlying theme behind the language debates and discussions analyzed in Chapter 3. In previous work (Soler 2013), I have discussed the difficulties that the Estonian language community seems to find itself in when it comes to producing less ethnolinguistic self-images, moving towards more open types of identity constructions (see also Ehala 2014).

Moving on, in Chapter 4 we saw and analyzed another set of positions and discourses around language policy issues in Estonian higher education, in this case those of members of the university community (namely teachers and researchers, as well as PhD students). For the sake of the analysis, participants were divided into two main groups: transnational scholars, on the one hand, and local researchers, on the other. While arbitrary, this division responds to the different sorts of consequences that the globalizing and nationalizing discourses have for the two groups, broadly defined. The chapter tried to trace possible connections between participants' disciplinary backgrounds and life trajectories, on the one hand, and their expressed stance in connection to language policy debates at the university, on the other. From the analysis presented in the chapter, important contradictions are apparent between the two broadly defined discourses, the globalizing and the nationalizing, and one could argue that individual members of the institution are at the receiving end of these contradictions. One important assumption behind the globalizing discourse is the need for universities to become more internationally appealing and become important poles of attraction for scholars from different countries. Some degree of adaptation from the host institution will be required for these scholars to function adequately and fulfil their duties and requirements effectively. How this adaptation translates in practical terms may vary, from complete laissez-faire policies to stricter requirements that need to be fulfilled in a particular language. For transnational scholars, this can be especially consequential. On the one hand, as long as they can hold a position of not having to engage actively and explicitly with Estonian, many will be happy to get by in other languages, primarily English. However, when certain important activities do need to be carried out in Estonian (obtaining credits for their doctoral training from courses taught only in Estonian, or writing the summary of their PhD thesis in Estonian), this will undoubtedly leave them in a more vulnerable position, especially if institutional measures are not in place and it is up to them to find out how to overcome these language-related obstacles.

Another assumption behind the globalizing discourse is that more courses and curricula need to be developed in foreign languages (i.e. English), which is a direct consequence of the previous assumption (the need to attract foreign students and staff). Here, the tensions can be more particularly felt by local scholars, especially those who hold more senior positions in their departments and who will be expected to explain and justify the inclusion of English-taught curricula, or those who will be expected to engage in the teaching of English-taught courses. The reasons behind the development and introduction of English-taught courses and programs are not the same across the university. At the medical faculty, it seems clear that the motivation is primarily economic, to generate increased revenue streams for the faculty (remembering that the yearly fee for students enrolled in the English track of the degree in medicine is 11,000 euros, substantially higher than any other English-taught program in the country). In the faculties of Social Sciences and the Humanities, by contrast, the main driver behind the introduction of English-taught degrees seems to be the dwindling number of (high-quality) students in their programs.

The consequences of introducing more English-taught degrees are also not homogeneous across the different faculties. In the Faculty of Medicine, the concern seems to be linked more to the actual delivery of an increasing number of courses in English: some of the teachers I interviewed wondered to what extent it will be sustainable to have two parallel study lines, one in Estonian and the other in English, for the entirety of the six-year medical degree. This will necessitate the involvement of more teaching staff, but at the time of the fieldwork, from the conversations I had with teachers in the faculty and with the English language instructor (who offered optional support courses for faculty members), it seemed that those who were most in need of attending language courses were not attending, for reasons that I could not fully uncover, given that I myself was not able to talk to them. In addition to that, the English-taught program in medicine in itself seems to generate the paradox of creating medical doctors who might be unable to engage with the local population professionally, if students do not invest enough time and effort in acquiring language skills in Estonian during their studies, something that might not be a priority for some (or indeed, many) of them, given that they may not see themselves as staying in the country after graduation. By contrast, in the Faculty of Humanities, in particular in the history department, the drive towards more English-taught courses might potentially lead to a solidification of an important problem that teachers have been encountering more frequently in recent times: students' lack of skills in other important languages such as German and Russian in order to conduct historical research in Estonia. In the medical faculty, then, teachers are wondering how they are going to deliver the increasing number of courses in English, and particularly how those colleagues in the faculty who might need more linguistic and pedagogical support are going to prepare themselves better for this upcoming requirement; while in the Faculty of Humanities, teachers are wondering how to prepare their students better, linguistically, in order to do good research in their discipline if more English is introduced for teaching purposes. These questions will likely persist and, once again, if institutional policies and initiatives do not address them in any meaningful way, it will be left up to the departments and their individual members to try to find appropriate arrangements.

Finally, Chapter 5 continued to uncover further contradictions and anxieties around language felt by relevant members of the university community (teachers and students), in this case by using the more indirect and implicit tool of participant observation in the case of the teachers, and with a survey and focus-group discussions to find out about students' attitudes towards learning in English. The analysis of the participant-observation data revealed an additional tension felt by teachers at the university: the view of 'academic English' as linguistic competence, associated entirely with fine-tuning their linguistic skills, as opposed to a view of it as pragmatic or communicative competence, the idea of becoming better communicators without necessarily having to aim at fully 'perfect' language proficiency. In this tension that I observed, the teacher naturally played a key role in shaping classroom discussions one way or another, but it was nevertheless revealing that, on several occasions at least and for some of the course participants, the idea of 'academic English' was strictly tied to linguistic competence. As for the attitudes of students, here too tensions were found, in the sense that they generally reported favourable opinions when it came to studying increasingly through the medium of English, but this was not always problem-free, particularly in mastering key terminology in their discipline and in writing extended assignments and essays. Here, the contradiction was more linguistically driven, with the friction being generated by the fact that the bulk of their course literature was in English, but they were expected to produce essays and engage in classroom discussions in Estonian. Chapter 5 also helped to contextualize the object of study further, looking at how different language regimes have evolved across different historical periods in Estonia. This historical contextualisation serves to emphasize that the current tensions, contradictions, and observed stances in connection to language in the context of higher education are a product of historical arrangements, and the current situation is inevitably leading towards future different arrangements with other kinds of assumptions about the role of language at university.

6.4 The sociolinguistics of higher education: A look from Estonia and a note for further research

Naturally, all (or at least the majority) of these tensions, ambiguities, and anxieties documented in the present volume are not exclusive to the Estonian case. In many respects, higher education institutions around the world, especially those in non-anglophone settings that operate with their own linguae academicae (cf. Vila 2015) present a number of similar paradoxes along the same lines (see also Haberland and Preisler 2015; Fabricius et al. 2017). These paradoxes include the idea that the more diversity, the more English might be used in higher education contexts, or the fact that state (national) and institutional policies might inadvertently push towards a more intense use of the English language (policies to include more English-taught courses, or to publish in more English-language outlets) (see Vila 2015: 203-204). Regardless of this set of (important) paradoxes and contradictions, Vila (2015: 206) concludes that those linguae academicae presently used in higher education settings (at least those included in the collection of essays he summarizes) are not likely to retreat from those settings, and he extends this conclusion to other linguae academicae that presently have a place in their respective university domains. From the analysis presented above, it seems safe to add Estonian to this group of linguae academicae that will continue to be used in higher education situations for the foreseeable future. However, it should also be clear that assessing the future sustainability of the Estonian language in higher education, as valid an exercize as it can be (see Klaas-Lang and Metslang 2015), was not the main objective of the analysis presented in this book.

Instead, with the current analysis, I hope to have illustrated the prevailing set of positions in the field of Estonian higher education held by a number of key social actors in it, the different ideological stances they can take, the discursive nature of the resources available to them, and the potential consequences of the current arrangements. Indeed, it is in the spirit of Heller (2011) and Mortensen and Haberland (2012) that I wanted to present my analysis as an account of the postnational university in Estonia and to see the discursive nature of the construction of the postnational university. As Heller (2011: 193) puts it, 'a critical ethnographic sociolinguistic analysis of post-nationalism can locate the discursive spaces and identify what resources are circulating, who has access to them and what they can make of them'. I have attempted to do precisely that, and in so doing, to highlight the fact that 'the changing language preferences of the university should not be examined in isolation from other factors, but rather be seen in relation to the developments in the underlying idea of the university, and, we may add, the ideological currents of the surrounding society' (Mortensen and Haberland 2012: 177).

Of course, a number of issues have had to be backgrounded, or simply left aside, given the inherent constraints of the project. In that sense, one key issue that I was not able to examine in as much detail as would be possible is the position of Russian speakers in Estonian universities. As was seen in the analysis of the policy documents and the material landscape (physical and online) of Estonian higher education, Russian is clearly absent from policy formulations and from the languages materially displayed at university. Although this is in line with the country's Estonianisation efforts, in place now for a couple of decades since re-independence in 1991 (Rannut 2008), more could and should be said about how graduates from Russian-language high schools adapt to and navigate the Estonian higher education system, which functions predominantly in Estonian. In that regard, Metslang and Šmõreitšik (2013) point out that students from Russian-medium schools form a clear minority in Estonian universities (about 6%), and although there appears to be room for improvement in some key areas (developing writing skills or learning specific terminology and vocabulary), the two authors find that the majority of Russian-speaking students cope sufficiently well with their university studies. However, where the authors do note that further action might be needed is around lecturers' attitudes towards these students. In their study, Metslang and Šmõreitšik find that in many instances, lecturers agree with the idea of helping these minority students to better cope with their studies, but a significant proportion of them (26%) do not believe that it is worthwhile to give these minority students some extra support. As we saw in Chapter 3, only one of my local informants, Ülle, felt prompted to raise the issue of the Russian-speaking minority in Estonian universities, adopting a critical view towards their poor level of Estonian while pointing out her openness to offer them further support.

Given the particular angle from which I approached the topic at hand, drawing on a project that explicitly sought to find out more about the role of English in the context of the internationalization of Estonian higher education, perhaps it was to some degree inevitable that I was not able to look into the role of the Russian language at the same time, and to find out more about its absence within that context. However, more can definitely be said about the Russian-speaking minority in Estonian higher education, both in terms of their learning and pedagogical needs (cf. Metslang and Šmõreitšik 2013) and in connection with the discursive tensions and ambiguities produced by and about them. In that respect, an interesting historical moment to look at, which would yield relevant data and revealing discussions, would be the developments that lead to the establishment of what was named Catherine's College (Katariina kolledž), a sub-unit of Tallinn University created in 2008. The explicit idea behind the college was to cater for students graduating from Russian-medium high schools in the country and to help them with a smoother transition into (Estonian-language) Estonian higher education (Mattisen and Männa 2007), offering degrees in liberal arts based on the American model. Additionally, the college had the further explicit mission of attracting Russian-speaking students from neighbouring countries, particularly Latvia and Russia, but also Ukraine and Moldova. For those students, as opposed to their Estonian peers, the transition would be made towards English-taught programs instead. Judging by some of the press coverage of the time (e.g. Delfi 2007; Postimees 2007), the general reception of the college by the public at large was not overwhelmingly positive, questioning why Russian-language graduates should be given Russian-language higher education, even if it was thought of as a transition towards Estonian-language higher education. It would seem, however, that Catherine's College is no longer operating, and while this may very well be the product of the deep structural reorganization that Tallinn University went through over the years 2013–2015, it would be interesting to find out about the fate of the college and what led to its apparent dissolution.

Inevitably, my particular approach and my take on the language issues within Estonian higher education drove me to leave aside all these potentially relevant points that would have complemented in significant ways the picture of the role of language(s) in the context of the internationalization of Estonian universities. This brings me to the last point I wish to mention in concluding, a note of reflexivity, which of late has become more central in applied linguistics debates (cf. Pérez-Milans 2016). Although I can only mention it at this point in passing, it does indeed seem important to be aware of the ways in which researchers may (a) affect the nature of the data that they collect and subsequently analyze, and (b) change the nexus of practice, an inevitable consequence of being part of the very same context that one wishes to investigate (Hult 2015: 225). On this latter point, I can only concur with Hult, but at the same time, I should also say that my involvement as a social actor in the context that I studied was only minor throughout the time of my fieldwork – although I did participate in meetings called by the university administration to discuss issues of the strategic plan which was under construction in late 2013, I did contribute to those meetings, voicing my views on the role of language in the internationalization efforts of the institution, and I did post messages in the online forum discussion to which university members were invited to contribute. Small as it may have been, though, it is important to acknowledge one's role in shaping discourses in the field under investigation (cf. Heller 2011), whether one believes it is a significant role or otherwise.

More important still, I feel it is absolutely crucial to acknowledge that as an ethnographer, one is part and parcel of the data that one is able to collect, and so, inevitably, one is both the analyst and the analyzed, carrying a particular set of tools, and having a number of possible impacts on the setting being studied. In that respect, needless to say, I did not come to the field of Estonian higher education as a *tabula rasa*, but I came with a specific set of discursive resources and affordances that allowed me to navigate that field in particular ways. I also had my own preconceived ideas about the Estonian sociolinguistic context, having lived there from 2005 to 2009, and I had some ideas in mind as to what to look for and what to find in the debates about language against the background of the internationalization of Estonian universities. This was back in 2012. With the passage of time, my reading, thinking, and writing about this topic have continued to shape my ideas about it, and what I have presented in this book is but my account of what I think I saw during the years that I spent between Tallinn and Tartu as a postdoctoral researcher. In this account, I hope I have been able to do justice to the many discussions, sometimes leading to intense collaboration, with colleagues in Estonia and abroad about the topic. With that in mind, I can only hope Estonian readers find this account credible and realistic, and that readers elsewhere will find potential resonances or dissonances with the contexts with which they might be more familiar. If neither is the case, however, I alone can be held accountable.

Bibliography

Ajsic, Adnan & Mary McGroarty. 2015. Mapping language ideologies. In Francis Hult & David C. Johnson (eds.), *Research methods in language policy and planning. A practical guide*, 181–192. Oxford: Blackwell.
Almann, Arno. 2012. EBSi rektor: äri õppimisel ainult eesti keeles puudub mõte [EBS's rector: Studying business only in Estonian makes no sense]. *juhtimine.ee*. 15 October.
Ammon, Ulrich (ed). 2001. *The dominance of English as a language of science*. Berlin: Walter de Gruyter.
Ball, Stephen. 1993. What is policy? Texts, trajectories and toolboxes. *Discourse: Studies in the Cultural Politics of Education* 13(2). 10–17.
Barakos, Elisabeth & Johann Unger (eds.). 2016. *Discursive approaches to language policy*. Basingstoke: Palgrave Macmillan.
Björkman, Beyza. 2013. *English as an academic lingua franca: An investigation of form and communicative effectiveness*. Berlin: Mouton de Gruyter.
Björkman, Beyza. 2014. Language ideology or language practice? An analysis of language policy documents at Swedish universities. *Multilingua* 33(3–4). 335–363.
Bernstein, Basil. 1999. Vertical and horizontal discourse: An essay. *British Journal of Sociology of Education* 20(2). 157–173.
Blommaert, Jan. 1999. The debate is open. In Jan Blommaert (ed.), *Language ideological debates*, 1–38. Berlin: Mouton de Gruyter.
Blommaert, Jan. 2005. *Discourse*. Cambridge: Cambridge University Press.
Blommaert, Jan. 2010. *The sociolinguistics of globalization*. Cambridge: Cambridge University Press.
Blommaert, Jan. 2013a. *Ethnography, superdiversity and linguistic landscapes. Chronicles of complexity*. Bristol: Multilingual Matters.
Blommaert, Jan. 2013b. Policy, policing and the ecology of social norms: Ethnographic monitoring revisited. *International Journal of the Sociology of Language* 219. 123–140.
Blommaert, Jan, Helen Kelly-Holmes, Pia Lane, Sirpa Leppänen, Máiread Moriarty, Sari Pietikäinen & Anna Piirainen-Marsh. 2009. Media, multilingualism, and language policing: An introduction. *Language Policy* 8(3). 203–207.
Bolton, Kingsley & Maria Kuteeva. 2012. English as an academic language at a Swedish university: Parallel language use and the 'threat' of English. *Journal of Multilingual and Multicultural Development* 33(5). 429–447.
Bretxa, Vanessa, Llorenç Comajoan & F. Xavier Vila. 2016. Is science really English monoglot? Language practices at a university research park in Barcelona. *Language Problems and Language Planning*, 40(1). 47–68.
Brown, Kara D., Kadri Koreinik & Maarja Siiner. 2017. Introductory chapter: Questioning borders. In Maarja Siiner, Kadri Koreinik & Kara D. Brown (eds.), *Language policy beyond the state*, 1–21. New York: Springer.
Bulajeva, Tatjana & Gabrielle Hogan-Brun. 2014. Internationalisation of higher education and nation building: Resolving language policy dilemmas in Lithuania. *Journal of Multilingual and Multicultural Development* 35(4). 318–331.
Bull, Tove. 2004. Dagens og gårdagens akademiske lingua franca. Eit historisk tilbakeblikk og eit globalt utsyn [The academic lingua franca of today and yesterday. A historical

retrospect and a global review]. In Dag F. Simonsen (ed.), *Språk i kunnskapssamfunnet. Engelsk – elitenes nye latin?* [Language in the knowledge society. English – the new Latin of the elites?], 35–45. Oslo: Gyldendal Norsk Forlag.
Bull, Tove. 2012. Against the mainstream: Universities with an alternative language policy. *International Journal of the Sociology of Language* 216. 55–73.
Busch, Brigitta. 2015. Linguistic repertoire and Spracherleben, the lived experience of language. *Working Papers in Urban Language and Literacies*, WP148.
Canagarajah, Suresh. 2006. Ethnographic methods in language policy. In Thomas Ricento (ed.), *An introduction to language policy: Theory and method*, 153–169. Oxford: Wiley Blackwell.
Coleman, James. 2006. English-medium teaching in European higher education. *Language Teaching* 39(1). 1–14.
Cooper, Robert. 1989. *Language planning and social change*. Cambridge: Cambridge University Press.
Cots, Josep M., Peter Garrett & Enric Llurda (eds.). 2014. Language policies and practices in the internationalization of higher education on the European margins. [Special issue]. *Journal of Multilingual and Multicultural Development* 35(4). 311–442.
Cots, Josep M., David Lasagabaster & Peter Garrett. 2012. Multilingual policies and practices of universities in three bilingual regions in Europe. *International Journal of the Sociology of Language* 216. 7–32.
Dafouz, Emma & Ute Smit. 2016. Towards a dynamic conceptual framework for English-medium education in multilingual university settings. *Applied Linguistics* 37(3). 397–415.
Delfi, 12 November, 2007. TLÜ lükkas Katariina kolledži loomise edasi [Tallinn University pushed the establishment of Catherine's College forward]. http://www.delfi.ee/news/paevauudised/eesti/tlu-lukkas-katariina-kolledzi-loomise-edasi?id=17407935 (accessed 9 December 2013).
Doiz, Aintzane, David Lasagabaster & Juan M. Sierra (eds.). 2013. *English-medium instruction at universities. Global challenges*. Bristol: Multilingual Matters.
Dörnyei. Zoltán. 2007. *Research methods in applied linguistics: Quantitative, qualitative, and mixed methods*. Oxford: Oxford University Press.
Ehala, Martin. 2014. Sustainability of the Estonian Language. In Marju Lauristin (ed.), *Development of the Estonian cultural space*, 191–198. Tallinn: Eesti Koostöö Kogu.
European Commission. 2012a. *Eurostat. Foreign language learning statistics*. September. epp.eurostat.ec.europa.eu/statistics_explained/index.php/Foreign_language_learning_statistics (accessed 9 December 2017).
European Commission. 2012b. *Special Eurobarometer 386. Europeans and their languages. Report*. June. ec.europa.eu/public_opinion/index_en.htm (accessed 9 December 2017).
Estonian Language Council. 2011. *Development plan of the Estonian language 2011–2017*. Tallinn: Estonian Language Foundation. Translated into Estonian from English by Enn Veldi.
Estonian Ministry of Education and Research. 2013. *Estonian Foreign Languages Strategy 2009–2015*. contactpoints.ecml.at/LinkClick.aspx?fileticket=8lWNTiRd1A4%3D&tabid=1319&language=en-GB (accessed 30 October 2018).
Fabricius, Anne, Janus Mortensen & Hartmut Haberland. 2017. The lure of internationalization: Paradoxical discourses of transnational student mobility, linguistic diversity and cross-cultural exchange. *Higher Education* 73(4). 577–595.

Fairclough, Norman. 1993. Critical discourse analysis and the marketization of public discourse: The universities. *Discourse & Society* 4(2). 133–168.
Gallego-Balsà, Lídia. 2014. *Language policy and internationalisation: The experience of international students at a Catalan university*. PhD dissertation, Universitat de Lleida.
Gallego-Balsà, Lídia & Josep M. Cots. 2016. 'Living to the rhythm of the city': Internationalisation of universities and tourism discourse. *Language, Culture and Curriculum* 29(1). 6–21.
Gee, James P. 1999. *An introduction to Discourse analysis: theory and method*. London and New York: Routledge.
Gerner, Kristian & Stefan Hedlund. 1993. *The Baltic states and the end of the Soviet empire*. London and New York: Routledge.
Gee, James P. 2011. *How to do discourse analysis: A toolkit*. London: Routledge.
Gorter, Durk. (ed.). 2006. *Linguistic landscape: A new approach to multilingualism*. Clevedon: Multilingual Matters.
Greenall, Annjo. 2012. Attracting international students by means of the web: Transadaptation, domestication and cultural suppression. *International Journal of the Sociology of Language* 216. 75–85.
Haberland, Hartmut. 2014. English from above and below, and from outside. In Anna Kristina Hultgren, Frans Gregersen & Jacob Thøgersen (eds.), *English in Nordic universities: Ideologies and practices*, 251–263. Amsterdam: John Benjamins.
Haberland, Hartmut & Bent Preisler. 2015. The position of Danish, English and other languages at Danish universities in the context of Danish society. In F. Xavier Vila & Vanessa Bretxa (eds.), *Language policy in higher education: The case of medium-sized languages*, 15–42. Bristol: Multilingual Matters.
Haberland, Hartmut & Janus Mortensen (eds.). 2012. Language and the international university. [Special issue]. *International Journal of the Sociology of Language* 216: 1–197.
Halonen, Mia, Pasi Ihalainen & Taina Saarinen (eds.). 2015. *Language policies in Finland and Sweden: Interdisciplinary and multi-sited comparisons*. Bristol: Multilingual Matters.
Hamel, Rainer. 2008. Les langues de la science: vers un modèle de diglossie gérable. In Jacques Maurais, Pierre Dumont, Jean-Marie Klinkenberg, Bruno Maurer & Patrick Chardenet (eds.), *L'avenir du français*, 87–94. Paris: AUF, Editions des archives contemporaines.
Han, Yawen, Peter De Costa, & Yaqiong Cui. 2016. Examining the English language policy for ethnic minority students in a Chinese university: A language ideology and language regime perspective. *Current Issues in Language Planning* 17(3–4). 311–331.
Harder, Peter. 2012. Parallel language use at the University of Copenhagen – An evolving commitment. Paper presented at CALPIU'12: Higher education across borders: Transcultural interaction and linguistic diversity, Roskilde, Denmark, 1–4 April.
Haugen, Einar. 1972. *The ecology of language*. Stanford: Stanford University Press.
Heller, Monica. 2011. *Paths to post-nationalism: A critical ethnography of language and identity*. Oxford: Oxford University Press.
Heller, Monica & Alexandre Duchêne (eds.). 2012. *Language in late capitalism. Pride and profit*. London and New York: Routledge.
Heller, Monica, Adam Jaworski & Crispin Thurlow. 2014. Introduction: Sociolinguistics and tourism – Mobilities, markets, multilingualism. *Journal of Sociolinguistics* 18(4). 425–458.
Hellekjær, Glenn Ole. 2010. Lecture comprehension in English-medium higher education. *Hermes – Journal of Language and Communication Studies* 45. 11–34.

Hélot, Christine & Muiris Ó Laorie. 2011. Introduction: From language education policy to a pedagogy of the possible. In Christine Hélot & Muiris Ó Laorie (eds.), *Language policy for the multilingual classroom: Pedagogy of the possible*, xi–xxv. Bristol: Multilingual Matters.

Hoffman, Michol. 2013. Sociolinguistic interviews. In Janet Holmes & Kirk Hazen (eds.), *Research methods in sociolinguistics: A practical guide*, 25–42. Malden, MA: John Wiley & Sons.

Hogan-Brun, Gabrielle, Uldis Ozolins, Meilute Ramoniene & M. Rannut. 2007. Language politics and practices in the Baltic states. *Current Issues in Language Planning* 8(4). 469–631.

Holborow, Marnie. 2015. *Language and neoliberalism*. London: Routledge.

Hornberger, Nancy H. & David C. Johnson. 2007. Slicing the onion ethnographically. Layers and spaces in multilingual language education policy and practice. *TESOL Quarterly* 41(3). 509–532.

Huisman, Jeroen, Paulo Santiago, Per Högselius, Maria José Lemaitre & William Thorn. 2007. *OECD reviews of terciary education. Estonia*. Paris: Organisation for Economic Co-operation and Development.

Hult, Francis. 2010. Analysis of language policy discourses across scales of space and time. *International Journal of the Sociology of Language* 202. 7–24.

Hult, Francis. 2012. English as a trans-cultural language in Swedish policy and practice. *TESOL Quarterly* 46(2). 230–257.

Hult, Francis. 2015. Making policy connections across scales using nexus analysis. In Francis Hult & David C. Johnson (eds.), *Research methods in language policy and planning: A practical guide*, 217–231. Oxford: Blackwell.

Hult, Francis & Marie Källkvist. 2016. Global flows in local language planning: Articulating parallel language use in Swedish university policies. *Current Issues in Language Planning* 17(1). 56–71.

Hultgren, Anna Kristina. 2014. Whose parallellingualism? Overt and covert ideologies in Danish university language policies. *Multilingua* 33(1–2). 61–87.

Hultgren, Anna Kristina. 2015. English as an international language of science and its effect on Nordic terminology: The view of scientists. In Andrew Linn, Neil Bermel & Gibson Ferguson (eds.), *Attitudes towards English in Europe*, 139–164. Berlin: De Gruyter Mouton.

Hultgren, Anna Kristina & Jacob Thøgersen. 2014. Englishization of Nordic universities. Policy and practice – A disconnect. *Language Problems and Language Planning* 38(3). 247–264.

Hultgren, Anna Kristina, Frans Gregersen & Jacob Thøgersen (eds.). 2014. *English in Nordic universities: Ideologies and practices*. Amsterdam: John Benjamins.

Hsieh, Hsiu-Fang & Sarah Shannon. 2005. Three approaches to qualitative content analysis. *Qualitative Health Research* 15(9). 1277–1288.

Irvine, Judith & Susan Gal. 2000. Language ideology and linguistic differentiation. In Paul V. Kroskrity (ed.), *Regimes of language: Ideologies, polities, and identities*, 35–84. Santa Fe: School of American Research Press.

Johnson, David C. 2009. Ethnography of language policy. *Language Policy* 8(2). 139–159.

Johnson, David C. 2013a. *Language policy*. Basingstoke: Palgrave Macmillan.

Johnson, David C. 2013b. Introduction: Ethnography of language policy. *International Journal of the Sociology of Language* 219. 1–6.

Johnson, David C. 2015. Intertextuality and language policy. In Francis Hult & David C. Johnson (eds.), *Research methods in language policy and planning: A practical guide*, 166–180. Oxford: Blackwell.

Johnson, David & Thomas Ricento. 2013. Conceptual and theoretical perspectives in language planning and policy: Situating the ethnography of language policy. *International Journal of the Sociology of Language* 219. 7–21.

Jürna, Merike. 2014. Linguistic realities at the University of Copenhagen: Parallel language use in practice as seen from the perspective of international staff. In Anna Kristina Hultgren, Frans Gregersen & Jacob Thøgersen (eds.), *English in Nordic universities: Ideologies and practices*, 215–249. Amsterdam: John Benjamins.

Kalm, Volli. 2012. Ahistavad keelehirmud [Oppressive language fears]. *Postimees. Arvamus.* 25 October.

Kaplan, Robert B. & Richard B. Baldauf. 1997. *Language planning: From theory to practice*. Clevedon: Multilingual Matters.

Kasekamp, Andres. 2010. *A history of the Baltic states*. Basingstoke: Palgrave Macmillan.

Kasik, Reet. 2011. *Stahli mantlipärjad. Eesti keele uurimise lugu* [Stahli's successors. The story of Estonian language research]. Tartu: Tartu University Press.

Kibbermann, Kerttu. 2017. Responses to the internationalization of higher education in language policies of Estonia and Latvia. *Journal of Estonian and Finno-Ugric Linguistics* 8(1). 97–113.

Kibbermann, Kerttu. 2014. Language Policy in Higher Education in Estonia and Latvia: Regulations and Practices. *Via Scientiarum* 2. 111–124.

Klaas-Lang, Birute & Helle Metslang. 2015. Language policy and sustainability of Estonian in higher education. In Gerhard Stickel & Cecilia Robustelli (eds.), *Language use in university teaching and research*, 161–177. Frankfurt: Peter Lang.

Kroskrity, Paul V. (2000). Regimes of language: Ideologies, polities, and identities. Santa Fe: School of American Research Press.

Kull, Kalevi. 2012. Eesti keel valitsegu eesti ülikooli [May the Estonian language govern the Estonian university]. *Postimees. Arvamus.* 18 October.

Kuteeva, Maria & Beyza Björkman. 2012. Difficult is difficult in any language: University students' perceptions of learning in English. Paper presented at CALPIU'12: Higher education across borders: Transcultural interaction and linguistic diversity, Roskilde University, 1–4 April.

Kuteeva, Maria. 2014. The parallel language use of Swedish and English: The question of 'nativeness' in university policies and practices. *Journal of Multilingual and Multicultural Development* 35(4). 332–344.

Kuteeva, Maria & John Airey. 2014. Disciplinary differences in the use of English in higher education: Reflections on recent language policy developments. *Higher Education* 67(5). 533–549.

Källkvist, Marie & Francis Hult. 2016. Discursive mechanisms and human agency in language policy formation: Negotiating bilingualism and parallel language use at a Swedish university. *International Journal of Bilingual Education and Bilingualism* 19(1). 1–17.

Lam, Queenie & Bernd Wächter. 2014. Executive summary. In Bend Wächter & Friedhelm Maiworm (eds.), *English-taught programs in European higher education. The state of play in 2014*, 15–24. Bonn: Lemmen.

Lane, Pia. 2010. "We did what we thought was best for our children": a nexus analysis of language shift in a Kven community. *International Journal of the Sociology of Language* 202. 63–78.

Lauristin, Marju, Esta Kaal, Laura Kirss, Tanja Kriger, Anu Masso, Kristi Nurmela, Külliki Seppel, Tiit Tammaru, Maiu Uus, Peeter Vihalemm & Triin Vihalemm. 2011. *Integration monitoring 2011. Summary*. Tartu: University of Tartu, AS Emor, Praxis Centre for Policy Studies.

Lehikoinen, Anita. 2004. Foreign-language-medium education as national strategy. In Robert Wilkinson (eds.), *Integrating content and language: Meeting the challenge of multilingual higher education*, 41–48. Maastricht: Maastricht University Press.

Liblik, L. (ed.). 1973. *Eesti NSV Teaduste Akadeemias Kaitstud Väitekirjad 1954–1970* [Estonian SSR Academy of Sciences defended theses 1954–1970]. Tallinn: ENSV Teaduste Akadeemia Teaduslik Raamatukogu.

Ljosland, Ragnhild. 2007. English in Norwegian academia: A step towards diglossia? *World Englishes* 26(4). 395–410.

Ljosland, Ragnhild. 2011. English as an academic lingua franca: Language policies and multilingual practices in a Norwegian university. *Journal of Pragmatics* 43(4). 991–1004.

Ljosland, Ragnhild. 2015. Policymaking as a multilayered activity. A case study from the higher education sector in Norway. *Higher Education* 70(4). 611–627.

Liddicoat, Anthony J. 2016. Language planning in universities: Teaching, research and administration. *Current Issues in Language Planning* 17(3–4). 231–241.

Linn, Andrew. 2010. Can parallelingualism save Norwegian from extinction? *Multilingua* 29(3–4). 289–305.

Llurda, Enric, Josep M. Cots & Lourdes Armengol. 2014. Views on multilingualism and internationalization in higher education: Administrative staff in the spotlight. *Journal of Multilingual and Multicultural Development* 35(4). 376–391.

Marten, Heiko. 2017. Negotiating a place for German in Estonia: Contemporary functions, attitudes and policies. In Maarja Siiner, Kadri Koreinik & Kara D. Brown (eds.), *Language policy beyond the state*, 143–162. New York: Springer.

Mattisen, Heli & Krista Männa. 2007. Tallinna Ülikooli senat kutsus kokku Katariina kolledži töörühma [Tallinn University Senate calls for the formation of Catherine's College working group]. http://www.tlu.ee/et/uudised/286/tallinna-ulikooli-senat-kutsus-kokku-katariina-kolledzi-tooruhma (accessed 9 December 2017).

Maurais, Jacques & Michael A. Morris (eds.). 2003. *Languages in a globalizing world*. Cambridge: Cambridge University Press.

Mayring, Philip. 2000. Qualitative content analysis. *Forum: Qualitative Social Research* 1 (2). Art. 20. http://www.qualitative-research.net/index.php/fqs/article/view/1089/2385 (accessed 9 December 2017).

McCarty, Theresa (ed.) 2011. *Ethnography and language policy*. New York & London: Routledge.

McCarty, Theresa. 2015. Ethnography in language planning and policy research. In Francis Hult & David C. Johnson (eds.), *Research methods in language policy and planning: A practical guide*, 81–93. Oxford: Wiley Blackwell.

Metslang, Helena & Šmõreitšik, Anastassia. 2013. How non-native speaker students cope in higher education: A case study of ethnic minority students in Estonia. In Ellu Saar & René Mõttus (eds.), *Higher education at a crossroad: The case of Estonia*. 165–195. Frankfurt: Peter Lang.

Miranda, Norbella, Martha Berdugo & Harvey Tejada. 2016. Conflicting views on language policy and planning at a Colombian university. *Current Issues in Language Planning* 17(3–4). 422–440.

Mortensen, Janus & Hartmut Haberland. 2012. English – The new Latin of academia? Danish universities as a case. *International Journal of the Sociology of Language* 216. 175–197.

Mortensen, Janus & Anne Fabricius. 2014. Language ideologies in Danish higher education: Exploring student perspectives. In Anna Kristina Hultgren, Frans Gregersen & Jacob Thøgersen (eds.), *English in Nordic universities: Ideologies and practices*, 193–224. Amsterdam: John Benjamins.

Niit, Jane. 2012. Estonglish kui uus sund Eesti kõrgharidusmaastikul? [Estonglish as a new direction in the Estonian higher education landscape?] *Postimees, Arvamus.* 08 November.

Nikula, Tarja, Taina Saarinen, Sari Pöyhönen & Teija Kangasvieri. 2012. Linguistic diversity as a problem and a resource – Multilingualism in European and Finnish policy documents. In Jan Blommaert, Sirpa Leppänen, Paivi Pahta & Tiina Räisänen (eds.), *Dangerous multilingualism: Northern perspectives on order, purity and normality*, 41–66. Basingstoke: Palgrave Macmillan.

Nokkala, Terhi. 2007. *Constructing the ideal university: The internationalization of higher education in the competitive knowledge society.* Tampere: Tampere University Press.

Oisaar, E. 1973. *Tartu Ülikoolis kaitstud väitekirjad 1802–1918: Bibliograafia* [Defended theses at the University of Tartu 1802–1918: A bibliography]. Tartu: Tartu Riiklik Ülikool Teaduslik Raamatukogu [The Scientific Library of Tartu State University].

Pennycook, Alastair. 2006. Postmodernism in language policy. In Thomas Ricento (ed.), *An introduction to language policy: Theory and method*, 60–76. Oxford: Wiley Blackwell.

Pérez-Milans, Miguel. 2016. Introduction: Reflexivity and social change in applied linguistics. *AILA Review* 29. 1–14.

Pérez-Milans, Miguel. 2018. Metapragmatics in the ethnography of language policy. In James Tollefson & Miguel Pérez-Milans (eds.), *Oxford handbook of language policy and planning* (forthcoming). Oxford: Oxford University Press.

Phillipson, Robert. 2015. "English as a threat or opportunity in European higher education." In Slobodanka Dimova, Anna Kristina Hultgren & Cristian Jensen (eds.), *The English language in teaching in European higher education*, 19–42. Berlin: Mouton de Gruyter.

Pietikäinen, Sari & Helen Kelly-Holmes. 2011. The local political economy of languages in a Sámi tourism destination: Authenticity and mobility in the labelling of souvenirs. *Journal of Sociolinguistics* 15(3). 323–346.

Piller, Ingrid & Jinhyun Cho. 2013. Neoliberalism as language policy. *Language in Society* 42(1). 23–44.

Postimees. 11 December 2007. ETV: Keelenõukogu hinnangul ei tohiks Katariina kolledži olla venekeelse õppekava [ETV: According to the Estonian Language Council, Catherine's College cannot offer Russian-medium programs]. https://www.postimees.ee/1734467/etv-keelenoukogu-hinnangul-ei-tohiks-katariina-kolled-olla-venekeelse-oppekavaga (accessed 9 December 2017).

Pärismaa, Sirje. 2013. Kui kaua kõlab ülikoolides veel eesti keel? [How long will Estonian still be heard in universities?] *Õpetajate Leht.* 01 March.

Pärnu Leadership Conference. 12 October 2012. https://www.konverentsid.ee/blog/ (accessed 9 December 2017).

Pöyhönen, Sari & Taina Saarinen. 2015. Constructions of bilingualism in Finnish government programmes and a newspaper discussion site debate. *Current Issues in Language Planning* 16(4). 392–408.

Qiang, Zha. 2003. Internationalization of higher education: Towards a conceptual framework. *Policy Futures in Education* 1(2). 248–270.

Rannut, Mart. 2004. Language policy in Estonia. *Noves SL. Revista de Sociolingüística* 2004(spring/summer). 1–17. http://www6.gencat.net/llengcat/noves/hm04primavera-estiu/rannut1_6.htm (accessed 9 December 2017).

Rannut, Mart. 2008. Estonianization efforts post-independence. *International Journal of Bilingual Education and Bilingualism* 11(3–4). 423–439.

Rhoades, Gary & Shelia Slaughter. 2004. Academic capitalism and the new economy: Challenges and choices. *American Academic* 1(1). 37–59.

Ricento, Thomas. 2000. *Ideology, politics and language policies: Focus on English*. Amsterdam & Philadelphia: John Benjamins.

Ricento, Thomas & Nancy H. Hornberger. 1996. Unpeeling the onion: Language planning and policy and the ELT professional. *TESOL Quarterly* 30(3). 401–427.

Ruiz, Richard. 1984. Orientations in language planning. *NABE Journal* 8(2). 15–34.

Saar, Ene & René Mõttus (eds.). 2013. *Higher education at a crossroad: The case of Estonia*. Frankfurt: Peter Lang.

Saarinen, Taina. 2012. Internationalization of Finnish higher education – Is language an issue? *International Journal of the Sociology of Language* 216. 157–173.

Saarinen, Taina. 2014. Language ideologies in Finnish higher education in the national and international context: A historical and contemporary outlook. In Anna Kristina Hultgren, Frans Gregersen & Jacob Thøgersen (eds.), *English in Nordic universities: Ideologies and practices*, 127–146. Amsterdam: John Benjamins.

Saarinen, Taina. 2017. Policy is what happens while you're busy doing something else: Introduction to special issue on 'language' indexing higher education policy. *Higher Education* 73(4). 553–560.

Saarinen, Taina & Tarja Nikula. 2013. Implicit policy, invisible language: Policies and practices of international degree programs in Finnish higher education. In Aintzane Doiz, David Lasagabaster & Juan M. Sierra (eds.), *English-medium instruction at universities. Global challenges*, 131–150. Bristol: Multilingual Matters.

Salö, Linus. 2014. Language ideology and shifting representations of linguistic threats: A Bourdieusian re-reading of the conceptual history of domain loss in Sweden's field of language planning. In Anna Kristina Hultgren, Frans Gregersen & Jacob Thøgersen (eds.), *English in Nordic universities: Ideologies and practices*, 83–110. Amsterdam: John Benjamins.

Salö, Linus. 2016. *Languages and linguistic exchanges in Swedish academia: Practices, processes, and globalizing markets*. Stockholm: Stockholm University PhD dissertation.

Scollon, Ron. 2008. *Analyzing public discourse: Discourse analysis in the making of public policy*. London: Routledge.

Scollon, Ron & Suzie Wong Scollon. 2004. *Nexus analysis: Discourse and the emerging Internet*. London: Routledge.

Scollon, Ron & Suzie Wong Scollon. 2003. *Discourses in place. Language in the material world*. London and New York: Routledge.

Scollon, Ron, Suzie Wong Scollon & Rodney H. Jones. 2012. *Intercultural communication: A discourse approach*. 3rd edition. Oxford: Wiley Blackwell.

Schieffelin, Bambi B., Kathryn A. Woolard & Paul V. Kroskrity (eds.). 1998. *Language ideologies: Practice and theory*. New York: Oxford University Press.

Shohamy, Elana. 2006. *Language policy: Hidden agendas and new approaches*. London & New York: Routledge.

Shohamy, Elana & Gorter, Durk (eds.). 2009. *Linguistic landscape: Expanding the scenery*. New York: Routledge.

Shohamy, Elana, Elizer Ben Rafael & Monica Barni (eds.). 2010. *Linguistic landscape in the city*. Bristol: Multilingual Matters.

Siiner, Maarja. 2016. University administrators as forced language policy agents. An institutional ethnography of parallel language strategy and practices at the University of Copenhagen. *Current Issues in Language Planning* 17(3–4). 441–458.

Siiner, Maarja, Kadri Koreinik & Kara D. Brown (eds.). 2017. *Language policy beyond the state*. New York: Springer.

Siiner, Maarja & Triin Vihalemm. 2011. Individual multilingualism in the Baltic states within the European context. In *Estonian human development report 2010/2011. Baltic ways of human development: Twenty years on*, 135–137. Tallinn: Eesti Koostöö Kogu.

Skerrett, Delaney M. 2010. Language and authoritarianism in the 20th century: The cases of Estonia and Catalonia. *Estonian Papers in Applied Linguistics* 6. 261–276.

Skerrett, Delaney M. 2014. The 2011 Estonian high school language reform in the context of critical language policy and planning. *Current Issues in Language Planning* 15(2). 174–200.

Slaughter, Sheila & Gary Rhoades. 2004. *Academic capitalism and the new economy. Markets, state, and higher education*. Baltimore and London: John Hopkins University Press.

Soler, Josep. 2013. The anonymity of Catalan and the authenticity of Estonian: Two paths for the development of medium-sized languages. *International Journal of Bilingual Education and Bilingualism* 16(2). 153–163.

Soler-Carbonell, Josep. 2014a. University language policies and language choice among Ph.D. graduates in Estonia: The (unbalanced) interplay between English and Estonian. *Multilingua* 33(3–4). 413–436.

Soler-Carbonell, Josep. 2014b. Emerging ELF as an intercultural resource: Language attitudes and ideologies. *Journal of English as a Lingua Franca* 3(2). 243–268.

Soler-Carbonell, Josep. 2015. Language policy in Estonian higher education: Internationalization and the tension over English. In Slobodanka Dimova, Anna Kristina Hultgren & Cristian Jensen (eds.), *The English language in teaching in European higher education*, 247–268. Berlin: Mouton de Gruyter.

Soler-Carbonell, Josep, Taina Saarinen & Kerttu Kibbermann. 2017. Multilayered perspectives on language policy in higher education: Finland, Estonia and Latvia in comparison. *Journal of Multilingual and Multicultural Development* 38(4). 301–314.

Soler, Josep & Virve-Anneli Vihman. 2018. Language ideology and language planning in Estonian higher education: Nationalizing and globalizing discourses. *Current Issues in Language Planning* 19(1). 22–41.

Soler, Josep, Beyza Björkman & Maria Kuteeva. 2018. University language policies in Estonia and Sweden: Exploring the interplay between English and national languages in higher education. *Journal of Multilingual and Multicultural Development* 39(1). 29–43.

Spolsky, Bernard. 2004. *Language policy*. Cambridge: Cambridge University Press.

Spolsky, Bernard. 2009. *Language management*. Cambridge: Cambridge University Press.

Statistics Estonia. www.stat.ee (accessed 9 December 2017).

Swaan, Abraham de. 2001. *Words of the world*. Cambridge: Polity Press.

Tamul, Sirje. n.d. Facts about the history of the University of Tartu. https://www.ut.ee/en/university/general/history (accessed 9 December 2017).

Thurlow, Crispin & Giorgia Aiello. 2007. National pride, global capital: A social semiotic analysis of transnational visual branding in the airline industry. *Visual Communication* 6(3). 305–344.

Tiik, L. (ed.). 1961. Tartu Riiklikus Ülikoolis 1946–1959 kaitstud väitekirjad: bibliograafia/ Диссертации защищенные в Тартуском государственном университете 1946–1959 [Tartu State University 1946–1959 defended theses: Bibliography]. Tartu: Tartu Riiklik Ülikool.

Tomusk, Voldemar. 2001. Higher education reform in Estonia: A legal perspective. *Higher Education Policy* 14. 201–212.

Vihalemm, Triin & Gabrielle Hogan-Brun. 2013. Language policies and practices across the Baltic: processes, challenges and prospects. *European Journal of Applied Linguistics* 1, 55–82.
Vaht, Gunnar, Liia Tüür & Ülla Kulassalu. 2010. *Higher education in Estonia*, 4th edn. Tallinn: Archimedes Foundation.
Veldre, Einar. 2012. Inglise keel pole võluvits [English is not a magic wand]. *Postimees, Arvamus*. 19 October.
Verschik, Anna. 2012. Practising receptive multilingualism: Estonian–Finnish communication in Tallinn. *International Journal of Bilingualism* 16(3). 265–286.
Verschik, Anna. 2005. The language situation in Estonia. *Journal of Baltic Studies* 36(3). 283–316.
Vihman, Virve-Anneli & Ülle Tensing. 2014. English-medium studies in the Estonian national university: Globalisation and organic change. In Lea Lepik (ed.), *Keelevahetus ülikoolis – probleem või võimalus?* [Language shift in the university: Problem or opportunity?] (Tartu Ülikooli ajaloo küsimusi, XLII). Tartu: Tartu Ülikooli Ajaloo Muuseum.
Vila, F. Xavier. 2015. Medium-sized languages as viable linguae academicae. In F. Xavier Vila & Vanessa Bretxa (eds.), *Language policy in higher education. The case of medium-sized languages*, 181–210. Bristol: Multilingual Matters.
Vila, F. Xavier & Vanessa Bretxa (eds.). 2015. *Language policy in higher education. The case of medium-sized languages*. Bristol: Multilingual Matters.
Willans, Fiona. 2016. Carving out institutional space for multilingualism in the world's most multilingual region: The role of Linguistics at the University of South Pacific. *Current Issues in Language Planning* 17(3–4). 351–368.
Wodak, Ruth. 2006. Linguistic analyzes in language policies. In Thomas Ricento (ed.), *An introduction to language policy: Theory and method*, 170–193. Oxford: Wiley Blackwell.
Woodfield, Steve. 2010. Europe. In Eva Egron-Polak & Ross Hudson (eds.), *Internationalization of higher education: Global trends, regional perspectives*, 170–178. Paris: International Association of Universities 3rd Global Survey Report.
Woolard, Kathryn A. 1998. Introduction: Language ideology as a field of inquiry. In Bambi B. Schieffelin, Kathryn A. Woolard & Paul V. Kroskrity (eds.), *Language ideologies: Practice and theory*, 3–47. New York: Oxford University Press.
Wächter, Bernd & Friedhelm Maiworm (eds.). 2014. *English-taught programs in European higher education. The state of play in 2014*. Bonn: Lemmens.
Zabrodskaja, Anastassia. 2014. Tallinn: Monolingual from above and multilingual from below. *International Journal of the Sociology of Language* 228. 105–130.
Zirnask, Mart. 2014. Estonian language and culture: Multilingual Estonian. *University of Tartu Vision Conference 2032* (UT Special Edition), 41–45. Tartu: University of Tartu Press.

Index

Aaviksoo, Jaak 57, 76, 131
academic capitalism 4
academic communication 130
academic English
– attitudes towards 130, 136, 137, 139, 151, 158
academic language 70
– attitudes towards 143, 145
Aiello, Giorgia 2, 5
Airey, John 8, 103
Almann, Arno 72
Altbach, Philip 2
Ammon, Ulrich 3, 6

Baldauf, Richard 10
Baltic states 26, 151
– demographics 43
Barakos, Elisabeth 10
Best, Randy 1
bilingualism in Estonia 16
bilingual signs 48
Björkman, Beyza 7, 8, 40, 63
Blommaert, Jan 9, 46, 72, 152, 153
Bolton, Kingsley 138
Bretxa, Vanessa 2, 6, 8, 127
Bulajeva 18, 39, 45
Bull, Tove 7, 115, 147
Busch, Brigitta 89

Canagarajah, Suresh 8, 12
Cho, Jinhyun 4
content analysis 63
Cooper, Robert 10
Cots, Josep Maria 2, 5, 6
critical sociolinguistics 153

Dafouz, Emma 7
Delfi 160
de Swaan, Abram 6
dialogicality 75
disciplinary differences 92, 103, 126, 146
discourses in place 58
– conceptual 25, 80
– material 41

discourse system 145
Doiz, Aintzane 6
Duchêne, Alexandre 2

Ehala, Martin 83, 155
English as an academic lingua franca 92
English-taught programs 19, 23, 32, 51, 54, 55, 61, 62, 69, 75, 107, 109, 137, 154, 156, 160
– economic reasons 104
– sociolinguistic consequences 156
Erasmus mobility in Estonia 86
Estonia
– demographics 15
– post-Soviet 17
– sociolinguistic context 14
Estonian Academy of Sciences 121
– languages used for publication purposes 121
– PhD theses 1950s to 1970s 121
Estonian higher education 14, 17, 19, 32
– historical development 114
– post-Soviet 58
– sociolinguistic regimes 115
Estonian Language Act 15, 43
Estonian Language Council 57, 154
Estonian-Russian students 108, 112, 159, 160
Estonian tongue twisters 97
ethnography of language policy 10, 12, 151, 153
Eurobarometer 16
European higher education arena 26
extended summaries of PhD theses in Estonian 94, 128, 156

Fabricius, Anne 5, 8, 158
Fairclough, Norman 3
Finnish language 29
focus group discussion 88
foreign language 29, 31, 32, 39, 40
– ambiguous label 111
foreign students 1, 5, 19, 24, 34, 103, 104, 110, 156

Gallego-Balsà, Lídia 5, 52
global English 7
Gorter, Durk 46

Haberland, Hartmut 2, 6, 7, 147, 158, 159
Halonen, Mia 10, 26
Hamel, Rainer Enrique 7
Harder, Peter 36, 39
Harro, Jaanus 78
Hellekjaer, Glenn Olle 138
Heller, Monica 2, 150, 152, 159, 161
higher education
– and English 6
– Baltic states 24, 41
– Denmark 25
– Estonia 31, 40
– EU 35
– Finland 29, 38
– Latvia 24, 33, 39
Hogan-Brun, Gabrielle 39, 42, 45
Holborow, Marnie 2, 3
home students 19
Hornberger, Nancy 11, 12
Hult, Francis 10, 13, 18, 26, 46, 80, 149, 161
Hultgren, Anna Kristina 2, 4, 18

Ilves, Toomas Hendrik 57
in-depth interviews 88
institutional websites 52
institutions in non-Anglophone contexts 4
international English 7
internationalization of higher
    education 1, 23
– and discursive contradictions 3, 5, 9, 39,
    45, 93, 149, 157
– and economic reasons 2
– and English 6, 7, 18, 23, 26, 32, 35, 39
– and globalizing discourses 7
– and language 2, 9
– and language ideological debates 72
– and language ideology 6, 25, 58, 85, 93
– and language policy 8
– and nationalizing discourses 7
– and Russian 33, 39, 53, 112
– and the 'normal' university 101, 108
– and the role of language 7
– and tourism 54

– demographic reasons 109
– nationalizing and globalizing
    discourses 81, 85, 108, 147
intertextuality 67, 68

Johnson, David Cassels 8, 10, 11, 151, 152
Jürna, Merike 86, 88

Källkvist, Marie 7
Kalm, Volli 1, 57, 72, 74, 76, 78, 155
Kaplan, Robert 10
Kasekamp, Andres 75
Kasik, Reet 119
Kibbermann, Kerttu 19, 24, 40
Klaas-Lang, Birute 19, 59, 159
Kroskrity, Paul V. 152
Kull, Kalevi 73
Kuteeva, Maria 4, 8, 103, 138

language and globalization 6
language attitudes 148
– and motivation towards Estonian 92
– negative attitudes towards Estonian 90
– positive attitudes towards Estonian 89
language correctness 131, 132, 134
language ideological debates 155, 156
language ideology 8, 152
language policy 5, 26
– and de facto practices 106
– and ethnography 152
– and governmentality 11, 14
– and language ideology 40, 41, 152
– as social action 9
– discursive turn 9, 10
– Estonianization efforts 159
– EU 36
– in Estonia 16
– institutional level 40
– macro and micro levels 11
– multilayered 86
– multilevel 41
– national level 40
language policy cycle 8
language survey 138
Latvian language 33
Latvian State Language Law 43
Liddicoat, Tony 6

linguae academicae 158
linguistic landscape 46, 154
Linn, Andrew 8
Lithuanian Law on the State Language 43
Ljosland, Ragnhild 9, 127
Llurda, Enric 7

Maiworm, Friedhelm 8, 18, 23
Männa, Krista 160
marketization of higher education 3
Mattisen, Heli 160
Maurais, Jacques 6
Mayring, Philipp 28
McCarty, Theresa 10
Metslang, Helena 159
Metslang, Helle 19, 59, 159
mobility
– students and staff 36
monolingual signs 48, 51
Morris, Michael 6
Mortensen, Janus 2, 6, 147, 159
Mõttus, René 17, 59
multilingual higher education 111
multilingual signs 50, 52

native/non-native speakers of English 7
native speakerism 132
native speakers
– and language ideology 132
neoliberalism 4
nexus analysis 9, 12, 149
– and language policy 9
– discourses in place 151
– historical body 151
Niit, Jane 74
Nikula, Tarja 36
Nordic countries 4, 18, 26, 151

parallel language use 4, 8, 40, 110
Pärnu Conference 2012 2, 72
participant observation 130
Pérez-Milans, Miguel 12, 152, 153, 161
Phillipson, Robert 35
Piller, Ingrid 4
policy documents 28
– A2008 - University of Tartu Strategic Plan 2008 63

– A2015 - The University of Tartu Strategic Plan 2009–2015 63
– A2020 - Strategic Plan for the University of Tartu 2015–2020 63
– Agreement on Good Practice in the Internationalization of Estonia's Higher Education Institutions 62
– Development Strategy of the Estonian Language 2011–2017 62
– Estonian Higher Education Strategy 2006–2015 62
– internationalization strategy 27, 28, 29, 36, 37, 111
– language principles 27, 28, 30, 31, 32, 37, 40, 63, 112
– state and institutional 62
– Strategy for the Internationalization of Estonian Higher Education 2006–2015 62
Postimees 160
post-nationalism 159
post-national university 2, 115, 159
Preisler, Bent 158

qualitative content analysis 28

Rannut, Mart 15, 42, 159
recontextualisation 75
reflexivity 160
Rhoades, Gary 4
Ricento, Thomas 10, 12

Saar, Elle 17, 59
Saarinen, Taina 2, 9, 25, 29, 38, 41
Salö, Linus 25, 127
Schiefelin, Bambi B. 152
Scollon, Ron 12, 46, 145
Scollon, Suzie Wong 12, 46
Shohamy, Elana 10, 46
Siiner, Maarja 7, 17, 42
Skerrett, Delaney 15
Slaughter, Sheila 4
Smit, Ute 7
Šmõreitšik, Anastassia 159
snow-ball technique 100
sociolinguistics of higher education 5, 18
– and tourism 5

soft multilingualism 39
Spolsky, Bernard 10, 152
subject-specific terminology 144, 158
Swedish language 29

Tallinn University 136
– Catherine's College 160
– fieldwork 137
– Focus group discussions 142
– history of 137
Tensing, ülle 19
Thurlow, Crispin 2, 5
transnational scholars 87
– Welcome Guide 98

Unger, Jonathan 10
Universities Act 44
University of Helsinki 27
– language policy 40
University of Latvia 27
– language policy 40
– linguistic landscape 46
University of Tartu 27
– English-medium programs 61
– fieldwork 87, 100, 129

– historical chronology 116
– history of the 44, 59
– Language Centre 104
– language policy 40
– linguistic landscape 46
– PhD theses 19th century 119
– PhD theses 1940s and 1950s 120
– PhD theses 1990s to present time 124
University of Tartu Act 66
university rankings 1, 4

Veldre, Eimar 74
Verschik, Anna 15, 44
Vihman, Virve-Anneli 19, 76
Vila, Xavier 2, 6, 158
Vilnius University
– history of the 44
– linguistic landscape 46

Wächter, Bernd 8, 18, 23
Wodak, Ruth 153
Woolard, Kathryn A. 152

Zabrodskaja, Anastassia 15

www.ingramcontent.com/pod-product-compliance
Lightning Source LLC
Chambersburg PA
CBHW050904160426
43194CB00011B/2287